# THE GUINNESS GUIDE TO

# SALTWATER ANGLING

## LIGHT TACKLE TECHNIQUE
## FOR BRITISH WATERS

# THE **GUINNESS** GUIDE TO

# SALTWATER ANGLING

## LIGHT TACKLE TECHNIQUE FOR BRITISH WATERS

# Brian Harris

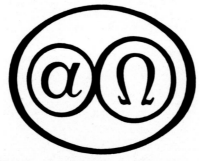

## GUINNESS SUPERLATIVES LIMITED
2 CECIL COURT, LONDON ROAD, ENFIELD, MIDDLESEX

**For Jean and Stuart**

Published in Great Britain by
Guinness Superlatives Ltd.
2 Cecil Court
London Road, Enfield, Middlesex

Set in Times 10/11
Printed and bound in Great Britain by
Hazell Watson & Viney Ltd, Aylesbury, Bucks

ISBN 0 900424 72 9

Guinness is a registered trade mark of
Arthur Guinness Son & Co. Ltd.

# ACKNOWLEDGEMENTS

Neil Nevison

**Editorial co-ordinator   Beatrice Frei**
**Design and layout   David Roberts**

**Illustrations**
Thanks are due to all who supplied photographs for this book, including Russ Symons, Bob Cox, Dave and Kay Steuart, John Darling, Ian Gillespie, John Cooper, Terry Hill, Keith Linsell, Reg Quest, the late Bill Keal and especially to Neil Nevison, whose professional skill, enthusiasm and patience are gratefully appreciated.

The author would also like to acknowledge the help and skill of many friends with whom so many happy angling hours have been spent.

Also to Anne Lewington, for unstinting work and forbearance – and for her excellent PR!

**Colour Illustrations supplied by:**
**John Cooper:** 87, 94, 210
**Bob Cox:** 82, 83, 134, 135, 138, 139, 178, 179, 186, 187, 190, 191
**John Darling:** 174, 175, 183 (top), 195, 207 (top right; bottom left, right)
**Ian Gillespie:** 202, 203, 206, 207 (top left)
**Terry Hill:** 154, 214
**Trevor Housby:** 106
**Keith Linsell:** 126, 127
**Neil Nevison:** 171, 183 (bottom), 223
**Reg Quest:** 107, 166
**Kay Steuart:** 118, 122, 123
**Russ Symons:** 98, 99, 103, 115, 147, 151, 158, 159, 182, 211, 218, 219
**The International Game Fish Association:** 228

# Contents

# Foreword

There is little doubt the sea angler is a hardy breed of sportsman. Throughout the year, regardless of weather conditions, he stands on desolate beaches, often at night, braving the biting wind and penetrating spray from heavy surf. Furthermore, with the quality of fishing improving considerably during autumn and winter months, a boat angler fares little better. On many occasions, often in open boats, he is tossed around from dawn to dusk, the only comfort a flask of coffee and sandwiches.

Even on more pleasant occasions I often wonder at the patience shown by the angler as he gazes intently at the rod tip, almost, it seems, willing a fish to take his bait. Little wonder therefore the angler is the butt of the cartoonist and considered slightly crazy by the general public.

Somewhat eccentric the sea angler may be, but the deep affection he has for this chosen sport allows him quickly to identify sound sincere angling writing.

There are journalists, often quite professional, who seem more concerned with the flow and arrangement of words, rather than the subject itself; often they attempt to write with authority on subjects well outside their experience. Such shallow words are quickly ignored by the sensible anglers.

On the other hand there is the true angling journalist, writers such as Brian Harris who have fished all their lives with dedication, affection and concern for the sport; such enthusiasm can be instantly recognised by the accuracy and sincerity of their words.

I remember Brian in his late teens fishing my patch from the steeply shelving beaches of Dungeness through to the rocky ledges of Winchelsea. Even in those days he had this enquiring mind bordering on the nuisance. My most enduring recollection is of him walking along the beach, spade and rod in one hand, with a bucket of worms, crabs and razor fish in the other.

From the practical down to earth task of bait digging to the Editor of a successful magazine in a few short years is no mean feat, and a sure indication of the Author's competence in the sea angling field. His obvious love of our sport is the reason I am happy to contribute a foreword to this excellent book 'The Guinness Guide to Saltwater Angling – Light tackle technique for British Waters'. The Author has not made the mistake of over stretching the subject matter but confines himself to discussing 25 of the most popular sporting saltwater fish in detail. The fish included are the most popular found around the British Isles. Their natural environment, methods of capture, including bait and tackle are described in depth. The amount of colour work with excellent photographs and line drawings, printed on high quality paper, are quite outstanding.

Brian Harris's approach to sea angling is very much my own, simple and direct. It is not always an easy task to explain on paper, at least in understandable terms, the important details that make the difference between the average and outstanding angler.

This book, however, is a distillation of a practical angler's knowledge that must prove invaluable to both beginners and experienced anglers alike.

Leslie J. Moncrieff

**Leslie Moncrieff.**

# Introduction

The rate at which mankind is consuming the world's natural resources continues to accelerate. Over-population and a widespread belief that an affluent society is the key to happiness have, together with greed and political factors, drained to an alarming level what land and sea are able to produce and provide.

Cousteau blames the trawl for most of the destruction of marine life and its environment. Add to the seabed slaughter the effects of pollution, sophisticated modern fish-location systems and equally refined fish-catching methods, and the dangerous situation may be envisaged.

Suddenly, world governments have become concerned, having ignored the warnings of their marine biologists for many years, and are imposing territorial fishery limits, though they cannot agree to a world-wide fishing policy. Some scientists believe it is already too late to save some fish species which have fallen in numbers to an extent that natural regeneration is impeded.

Against this background sportfishing is an important and growing part of saltwater angling. The sportfisher, appreciating that there are fewer fish to catch, is content to catch fewer than many other heavy-tackle anglers, but makes sure he gets maximum enjoyment from each fish. It is a natural sequence of events, therefore, for him to decide that some fish fight harder than others, some are more demanding of skill to catch than are others, and that henceforth he will choose to fish only with light and sporting tackle for the kinds of fish that fulfil his requirements.

This book aims to encourage more saltwater anglers to adopt the sportfisher's attitude since this will be both a move towards conservation and – due to the self-imposed problems that have to be overcome – it leads to lasting interest and fulfilment.

Sportfishing elevates what has for too long been regarded as a 'thick-eared branch of angling' to something of an art.

Brian Harris

# Part I

## Attitude and principles: tackle and baits

# 1

# Sport-fishing principles

Sheer size or weight in a fish is of little importance to the sportfisher in his assessment of whether it qualifies for his interest or not. For example, the fighting abilities of a 3 lb (1·3 kg) grey mullet and a 3 lb whiting, both hooked on the same tackle, are inarguably so far apart that any experienced sea angler who has taken plenty of both species will find even the suggestion of a comparison laughable. The poor old whiting is not in the same league, neither would it be were the comparison to be made between a 3 lb grey mullet and a 6 lb (2·7 kg) whiting.

When considering which fish rate the interest of sportfishermen, it is generally accepted that the round fish rather than the flat fish are more popular. This is to be expected since fish with a fusiform body shape are agile, fast swimmers while those with bodies

**A fast-taper 2–3 oz (56·5–85 g) casting bass rod bends over as Hampshire angler Jack Austin drags a nice bass through the swash at Inch Strand, County Kerry, Ireland.**

flattened in a horizontal plane are more fitted to lying on or being partially buried in the sea-bed, the tidal flow passing over them easily.

A number of flatfish do earn the sportfishers' interest and are included in this book, while there are omissions of a number of round-bodied fish, the whiting being one, of course, which cannot be of interest. While sheer size or weight of a fish is of little importance when giving it a rating as a sporting fish, there are some species which do depend upon their size to a certain extent as to whether they are fished for. For example, a 3 lb codling (cod under about 5 lb (2·2 kg) are called codling in most parts of Britain) would not be a very interesting proposition for a sportfisher, but a cod of 10 lb (4·5 kg) or more would be, since its extra weight helps it resist the tackle.

The speed at which a fish can swim, the speed and the depth of its dives, whether it leaps from the water, or whether it can stay deep in the water and resist by dogged pulling the resistance exerted by the angler's rod and line, are all characteristics by which sporting species are judged. Aesthetic appeal enters the picture, too: whether a fish is beautiful to look at or just 'plain ugly.' Paradoxically, one or two ugly customers are included in these pages because they can swim fast and pull, or both.

Here, then, is our list of sporting saltwater fish that may be caught in their seasons round the shores of the British Isles and the Irish Republic, as well as in other parts of north-west Europe: porbeagle shark, blue shark, mako shark, thresher shark, tope, smooth-hound, conger eel, common skate, stingray, cod, pollack, coalfish, halibut, bass, thick-lipped grey mullet, thin-lipped grey mullet, ballan wrasse, black bream, red bream, mackerel, garfish, plaice, flounder, twaite shad and allis shad.

Twenty-five species. Many saltwater anglers no doubt feel that some of these should not be listed, while others should. The blue shark, for example, is a borderline case and is included on the grounds that, though it fights less well than even the tope or smooth-hound, size for size, it is prolific, grows to a good size and can be quite fun on light tackle. Haddock might have been included but the species has a very limited range and reaches no great size. Species that attain

Even youngsters can bring big fish to the boat on light gear. This 26 lb (11·7 kg) cod was beaten on 15 lb (6·8 kg) test line in a strong tidal stream by the author's son Stuart, then aged 12.

heavy weights, such as monkfish and anglerfish, both capable of being taken frequently at weights of 30–40 lb (13·6–18·1 kg) are both dour on the hook and among the ugliest fish in our seas.

To make catching the 25 selected species consistently interesting and enjoyable and, to a certain extent, difficult (in that clumsiness in tackle handling will weigh against success) it is necessary to use tackle that is light in weight and of a strength that makes fighting an average size specimen a relatively equal contest, yet will still enable an angler to exercise skill in overcoming the occasional fish that is well above average size. Balanced tackle is the term used to describe the gear used by sportfishers in the sea. It is nothing new, yet strangely enough, fewer than half the anglers in Britain have discovered the delights of using balanced, lightweight tackle.

There is a great deal of misunderstanding about light tackle fishing in the sea: old habits die hard and in spite of the fact, for example, that enlightened anglers have regularly been catching cod to 30 lb (13·6 kg) on light rods and lines of 15 lb (6·8 kg) test and conger eels of up to 80 lb (36·2 kg) on 30 lb test lines, many will not try the system. They continue to haul up their multi-hooked paternosters, each hook adorned with an almost undetectable pouting or dab, on rods and lines twice as stiff and as strong as those used by anglers catching the big cod or congers.

Some of the resistance to light tackle sportfishing in the sea has been brought about by a few light tackle addicts taking their technique too far, such as seeking to catch cod with weights in double figures on line testing 5 lb (2·2 kg), or porbeagle sharks known to average well over 100 lb (45·3 kg) on lines of 10 lb (4·5 kg) test. The author, having been guilty a time or two of trying the latter smart trick, now believes that 25 lb (11·3 kg) test is more suitable to handle porbeagles that may be expected to range between weights of 80–200 lb (36–90 kg) in the hands of a skilled angler.

Using ridiculously light tackle does lead to criticism, and with justification. Quite apart from the fact that it is not clever to leave fish swimming around with hooks, leads and yards of line trailing from their mouths, there is the matter of such tackle interfering with the pleasure of fellow anglers near whom one is fishing. Nothing can be more relied upon to get tempers flaring, than an angler in a party of eight or so on a 30-foot (9·1 m) plus boat, who is using tackle much lighter than that which his fellows deem necessary to hold bottom. His gear drifts and tangles, unless he is made to fish at the extreme stern of an anchored boat, or he spends so much time playing each fish he hooks, that his companions have to spend much of their time with their tackle out of the water and out of his way; and, of course, out of the fish's way!

Thus it may be seen that light-tackle sportfishing on

A good place to pull in the gaff on a cod is near the gill covers, since edible meat is not spoiled and lifting against water resistance is easy.

a boat has to be carefully planned: either one goes with a party of like-minded friends, all of whom realise that fishing time is wasted when one of the party is playing a good fish, or, if the intent is to fish really light – for example with 25 lb (11·3 kg) test line for big porbeagle sharks – then only one or two anglers may fish. That makes the cost of a day's sport very expensive indeed. In fact, such fishing really calls for a special type of boat and experienced skipper, of which more in chapter 5.

Sportfishing then, as it is described in this book is demanding of skill, a suitable mental attitude and the knowledge that it is either necessary to pick your boat fishing companions with care, or spend a lot more than most non-specialist sea anglers do on charter-boat fees. Your tackle, too, will tend to cost more, though there are many items, including rods, that may be made at home and thus save a great deal of money.

It is necessary to pay a great deal of attention to the choice of tackle for sportfishing and its maintenance. The various items needed to cover the whole scene are the subject of the next chapter.

An angler playing his first shark on light tackle, in this case a 30 lb (13·6 kg) combination. This is the stern of the Q22 craft designed on the Isle of Wight and ideal for shark fishing in those waters.

# 2
# Tackle and accessories

The Atlantic strands of County Kerry can provide magnificent surf for the bass angler, and solitude in beautiful surroundings. This is Derrynane, where there is also fine rock fishing for pollack, tope, wrasse, conger eels, mackerel and garfish.

Because the sportfisher's chosen species vary so widely in average weight – from about 1 lb for mackerel up to well over 100 lb for some of the sharks and common skate – anybody who wishes to fish for all the species dealt with in this book will need to acquire a considerable collection of specialised tackle. In addition to the wide differences in the fish sought, tackle has to be selected to deal with a wide range of fishing conditions and locations: wild Atlantic surf beaches, steep shingle beaches, rocky points, piers, gantries, harbour walls, muddy tidal flats, the shores of many types of estuary, the banks of non-tidal rivers miles inland, the inshore areas from a small boat, the depths of the ocean perhaps 50 miles (80·4 km) from land in a big trawler.

Action from a large trawler off Ireland's South-West coast as an angler bends into a fish deep down in a rocky gully between rock pinnacles.

About a mile up the estuary of the Hampshire Avon there is excellent fishing for thick-lipped grey mullet. This is best done from a dinghy. This lad has just beaten a good mullet on light float tackle.

A total of 11 rods and reels will be suggested to cover all species and all situations, but obviously it is possible to reduce that number if one chooses only some of the species and locations, or if one needs to make do for budget reasons – a very serious consideration today.

Before going into detail concerning the rods, reels (and accessories) and lines, it is necessary to compare what this suggested mountain of fine tackle will achieve when set against the one rod and reel used by so many sea anglers today. In general, the man who owns only one rod or reel (either for boat fishing or shore fishing) will choose a stiff, heavy rod, big, budget-price reel and line of about 25 lb (11·3 kg) test for all shore fishing and 40 lb (18·1 kg) test for all boat fishing.

The boat rod, for example, will be used in summer and winter, together with the same reel and line, for catching dabs and whiting of less than 1 lb (450 g) each, to conger and ling of 40–25 lb (18·1–11·3 kg) respectively. It is obvious that the outfit cannot be properly geared to either extreme: to bring the 40 lb congers to boat the angler needs little skill on 40 lb line; the 1 lb dabs, even four at a time on the customary paternoster tackle used by single outfit anglers, are hardly able to make their presence felt as the line is reeled in. In addition, heavy line has its disadvantages in actual fishing techniques, which are dealt with throughout these pages.

Let us now see what the sportfisher would use for catching comparable fish. He would be unlikely to fish for dabs and whiting, since they do not fight, but for flounders averaging 1½ lb (600 g) from a boat he might choose a freshwater baitcasting rod and a tiny multiplying reel holding line of 4–6 lb (1·8–2·7 kg) test, depending on tidal conditions and the size of fish expected in the area. On that rod a 2 lb (900 g) flounder will put a satisfying bend in the little rod and even drag line from the reel: a 3 lb (1·3 kg) flounder or a plaice of 4 lb (1·8 kg) that may come along is quite capable of breaking the line if the angler's reel is incorrectly adjusted or he fails to do the right thing when the fish makes a determined dive. Skill becomes of great importance; the sport calls for dexterity, delicacy, artistry. It is a rebuff against the accusation that all saltwater angling is 'thick eared'.

# Sporting saltwater tackle; recent developments

About 95 per cent of saltwater fishing rods are today made from glass fibre. It is a very suitable material that has been in use for making fishing rods for the past 20 years or so and refined to a very high standard. In simple terms filaments of glass, finer than human hair, are stuck together with modern resins to form strong and resilient rods. The best rods are made in the form of tapered tubes, and these are constructed by first producing a cloth woven from glass filaments, then impregnating it with a sticky resin, which may be of three main types: phenolic, epoxy or polyester. The cloth is cut on a steel-topped table to an elongated triangle and then wrapped round a steel mandrel whose length and external size and rate of taper have been carefully calculated. The mandrel is then baked in an oven, which cures the resin and changes the sticky roll of cloth into a flexible, strong and light tube.

Of course, there is much more to it than that. It is desirable that a high proportion of the glass filaments run along the axis of the tube for tensile strength, a few being circumferential to hold the tube together. Before the mandrel is baked, the glass cloth is taped firmly with cellophane to force out any air and compress the cloth and synthetic resin into a thin, dense mass. Glass bonded with phenolic resin is said to be superior to other systems, but some very good rods are made, using the other two resins.

Hollow glass rods are best, being strong and light to hold. They resist great strains in casting and bending to big fish, but they do not take kindly to crushing. However, a case can be made for using solid glass rods in some forms of heavier boat fishing. Solid glass rods are made from glass filaments running longitudinally, impregnated with resin and compressed and cured, as is the tubular construction. This results in a much heavier rod to do a comparable task but it does resist damage by crushing.

**Hollow glass surfcasting rods can absorb tremendous strain without breaking. Here the author punches out light tackle on a Kentish cod beach in autumn. Note the short distance between the hands.**

Saltwater reels today are superb, the best ones being made of light alloys, corrosion-proofed, free running, with ball bearings, smooth working braking systems for playing fish, aesthetically designed . . . and many of them costing a fortune! Three types of reel are included in the sportfisher's armoury: the multiplier, the fixed-spool reel and the ordinary, so-called single action centrepin or Nottingham reel in two forms: a fly reel and a freshwater trotting reel.

The multiplier is used on top of the rod. This is a Policansky Monitor Number 4 lever-drag reel firmly anchored with braces to a 30 lb (13·6 kg) class rod. The butt cap of the rod is slotted and fits into the bar on the groin protector, which prevents the rod from turning when playing a fish.

Glass fibre, then, is the workhorse of the modern sea angler. Given reasonable care it will last for many years of hard work and it is almost impervious to water, and resistant to remaining bent, 'taking a set', as rods of wood and metal are prone to do. Saltwater fishing, be it on a boat or from beach, pier and rocks, is a rugged sport, and no matter how careful one is, a rod is sooner or later going to get dropped, banged or dragged along hard, rough surfaces. The glass rod resists such treatment extremely well.

During 1975 a new material, originally invented in Britain, then developed in America, came on to the British angling scene: carbon fibre, or graphite, as the Americans prefer to call it. Seven times the cost of a comparable rod blank in glass fibre, carbon fibre is yet (at the time of writing in summer 1976) an untried material for saltwater angling. It has proved exceptionally suitable for fly rods due to the fact that the material is stiff and can perform angling tasks that would need a glass rod of nearly twice the weight in some cases. Perhaps it will be of greatest use to saltwater anglers in some forms of light shore fishing in which the rod must cast well yet be constantly held. At present, though, such a finished rod would cost about £150, while a comparable hollow glass rod would cost about £25.

The multiplier is the most used saltwater reel. It is used on top of the rod while the other types of reel are used below the rod handle. The multiplier features a wide spool set inside a frame consisting of two endplates joined by crossbars. The centre of each endplate contains a bearing in which the ends of the spindle, which passes through the spool, run easily.

There are gears and a handle at one side, usually the right side, of the reel when it is on top of the rod handle. The comparatively small diameter of the spool is compensated for by the gears, which may vary from about $2\frac{1}{2}$ revolutions of the spool to one turn of the handle up to a ratio of more than 5:1. Usually the low ratio rate of retrieve is found on big multipliers for boat fishing for big fish and the high rate on multipliers of a small size designed for casting from the shore: it is impossible for a boat angler to recover line against the strain of a heavy fish with a reel having a high gear ratio. Most of the fish found in the waters of northwest Europe are fairly slow moving when compared to tropical water species and resist by ponderous weight and doggedness.

Spools of the bigger multipliers – those which can hold about 400 yd (365·7 m) of 50 lb (22·6 kg) test nylon monofilament line – are usually of either strong aluminium alloy, bronze or chrome-plated brass or glass fibre, to resist the crushing pressures of line rewound under tension and which then contracts, each coil adding its strain, and can smash even some apparently robust metal spools. It is best, and naturally most expensive, if the boat reel spool is actually turned from a solid block of metal rather than pressed from sheets which are fitted to the central hub.

On multipliers for shore casting long distances the spools are not primarily made for strength, though strength is important to some extent, but for lightness and free running qualities. We are now discussing the smaller sizes of reel, those holding about 200 yd (180 m) of 15 lb (6·8 kg) test nylon monofilament and others holding up to 400 yd (365·7 m) of the same line.

The fixed-spool reel's prime part in our scene is to permit very light lures or baits to be cast long distances with thin line. It can do this because the small spool lies at right angles to the axis of the rod, the line leaving the front of the spool in small coils (as one can pull cotton from a reel held by one side in the other hand), while the spool is stationary. The line is rewound by a pick-up arm fitted into a geared rotating flyer, a system by which twisted line is avoided.

The centrepin or Nottingham freshwater reel is one that may be done without, although it is very pleasant to use for light float-fishing for mullet in rivers or for some very light boat techniques. However, the small multiplier may be used for the light boat work and the fixed-spool reel for the river mullet. If one is used ensure that it is a good one; names will be mentioned later in this chapter when the various rod and reel combinations are set out.

Finally, and perhaps of some surprise to many sea anglers, the fly reel. Fly fishing has not been done in British saltwater to anything like the extent it is done in warmer waters, mainly because the temperate and cold water species we have do not generally lend themselves to such an approach. However, several species do succumb to the kind of fly tackle normally used to catch trout in big reservoirs. The main points to watch in such a reel are that it must be big enough to hold the fly line and at least 50 yd (46 m) of backing – in a few specialised instances much more backing of a stronger (25 lb test (11·3 kg)) type – and it must be robustly made and reasonably proof against the inroads of corrosion.

In the following pages constant mention will be made of corrosion and the need to use gear that does not suffer, or how to prevent it. This is because sea water is one of the most corrosive agents known to man. To ignore its inroads is foolhardy and very expensive. Plastics, glass fibre, brass, bronze, stainless steel, and properly chrome plated brass and properly anodized aluminium alloys will resist corrosion. The only non-stainless steel to consider in any part of salt-water equipment, apart from hooks, is that which has been galvanized or cadmium plated.

Now for a look in detail at the main items of tackle.

# Rods for shore fishing

Six of the total of 11 rods suggested are for shore fishing, which includes the banks of estuaries, non-tidal reaches of rivers, piers and rocks. Three of the six may be used from a boat from time to time, but the shore is their prime hunting ground. Let us identify each rod by the numerals 1 to 6.

Rod 1 is a powerful surfcasting weapon, able in competent hands to launch up to 6 oz (170 g) of lead weight – or 4 oz (113·3 g) of lead and 2 oz (56·6 g) or 3 oz (85 g) of bait – distances of 80–150 yd (73·1–137·1 m), depending on how much air resistance there is in the bait. It has two main jobs to do: cast a long way and subdue big, hard-fighting fish. It must have other attributes but they are secondary.

This rod's main quarry will be cod, tope, conger, stingray and even the occasional common skate in places where they come within range of the shore. Length of the rod will depend on the strength and build of the angler, but between 11 ft and 12½ ft (3·3–3·8 m) will usually be found suitable. It is surprising to many people that such a rod may be very slim indeed, perhaps a shade over ⅛ in (3 mm) at the extreme tip to about an inch or 1⅛ in (29 mm) at the butt end, depending on the type of taper and the thickness of the walls. There are glass blanks made for producing such rods that have a fast taper (very slim tip, thick butt), medium taper (thicker tip and less thick butt) and slow taper (thickish tip and slim butt). A few rods are made in which the butt tapers from where the reel is fitted to the rod to the extreme butt end, called reverse taper rods. However, their use is declining since the reason for their original design – to stop casting tangles or backlashes with multiplying reels – has been made history by vast

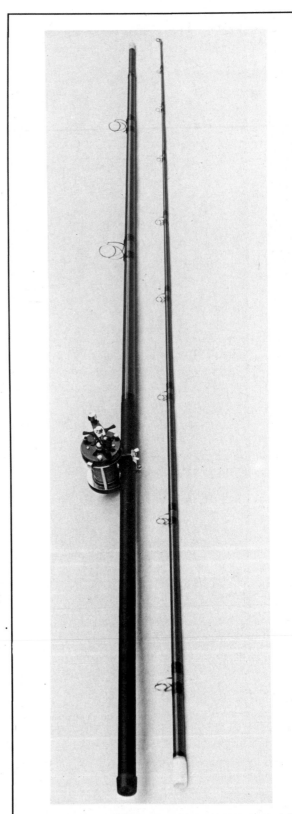

Rod 1, the powerful surfcasting rod, with one of the matching reels suggested, the ABU Ambassadeur 7000. This rod casts up to 6 oz (170 g) long distances for cod, tope, conger, stingray and even common skate on occasions.

A sound design of lightweight ring for surfcasting rods is this centre-supported model with a hard chromed finish that resists both line abrasion and corrosion by saltwater. It is also very strong.

improvements in reel design, which achieves the same object.

When fitted with a set of light, hard-chrome rings, a screw reel fitting when necessary, and some slim handle covering for a comfortable grip in wet or cold conditions, such a rod need weigh no more than 20 oz (566 g). But most of these ready-built rods to do comparable work that you see in the shops, will weigh as much as 2 lb (907 g) due to their having unnecessary or too heavy metal fittings. A shop-bought rod may cost about £32; it is so easy to buy the blank and the bits to make it into a rod that it is amazing to find people still paying out good money for such rods. Making the rod at home will cost in the region of £15 and not only saves money but enables you to fit the rod to yourself, making the reel come at the correct point on the handle so as not to have to stretch or confine your hands on a rod bought 'off the peg'.

However, for those who do not want to make the rod, good brand-names to buy include Hardy, ABU, Modern Arms Company, and specialist custom makers, such as Going Brothers of Southend-on-Sea and Essex Angling Centre, Leigh-on-Sea, Essex.

Good blanks for this kind of rod are produced by Fibatube, Carroll-McManus, Sportex, Conolon and Fenwick. Many such blanks are supplied either in one length or in two equal parts for easy carriage and joined by a hollow glass spigot. This is fitted and glued into the top end of the lower section and has some 4–6 in (10–15 cm) protruding to fit up inside the thick end of the tip section. You can carry an uncut rod on the roof rack of a car or in special rod clips that fit into

car roof gutters. Storage in the garage is relatively simple and in truth, this is the very best surfcasting rod of all, having no weak points and an uninterrupted curve.

A spigot joint on a hollow glass bass rod is fitted together. The gap left when assembled is to permit the joint to remain stable after the glass wears a little with years of use. The whippings are made very firmly to prevent casting and fishing stresses splitting the rod blank.

Long, unjointed surfcasting rods – or jointed rods assembled – may be carried on a variety of racks that fit to roof gutters on cars.

# Tackle and accessories

To make the spigot-joined rod or the uncut blank is the work of one evening at home. You need about 10 hard-chromed, centre-supported, light-weight rings, the biggest having a ring inside diameter of about 1 in (25·4 mm); the tip ring and the ring next to it should have an inside diameter of about $\frac{1}{4}$ in (6 mm). Decide the position of your reel – something between 23–30 in (58·4–76 cm) up from the butt end is generally accepted to be right these days. They used to be excessive distances which spread the hands too far apart and reduced casting efficiency, as well as making the long butt awkward when fighting a big fish. The first ring up the rod needs to be about 2 ft (60 cm) from the reel, after which gradually decreasing gaps are left between subsequent rings, the one next to the tip ring being about 5 in (12·7 cm) from it.

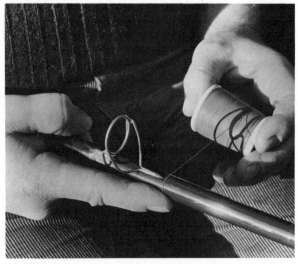

1. Whipping on a ring. Begin by moistening the first three inches with saliva, which prevents the threads from slipping on the shiny blank, then lay the thread on the rod just ahead of the sloping ring leg, holding it with the forefinger.

2. Rotate the blank, holding down the end of the thread, and trap the end with the first turn of the thread round the blank. Use plenty of tension, both with the thread and with finger pressure on the tag of thread.

3. Continue to turn the blank, keeping the spool of thread under considerable tension for a tight whipping. At this stage the trapped tag end may be cut off by see-sawing across it on the glass surface with a very sharp scalpel or knife.

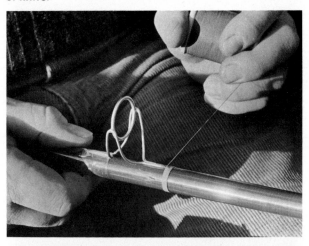

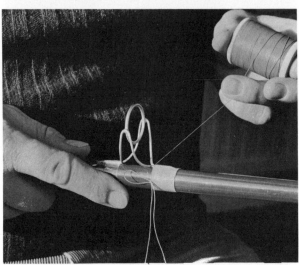

4. About six turns from the point at which the whipping will end, insert a loop made from a separate piece of thread.

5. When the remaining turns of whipping have been completed, keep all the turns firmly anchored by finger pressure and tuck the end of the thread – after cutting off from the spool – through the loop.

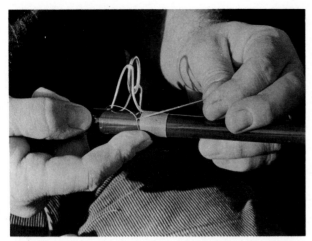

6. Pull on the ends of the loop, still holding all whipping turns secure, to drag the tag end under the tight turns of thread.

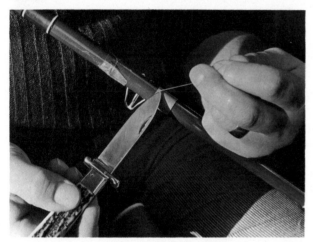

7. Pull the tag end firmly at a right angle and trim flush with the surface of the whipping.

Having ground or filed each leg of the ring to a fine feather edge so that no bump exists where it meets the surface of the blank, you stick one leg down with sticky tape and whip on the other leg firmly using nylon or Terylene thread. Gudebrod or Celebrated Talbot's are dependable whipping threads; maroon, dark orange, black or green look well on most glass.

Holding one finger on the tag end of the thread, begin whipping over it to secure it by about six turns before the thread comes up to the beginning of the upward slope of the leg, then cut off the spare tag-end. Continue whipping up the slope of the leg, each turn touching the next, turning the rod slowly away from your body and holding the thread by the spool under tension. It is easy but may take a little practice.

When about six turns of thread remain to be made before reaching the point where the ring-supporting wires leave the base leg, insert a loop made from 6 in (15·2 cm) of thread doubled, so that the open end of the loop faces away from the direction towards which the whipping is progressing. Holding all secure, whip over the loop of thread and cut off the working thread to leave a 6 in tag when the support strut is reached.

Pass the tag through the separate loop you inserted and, still holding the final few turns of the whipping securely, pull firmly on the free ends of the loop. This draws the end of the whipping back under the last six turns, after which it may be trimmed flush with the surface of the whipping by holding it at a right-angle under tension and slicing with a razor blade or sharp knife.

Having fitted all the rings, push all the turns of whipping firmly together with a thumb nail. Now give them a coat of varnish with a soft brush, afterwards rubbing the varnish into the thread with a forefinger. Yacht varnish is good. Give each whipping at least four subsequent coats with a brush, working round the whipping, making sure each previous coat is perfectly dry. Plenty of varnish protects the thread from being frayed or bruised, then becoming loose.

For something comfortable to hold you can wrap the handle area with rubber strip, such as that which is sold for making wet-suits. Roughen the glossy finish of the glass with abrasive paper, then coat the glass thinly with a two-part epoxy adhesive, such as Araldite, over the area from the butt extremity to a point 6 in (15·2 cm) or so in front of where the reel will go. Then, having cut a long taper on the outer edge of the end of the tape so that it lies straight across the rod, wind it carefully down the glass, making sure each turn is tightly butted up to the last. Hold the first inch or two firmly – by hand at first, but then tape it tightly with Sellotape so that all is secure as the handle covering progresses.

When the butt extremity is reached, simply let the rubber overhang, all turns tightly butted, and tape it firmly to the very end of the rod. Check back over the whole length for any gaps, and twist the rubber so that such gaps are closed by the turns, the rubber being tightened, and allow to set hard for 24 hours. After that trim off the overlap at the butt end using sharp scissors, then fit a rubber cap such as are supplied for non-slip tips to invalids' crutches or walking sticks.

It may be felt that the job could be done better with an impact adhesive, but it will be found that once the adhesive takes hold, it is not easy to manipulate the rubber to close any gaps. Gaps cause weaknesses where constant use and abrasion can cause the rubber to lift and then the handle can be ruined.

Some anglers use a plastic material called 'shrink tube' which may be bought in black and several colours. Choose it a little oversize of the glass blank. It is trimmed to the required length and slipped over the area to be covered, then warmed over a mild heat. Heat contracts the plastic to fit tightly to the glass, but the resulting handle is slippery and cold, and not as good as the neoprene rubber strip.

Now all you need do is consider the fitting of the reel to the rod. Some of the reels later to be suggested as a partner to this rod are supplied with special clamps that permit the reel to be held without the need for any reel fitting on the rod. Should this be the case, all that is necessary is to have either an extra layer of the rubber strip over about 4 in (10 cm) where the reel will be clamped (to protect the rod from crushing while permitting the reel clamps to be tightened firmly enough to prevent the reel from turning on the rod) or to roll over the handle a short length of the black rubber tube used to cover cricket bat handles etc.

If a reel without its own rod clamps is chosen, then the lightest and most effective way of fitting reel firmly to rod is with a Japanese Fuji reel seat. These are made from stainless steel, are relatively cheap, and one type is simply whipped very firmly at front and rear lugs and across a central recess to the rod handle at the selected point. A sliding clip on a ratchet holds the reel onto the rod and it is a good idea again to put a rubber buffer on the rod butt under the point where the reel clip is bound to the rod, since the clip is made of metal and the blank of glass, one result being a loud crack as each cast is made, glass bending, steel resisting. It could eventually cause the glass to fracture against the hard metal edge, but the rubber buffers the fitting. Fuji fittings with tubular bases are also available. These are slid on the blank and glued with Araldite.

One point to remember is that if the rod blank is purchased in two parts, with a spigot joint already fitted, then it is necessary to whip tightly over the ends of the blank, at the open end of the tip section and the point at which the spigot emerges from the butt section, to prevent the glass tube splitting under stress. Whippings of $\frac{1}{2}$–1 in (1·2–2·54 cm) in length will be about right.

Rod 2 is actually a lighter version of rod 1. It is of exactly the same type of construction, but its power and actual weight is less; the length may also be a little less, between $10\frac{1}{2}$ and $11\frac{1}{2}$ ft (3·2 and 3·5 m).

Some reels come equipped with clamps with which they may be firmly attached to the rod; an Ambassadeur 7000.

An excellent light but inexpensive reel fitting, this Fuji clip is whipped firmly to the handle of the bass rod.

This light surf rod (rod 2 in the list) is uncluttered with 'hardware' and weighs just over 12 oz (340 g). The only luxury is a length of rubbery plastic to hold. The butt is equipped with a rubber walking stick pad. The matching reel is an Ambassadeur 6000C.

When fishing for bass in the Atlantic surf there is nowhere to rest the rod, since one is standing in the surf most of the time. A light rod tires the angler less than a heavy one and adds to both fish-fighting enjoyment and ease of handling.

This rod's main purpose will be to cast weights of 2–3 oz (56·5–85 g) distances up to 100 yd (91·4 m) using lines of 10–15 lb (4·5–6·8 kg) test. The main quarry will be bass, both in the surf and from the rocks, but as it will be seen later in the book, it has other uses as well.

Fortunately there are more good rods of this type to be bought ready made than there are of rod 1, Modern Arms Co, Don's of Edmonton, Hardy, Milbro Sport Ltd, ABU, Going Brothers, Shakespeare being among the makers. Even so, most shop-bought rods of this type are encumbered by unnecessarily heavy metalwork and cost more than the home-made rod. The weight of a rod of this type should be between 11–16 oz (311–453 g). The author's current favourite he made from a Fibatube No. 132 11 ft (3·3 m) blank of medium fast taper weighs just over 12 oz (340 g). Eight light-weight centre-support rings are sufficient for a rod of this length and the distance from the butt extremity to the place where the reel sits may be shorter for fishing and fighting comfort, since this rod is not going to be used to hurl heavy leads or big baits a long way.

Shop prices will vary between about £22 and £30, whereas the home-built rod will cost as little as £15.

Rod 3 is a spinning-cum-float-fishing-cum-many other-light-tackle-tactics rod, and it may be 9–10 ft (2·7–3 m) in length. In fact, it is the same rod as one would buy or make for salmon spinning in spring, spinning for pike or fishing for big carp. It will be used with two different types of reel with lines of about 7–12 lb (3·1–5·4 kg) test for spinning, float-fishing and some light bottom fishing from the shore, and for spinning and drifting a bait from a boat.

There are many excellent rods of this type on the market ready made and at prices ranging from about £15–£22. Choose one with a light screw reel fitting, not with universal sliding rings which will not hold a multiplier securely. Buy only rods with hard chrome plated rings, or with aluminium oxide linings, as made by Fuji. Hardy, ABU, Modern Arms Company, Milbro Sport, Bruce and Walker, Shakespeare and some of the small custom builders make good rods of this type. Weight: 9–14 oz (255–396 g).

To make the rod at home will cost about £10. The only new thing you'll need to learn about is that of making a cork handle. It really is simple. Cork rings – or lengths of shaped, drilled cork – are stuck onto the blank with epoxy resin adhesive, being pushed on tightly from the narrow end. Glue them to the blank and to each other. They are then shaped with a Surform or similar tool, applied longitudinally, while rolling the handle on a worktop to retain its round shape. Various grades of glasspaper used on a sanding block are then applied to get the right dimensions. Start using very fine grade paper before you expect it to be necessary – cork has to be worked gently for a smooth finish.

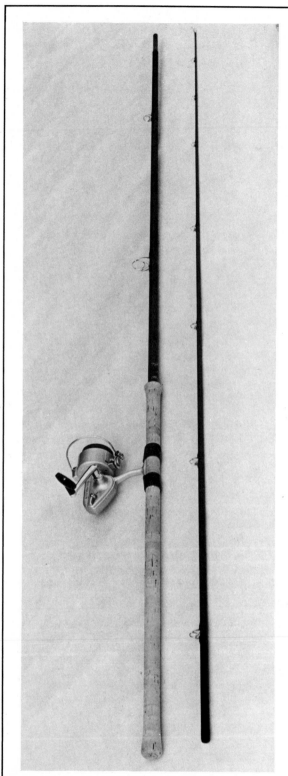

Rod 3 is a 9–10 ft (2·7–3 m) weapon of the salmon (spring) spinning or carp type. This one is excellent, though it would be better with a screw reel fitting instead of the sliding rings. The rings are, in fact, of nylon and therefore not subject to corrosion. The reel is a medium size fixed-spool type of Japanese origin.

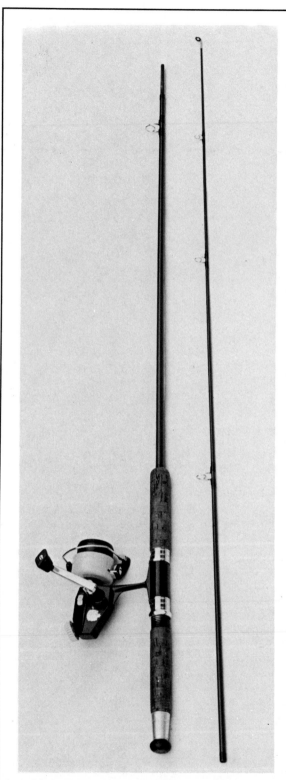

Rod 4 with a matching ABU Cardinal 44X fixed-spool reel. The rod in this case is 7 ft (2·1 m) long and was made from a fly rod blank. It weighs 4 oz (113·3 g) and has been used by the author to catch bonefish in the Bahamas, seatrout, mackerel, pollack, black bream and mullet in Britain. Its rings, now 12 years old, have never needed replacement. They are Pezon et Michel Chromex.

The screw reel fitting, with the stationary clip facing towards the butt end, is fitted on in the desired position over a bedding of cork rings or drilled wood, before the corks that will go on in front of it are stuck on and shaped.

Rod 4 is a trout spinning rod 7–8 ft (2·1–2·4 m) long, of hollow glass and in two sections joined by a spigot ferrule. It will be used with lines of 3–6 lb (1·3–2·7 kg) test for very light spinning from rocks and similar vantage points and also from small boats. Mackerel, small bass (and maybe big ones), shad and garfish are its main quarry, mullet at times.

The same advice as given for rod 3 holds for this one. It should weigh no more than $4\frac{1}{2}$ oz (128 g) and cost about £12 ready made, or a little less to build at home.

Rod 5 is yet another freshwater rod – an Avon-type trotting rod of about 11 ft (3·3 m) to a maximum of 12 ft (3·6 m) length. It is made of hollow glass, again, and weighs no more than 9–10 oz (255–283 g), the taper being described as medium fast. It should bend to a point about 18 in (45·7 cm) in front of the cork handle when pulled into a quarter circle. The lines are 3–6 lb (1·3–2·7 kg) test.

This is a mullet rod, for use in light float fishing in harbours, creeks, marinas and up in freshwater areas of river and dykes where the fish go. It will also be used for garfish, flounders, mackerel and shad, perhaps. It can have sliding universal reel fittings and the rings must be of High Bells Life stand-off pattern, hard chrome plated, which will permit trouble-free casting and fishing in wet weather, when fine nylon line tends to stick to the wet rod. Good ones are available from these makers – Hardy, Bruce and Walker, Milbro Sport Ltd, Modern Arms Company, ABU, Shakespeare, as well as custom rod builders. One

**The High Bells Life ring, best for the mullet-type rod.**

Rod 5, the freshwater Avon type, for mullet etc. It is used in the open sea, in brackish water, even in pure freshwater for thin-lipped grey mullet. The reels are a Black Cat open centrepin (on the rod), a Rapidex caged centrepin, and a Mitchell 300 fixed-spool reel.

would expect to pay between £16–£25. Making them at home from kit or blanks will save in the usual proportions, say a minimum of £10. Most of these rods are in two pieces, though some 12-footers (3·6 m) are in three pieces, often two long rod sections, the cork handle being made as a separate part.

Rod 6 – the last of our main shore armoury, though it, too, is often used from a small boat – is the fly rod. Many of the reservoir fly rods of 9–10½ ft (2·7–3·2 m) and matched to line sizes 7–9 will do the job, which is casting hair and feather lures up to about 3 in (7·6 cm) long to ranges of about 30 yd (27·4 m) even with adverse wind and cramped conditions. The rod should be hollow glass (carbon fibre would be at risk in the rough and tough game of the sea) and spigot-jointed, in two pieces and weighing 4–5½ oz (113·3–155·9 g).

If there is a screw reel fitting, which is advised, to hold the reel firmly, make sure it is anodised aluminium alloy, for lightness and corrosion resistance.

Good makers of such rods include Hardy, Bruce and Walker, Modern Arms Company, Shakespeare, Sharpes of Aberdeen, Masterline, Milbro Sport Ltd, and trout-orientated custom builders.

Try to get a rod with hard chrome plated or aluminium oxide butt and tip rings, with all the other rings wide snake type (also hard chromed) or lined with aluminium oxide. The single-legged Fuji type are excellent.

Expect to pay between £17 and £25 for a good fly rod; the usual saving obtains for home building

them. Reliable blanks, should you decide on this course, are made by Fibatube, Sportex and Fenwick.

This rod is used for bass, mackerel and garfish.

# Rods for boat fishing

There are five rods in this section of the weaponry, but only three of them are what are usually described as boat rods; the other two are a bit unusual in this country: a freshwater baitcaster and a special type of rod used for legering from a boat by casting uptide and out from an anchored position.

Most boat rods are between 6½–7 ft (1·9–2·1 m) in length. One single length of glass forms the tip or working part of the rod and is connected to the butt section by plugging into the strong chrome-plated brass tube that forms the screw reel fitting. A locking ring screws into position to secure the two parts. There is usually a cork foregrip on the tip section just above the ferrule which plugs into the butt. This may also be of firm cellular rubber composition, or something similar covered with waterproof leather, like that used on tennis rackets.

The sportfisherman really needs three such rods, which may be identical so far as the butts are concerned. The tips range from a very flexible one that will bend into a quarter circle (the tip at right angles to the butt) when a weight of about 2 lb (900 g) is hung on the tip ring, through one that will behave similarly with a weight of about 4 lb (1·8 kg) and a third to hold about 6 lb (2·7 kg).

The curve of the rod, when the tip is at 90 degrees to the butt, is known as its test curve and it is at this state that the rod is exerting its maximum safe resistance to a strain imposed upon it. Once the test curve of a rod is known it will be safe to use it with a line about five times the test curve in resistance: thus the above rod that will support the 2 lb (900 g) weight will be safe when pulled into a quarter circle with line of about 10 lb (4·5 kg) test. The rod holding up the 4 lb (1·8 kg) weight will be safe with 20 lb (9·0 kg) test line, and the third rod with 30 lb (13·6 kg) test line.

**Opposite top:** The 30 lb (13·6 kg) class boat rod and a matching reel: the rod is an American Berkley Regulation model, the reel the Policansky Monitor Number 4. The slots in the butt cap of the rod may be clearly seen: they fit into a crossbar in the groin protector to prevent the rod from rolling when fighting fish.

**Opposite bottom:** A lighter boat combination, the 20 lb (9·0 kg) class rod and a suitable matching reel: the ABU Ambassadeur 9000C. The rod is a Puma by Martin Ashby of Going Brothers, the specialist Southend-on-Sea tackle shop. Only butt and tip rollers are fitted, but rollers throughout are fitted on request at extra cost.

This still-water trout fly rod has big hard chromed snake rings on it to facilitate line shooting when casting for distance with shooting-head lines. The reel is an Intrepid Rimfly with all the paint stripped off and the aluminium alloy polished. It is washed after use and wiped with a soft cloth soaked with WD40.

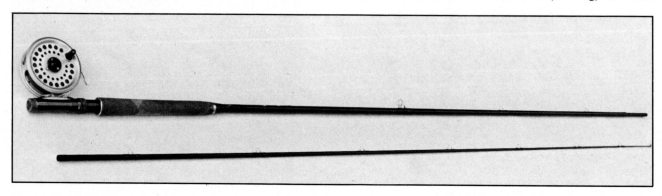

These figures are not critical and the line tests used may vary by about 30 per cent either way.

Now, it just so happens that the International Game Fish Association, based in Fort Lauderdale, Florida, administers the world record list of marine fish taken on various closely defined rod, line and tackle set-ups. Each set of tackle is called a class; the classes begin at 6 lb (2·7 kg) and rise through the following weights: 12, 20, 30, 50, 80, to 130 lb (5·4, 9·0, 13·6, 22·6, 36·2 to 58·9 kg). Various other restrictions on the tackle are imposed, but for the moment it is only necessary to state that the line, if fish weighed in are to be accepted for new record claims, be tested by a special machine and it must not resist a strain, when wet, of more than the stated class tests. For example, in the 12 lb (5·4 kg) class, the line must break at 12 lb (5·4 kg) or under; even a fraction over that and the claim would be dismissed. It is for this reason that line makers produce special lines guaranteed to break at no more than the various IGFA classes.

So, our three sportfishing rods are IGFA classes 12, 20 and 30, and to enable any captures made on them to be accepted by IGFA as a world class record, it is necessary to use lines of a little below the maximum permitted test to be sure they break below the limits. Nylon monofilament line loses approximately 15 per cent of its resistance to breaking when it is completely saturated with water, but since complete saturation is not reached until after about 24 hours of immersion (as a minimum) it is not necessary to be much concerned on that score, although knots also weaken lines.

To get to the point quickly, it is only necessary to say that our 12, 20 and 30 lb rods will be very nicely matched to lines of tests 10 lb (4·5 kg), 17 lb (7·7 kg) and 27 lb (12·2 kg) (if we want to fish always with a world line-class record in mind) but that the 12 lb rod may be used with 15 lb (6·8 kg) line, the 20 lb with 25 lb (11·3 kg) line and the 30 lb with up to 35 lb (15·8 kg) line. This is because the test curve system, worked out by the doyen of freshwater anglers, Dick Walker, was based on split bamboo fishing rods. These are delicate instruments, whereas glass rods are much less delicate and will withstand far more bending than will split bamboo, without damage.

Back to our three boat rods. . . .

It is as well to have all three tips the same length, around 5 ft (1·5 m) or even 6 ft (1·8 m). It is, in fact, possible to have one butt that will enable all three tips to be used with it – except that it will be found, quite often, that it is a good plan to have more than one rod and reel combination made up at the same time to cope with different situations during one fishing session. This just isn't possible with one butt.

Good 12, 20 and 30 lb rods are made by such firms as Hardy, Going Brothers, Shakespeare, and ABU, though the availability of the 12 lb rod is undependable since so few British anglers use them. Some of the prices charged are quite unjustified: some rods imported from America have been offered at £70 or so, about twice as much as they are worth! Good rods of this type should cost between £25–£30 in the three classes listed.

Boat rods are very easy to make. Fibatube, Sportex and Carroll-McManus make good blanks that are

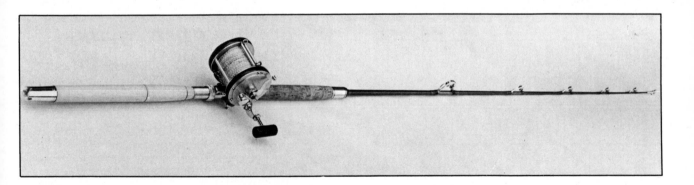

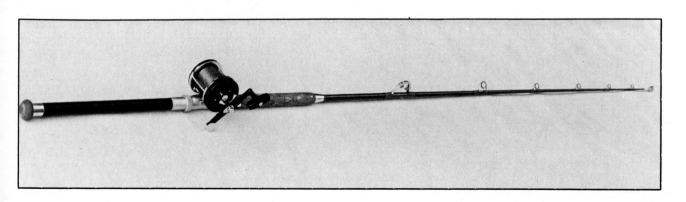

freely available in the UK. Simply fit the special locking ferrule (which plugs into and screws up to the screw reel fitting) to the butt end of the blank with Araldite adhesive, or similar, using a wooden plug or offcut of hollow glass, where necessary, to get the slim glass to fill out the bore of the ferrule. Often such gap-fillers are supplied with rod-making kits.

The actual butt, which need be about 16–18 in (40·6–45·7 cm) overall when the reel fitting has been fixed to one end, can be built on to a parallel length of strong, thick-walled glass-fibre tube, sold for the purpose, or high tensile aircraft quality alloy tube. The reel fitting is stuck on one end with Araldite, making sure the fit is accurate by slim packing with string over adhesive if necessary, then the rest of the butt may be covered with plastic shrink-tube, a stuck-on wrapping of neoprene rubber, as for the surfcasting rods, or left bare if it is glass. Alloy is best covered for corrosion resistance. A parallel chromed brass butt cap to take a screw-in rubber button about 1¼ in (3 cm) diameter should be glued on.

When the ferrule is fitted to the base of the glass tip, make sure that the transverse bar located in the reel fitting engages in the notch in the base of the ferrule; while doing this (before the glue is set) check that the rod and butt fit together in a straight plane and that any bend in the glass is with its convex side down when lined up with the fixed clip of the reel fitting facing up. This means that the rod will be straight in the fishing position when the multiplier reel is fitted into the clips and screwed up on top of the rod.

All three tips need roller rings at the butt and tip, and the 20 and 30 lb (9·0 and 13·6 kg) rods need rollers throughout. Only one make of roller rings has stood the test of time: AFTCO, made in America. They are freely available in the UK but quite expensive.

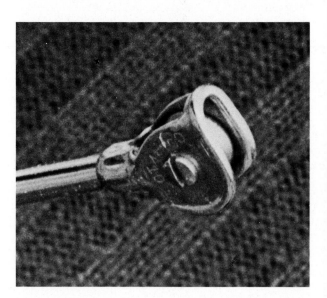

A single roller tip ring, a double roller butt ring and no less than seven intermediate rings of the hard chromed plated type will be required for the 12 lb rod; the 20 and 30 lb rods will need four ordinary roller rings in addition to the butt and tip rings.

Above: Typical construction of the tip to butt junction of a well made boat rod. The Vee in the tube on the tip locates into a transverse bar inside the reel fitting, the two then being locked by the knurled collar shown up against the cork foregrip. This construction is very strong and stops the tip from turning in the butt section when using a multiplier and there is tension from a big fish.

Top right: Detail of the single roller tip ring on the Puma 20 lb (9·0 kg) class rod.

Bottom right: Roller butt ring for a light tackle boat rod, showing the way in which the line should be passed through. The reel is on the left out of the photograph. The underwhipping can be clearly seen.

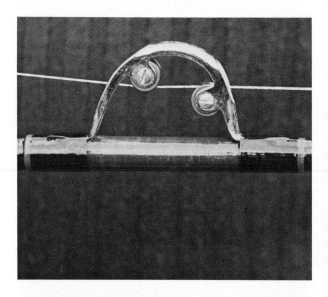

Roller tip rings are fitted simply by gluing the tube, on which they are built (of various bores to fit most tips), to the rod tip, making sure the tip reaches to the end of the tube. Do not fit the tip ring until the other rings are whipped on. To do this assemble butt and tip, put the reel on and screw up the fittings tight. Fit the butt roller in position with tape at a point about 18–20 in (45·7–50·7 cm) from the front of the reel.

Tape the rest of the rings in their positions at distances of $10\frac{1}{2}$ in (26·6 cm) from the butt ring and then $9\frac{1}{2}$, $8\frac{1}{2}$ and 7 in (24·1, 21·5 and 17·7 cm) from each respectively in the case of the remaining rings. Distances are measured from the centre of each bridge that carries the roller or the actual ring in the case of ordinary rod rings.

Now mark with a pencil a circle round the rod, $\frac{1}{4}$ in (6 mm) from each side of the legs of each ring, then remove each ring. The space between each of the pencilled circles – a distance of about $4\frac{1}{4}$ in (11 cm) for the butt ring – has now to be whipped firmly and closely with heavy grade nylon or Terylene rod thread. When all five spaces have been whipped, rub in with a forefinger some yacht varnish and set aside to dry for eight hours. Now tape on the butt ring and, having filed down each leg to a smooth feather edge, whip from the rod up on to the leg as for the surfcasting rods. Take the tape from the free leg and whip that too. Carry on whipping on the other rings, lining up each one with the butt ring.

The purpose of first putting on the layer of thread on which to whip the legs of the roller rings is to prevent the rings, which are on supports set high off the rod, being dragged round by the stresses imposed on the line by a hard-fighting fish. The whipping made over the legs beds the legs firmly into the under-whippings. It is very important that boat rod rings, rollers in particular, are whipped very tightly. It is common to find that rods whipped by the usual teams of women in factories – or female out-workers – are not tightly whipped and will move round when stress is applied.

Give each whipping a coat of yacht varnish, well rubbed in with a forefinger, when the whole rod has been completed. Allow to dry for eight hours, then wipe down the whole rod with a cloth moistened with white spirit to remove grease. Varnish the whole rod,

paying special attention to the gaps under the rings where the ring legs emerge from the whippings: daub the varnish into the gaps with a slim sable brush.

The glass needs about two coats of varnish, the first one gently flatted with fine silicon-carbide paper, used wet. The rod is then washed with clean water and dried before the second coat is applied. And because boat rods, no matter how careful one is when using them, get knocked about on board, it pays to give the whippings at least six thin coats over a period of several weeks, which will prevent the thread being worn.

The fourth of our sporting boat rods is, in fact, nothing more nor less than a freshwater baitcaster, meant for use with a small multiplier or closed-face reel fished on top of the rod to throw plugs and other artificial lures for pike, perch, American black bass and many other foreign species.

**The baitcaster, shown with a suitable reel: the Ambassadeur 5000C. This combination is excellent for black bream, red bream, plaice and smooth-hounds from a boat.**

**Even a roller tip ring helps make pumping up a fish easier, reducing friction at the angle of rod and line.**

Freshwater baitcasting rods come in a wide range of strengths, for use with lines as light as 5 lb (2·6 kg) test or as heavy as 15 lb (6·8 kg). We are now discussing the short baitcasters rather than the double-handed salmon rods presently available. Our baitcaster will be no more than 6½ ft (1·9 m) overall, which includes its little crank handle, which is sometimes permanently fixed to the actual blank or may be demountable through a collet and chuck system.

Good rods of this type are thin on the ground, because British anglers are extremely conservative and do not take kindly to 'new-fangled gadgets thought up by Yanks', as one man was heard to put it when asked if he used a baitcaster! Good baitcasters come from ABU, Berkley and Shakespeare, the ABU range being most easily acquired. Choose a rod that will lift a 1 lb (450 g) weight when its tip is pulled into a right angle with the butt – or very nearly such a specification. The rod may be used for light bottom fishing with lines of 4–7 lb (1·8–3·1 kg) test for flounders, plaice, black and red bream, bass, spinning and driftlining: it may even be pitted against bigger and tougher opponents from time to time, which is living dangerously but great fun when one is sufficiently skilled not to continuously break-off on such fish.

It really isn't worthwhile making up a baitcaster as a good one will cost from £10 to £15 or so. But if you wish to make one, the only crank handle sold is that made by ABU, who also supply collets to fit suitable tips.

Finally, then, the *boat*caster. Over the past few years a type of fishing from boats over shallow water has been refined by a few anglers and boat skippers fishing in the Thames Estuary and along the neighbouring Essex coastline. The technique involves casting up and across the run of the tide, to get the bait away from the shadow and noise of the boat and its crew, also to hold the bottom with a light anchor-lead in a strong current and to fish a wide area of the seabed. This type of fishing is not absolutely new, it having been done certainly 20 or so years ago, but it has been cleverly developed in the Thames' mouth.

Now, a cast is possible with the 6–6½ ft (1·8–1·9 m) boat rod, but it is not so easily done as with a rod of around 8½–9 ft (2·5–2·7 m). Such a rod may be made in one piece by using a 9 ft (2·5 m) surfcasting rod blank and going through the same building procedure as for the casting rods mentioned.

The rod needs to cast 3–5 oz (85–141·7 g), and use lines of 12–15 lb (5·4–6·8 kg) test. Unless you do make it yourself, the only currently made rods from a commercial source are those from the Essex Angling Centre at Leigh-on-Sea, or Rod and Line at Lewisham.

---

Stuart Harris plays a 26 lb (11·8 kg) cod on sporting tackle from a boat – the fish he is shown holding earlier in the book.

---

# Reels for shore fishing

Luckily, although there are six rods in the shore fishing armoury, there need be only four reels to use with them.

For casting long distances with leads of 4–6 oz (113·3–170 g) – for winter cod or summer tope, for example – a reel capable of holding 400 yd (365·7 m) of 15 lb (6·8 kg) test monofilament line is required. Of course, it is necessary to have only about 200 yd (182·8 m) of line for cod, since they do not make long runs like tope, but it will be found better to use such a rugged reel than a smaller, lighter one, such as will be next on the list, to take the strains some winter cod fishing imposes.

Good examples of reel number 1 include: ABU's Ambassadeurs 9000, 9000C, 7000, Mitchell's 600P and 600AP, Penn's Surfcast 200 and the wide-spool Squidder. Prices range from about £45 down to about £12.

This is the position for the thumb when controlling the spinning spool of a multiplier during the cast. The edge of the ball of the thumb rests on the edge of the spool when the lead is in flight, so avoiding friction-induced line or skin burns.

The reasons for listing the above reels, which are quite big for shore fishing, is that they combine adequate line capacity (for shore tope, which may run more than 200 yd (182·8 m) in one attempt at escape) with light spools of aluminium alloys or plastic, and strength in the spools, drag and gear mechanisms, for dealing with big dour fish like conger or stingrays or even the occasional common skate. If the reel were to be used only for long casting for cod, then it would be possible to use the next reel on the list, since casting distance is the main requirement for cod, and they do not usually take more than 30 yd (27·4 m) of line from the reel in one run.

Number 2 reel, then, is for the number 2 rod: for surfcasting and rock fishing for bass in the first instance, but useful in other spheres too. This reel must hold at least 150 yd (137 m) of 15 lb (6·8 kg) test line and will be used with lines of 10–15 lb (4·5–6·8 kg) test.

The reel needs to be reasonably compact and light, yet with adequate strength. Casts of up to 100 yd (91·4 m) using 2–3 oz (56·6–85 g) of lead will be made at times, and the spool must be very light to cast light leads easily. A smooth drag is desirable, but, even though the reel will be used for fish that run faster and farther than bass (for 50 or so yards (45·7 m), perhaps), it will not have to cope with such long runs as the number 1 reel.

Good examples include ABU's Ambassadeurs 6000, 6000C, 6500C, 5000, 5000C, Mitchell's 602P, 602AP, Penn's Surfmaster 100, Baymaster, Squidder Junior, Daiwa's Millionaire and DAM's Quick 800B Champion High Speed. The last reel on the list is very good in most respects but has a drag that can be jerky. The letter C after the Ambassadeur numbers signifies that the spool runs on ball races. The prices of these reels run from about £11 up to £38 for the best Ambassadeurs.

Some anglers cannot master a multiplying casting reel; and for those the fixed-spool reel that will carry 400 yd (365·7 m) of 15 lb (6·8 kg) test monofil is a substitute to use with rod 1 (the need for the large line capacity comes only if tope are to be hunted, of course) and a smaller reel with 200 yd (182·8 m) of 15 lb (6·8 kg) test capacity for use with the bass rod.

It is important that any fixed-spool reel to be used for saltwater fishing is chosen for strength and resistance to corrosion; there must be a free-turning bollard or roller in the pick-up arm for easy line recovery and yield against tension, and the drag mechanism must be widely variable and operate to yield line smoothly, even when the line is being pulled off at high speed. Such reels will cost between about £18–£25. Good ones are made by ABU, DAM, Mitchell, Shakespeare, Penn, Daiwa.

When tope fishing from the shore, especially in shallow water, and a fixed-spool reel is used, it must have a free-turning line roller or bollard in the pick-up and a spool capacity of about 400 yd (365·7 m) of 15 lb (6·8 kg) line.

To match rod 3 – the spinning, float-fishing etc rod – the choice of reel may be either a small multiplier or a medium fixed-spool reel. So long as it contains the necessary amount of monofil – 150 yd (137 m) of any test chosen between about 7 lb and 12 lb (3·1–5·4 kg) – it will do the job, the qualifications listed for the other fixed-spool reel applying, of course. All the firms listed above make good ones of this size too.

If a multiplier is chosen, it may be the ABU Ambassadeurs 5000 and 6000, standard, C or the 5500 and 6500 fast retrieve models, a Daiwa Millionaire – which you may already have for use with rods 1 and 2.

The next rod to arm with a suitable reel is the light spinning rod for lines between 3–6 lb (1·3–2·7 kg) test. Since very light baits will need to be cast up to approximately 50 yd (45·7 m) on some occasions, it must be a fixed-spool reel, since even the most avid user of a multiplier must admit that the reel cannot attain the distances of the 'mincing machine' with very light lures. So, a trout/coarse fishing size reel is the answer, and it will pay to have a spare spool with a different line capacity to fit it. One spool should be loaded with 150 yd (137 m) of 3–4 lb (1·3–1·8 kg) test monofil, the other with the same amount of 5–6 lb (2·6–2·7 kg) test.

Again, the same companies make the best ones, the only consideration being corrosion resistance and robustness. In this type Mitchell reels, for example, will soon corrode badly, even when given regular maintenance, whereas the ABU Cardinal reels, DAM Quick and Shakespeare BB Wondereels do not suffer such damage. Mitchell's larger fixed-spool reels made specifically for sea angling, are more resistant to such damage than the 300, 410 and similar small models.

Prices range from about £11 to over £20.

Now for the Avon-type freshwater rod's partner. This rod will be used mainly for float-fishing with lines of 3–6 lb (1·3–2·7 kg) test, in harbours, estuaries, creeks and even the open sea for mullet, garfish, mackerel, flounders and shad. The same fixed-spool

**Thumb control by a right handed angler on the edge of the drum of the fine Black Cat centrepin reel in use when trotting a bait for mullet, shad or garfish.**

reel as used for rod 4, the lightweight spinning rod, will be very suitable, making long casts with the light terminal tackle. However, many anglers prefer the centrepin trotting reel for pleasurable playing of fish by direct manual control without going through a gear train or drag system. A really competent freshwater angler will cast light float gear 20 yd (18·2 m) or so with the centrepin reel, using a cast that demands dexterity in spinning the drum and *then controlling the flow of line*, the so-called Avon cast or a derivative.

Suitable reels must have a caged drum, two or three bars across the frame that holds the works and spindle, to prevent line spilling out and getting tangled round the foot of the reel or elsewhere. Suitable reels are now only available second hand and fetch prices four times what they cost when new a few years ago: Rapidex, Flick'em, Eureka, Silex are among suitable reels. Expect to have to pay £10–£30!

Finally, to complete our shore reels, comes the fly reel. It will not be worthwhile paying a lot of money for a good reel since corrosion will soon ruin it. The writer has used a cheap but excellent British reel, the Intrepid King Size Rimfly, and found it surprisingly resistant to corrosion when washed in fresh water after use. It even stood up to the tremendous strains of catching bonefish on the flats of the Bahamas. This reel is the best buy of all at only about £5.

# Reels for boat fishing

For the so-called boatcaster rod, one can make use of the bigger shorecasting reels already listed for shore rods 1 and 2, which is a saving. Similarly, the multiplying reels listed for shore rod 2: the Ambassadeurs 5000, 6000 etc and the Millionaire and DAM Quick 800B Champion can be used with the little baitcaster (to be used for light bottom fishing and some driftlining and spinning, perhaps).

For the two lighter, conventional boat rods, the 12 and 20 lb (5·4 and 9 kg) class rods, it is also possible to use reels from the shore range, provided that one is not going to, for example, fish for porbeagle sharks with the outfits, in which case vast line capacities and special game reels are called for. The Ambassadeurs 9000, 9000C, 7000 are very suitable for use with the 30 lb and 20 lb rods, for all fish other than big sharks – over 100 lb (45·3 kg). The 9000 and 9000C are also fine for the 12 lb rod when fishing for very big tope, say, in the shallows where long runs are predictable, or for anybody who wishes to fish 12 lb class for blue sharks that do not run much more than 70 lb (31·7 kg). For normal 12 lb class fishing the Ambassadeurs in the 6000 and 5000 range, plus the Millionaire and Quick 800B will hold enough line; that is 10–11 lb (4·5–4·9 kg) test, usually.

Other reels suitable for the 20 and 30 lb rods and non-shark fishing include Penn Senator 2/0, Long Beach, Sailfisher, Super Mariner and Leveline; Mitchells 624 and 622; ABU Ambassadeur 8500 and Ambassadeur 12. All reels for boat fishing should have metal spools, either of aircraft quality aluminium alloy, bronze or strong brass, chrome plated, and preferably turned, instead of pressed, into shape. The spools must resist the crushing pressure of the line rewound under tension when playing big fish or fishing in strong tides; no spool of plastic has yet been made that is truly reliable in this respect.

There are no doubt other reels not listed here but suitable for the job, some Japanese and American reels, as well as German and Australian, are good, but the author has not had personal use of them in the 'field'.

Very special reels have to be used if it is decided to really live dangerously and fish with the 20 and 30 lb class rods for big sharks, porbeagles, big blues – over 100 lb (45·3 kg) at least – threshers and makos, as well as a regular date with big congers – 40 lb (18 kg) plus – or big coalfish.

The lever-drag is simple to use and gives quick, sensitive adjustment while still holding the reel handle.

All these fish demand that extra something from the reel: in throwing down the gauntlet to these species, which are either very heavy and can pull, or fairly heavy and can swim and dive at very great speed, for long distances, the angler is knowingly putting himself and his tackle to its greatest test. If the angler or the tackle is not at peak condition then, in the words of the song . . . 'Something's got to give'.

Long fights with large, heavy and hard-pulling fish impose strains on both angler and tackle far outside the norm. The tackle itself is weak by comparison with the fish; but used with skill it can, in extreme cases, wear down fish that are 20 times the tensile test of the line. For example, world records captured on 20 lb (9 kg) line class include a great white shark of 1068 lb (484·4 kg), an Atlantic blue marlin of 430 lb

(195 kg) and, to get a bit nearer home, porbeagle, mako and blue sharks of 180, 242¾ and 218 lb 2 oz (81·6, 110·1 and 98·8 kg) respectively! Some slightly heavier fish have been taken on 30 lb (13·6 kg) class tackle.

Although some multiplying reels for boat work have excellent star-type drag mechanisms that add pressure in small amounts and yield line smoothly, even against strong pressure (the ABU Ambassadeur 9000 and 9000C reels being the best examples) for absolute precision in this field there is little doubt that the lever-drag, bearing on a wide surface – such as the whole of the circumference of the spool flange – is smoother and more delicate. That is why the anglers of experience, who deliberately hunt big, wild fish with light tackle, nearly always choose lever-drag reels.

There are a number of reels from which to choose, should you wish to get involved in this kind of fishing. However, some are so expensive that few can afford them: £350 or more each! Here, then, are a few less expensive ones, but they still give excellent results; the least expensive is, in this case, the best – and this is the view not only of the author but of other anglers, such as Leslie Moncrieff, John Goddard, and the big-conger-on-light-tackle man, Ray Rush.

The Policansky Monitor Number 2 is a fine reel for heavy shore fish, such as conger and common skate. It will cast 6 oz (170 g) up to 100 yd (91·4 m) but is not a long-distance reel. It is also a good light tackle boat reel.

The reel is the South African Policansky Monitor, available in two sizes, 2 and 4, and at the time of writing costing about £35 and £57 respectively. The No. 2 holds about 450 yd (204 m) of 20 lb class monofil, the No. 4 about 550 yd (249 m) of 30 lb class. The reel is beautifully made and cannot be faulted: the No. 2 has a fast recovery (some say a little too fast for adequate recovery power) of about 5:1; the No. 4 ratio is 2½:1, which is better for the job.

ABU have recently produced two excellent game reels for 20 and 30 lb class outfits; they have lever-drags, too, and cost about £90 and £95 respectively.

Other worthwhile lever-drag reels include the Roddy Dominator (Japanese) and the Penn International range, the latter being in the more expensive class. There are other Japanese lever-drag reels, as well as a Mitchell and an Italian model, of which the writer has no personal experience.

# Lines

Three types of line are used in the sea: nylon monofilament, braided lines, produced from nylon or Terylene (Dacron in America) and wire. For all shore fishing the monofilament has the advantage. It is much cheaper, less visible to fish, and can take abrasion and knocks without suffering too much damage. It may be easily, very quickly and reliably joined by special knots.

However, nylon monofilament has its faults. It stretches considerably. This is more apparent in the limp, soft types; while the hard, wiry monofilaments stretch least. A monofil that is in between these extremes usually proves best. Stretch hampers the strike of the angler and if there is too much of it the

When a fish gives a slack-line bite on a beach and the angler has cast 140 yd (128 m) or so, it is essential that a running strike is made to take up the slack and sink the barb. John Darling demonstrates on long range bass at Dungeness, Kent.

hook may not penetrate the fish's mouth properly; naturally the more line there is between rod tip and fish the more stretch there will be. In addition, monofilament nylon possesses memory, in that it returns to its normal state after being stretched. If that occurs when the line has been rewound on the reel spool under considerable tension (in fighting a big fish, heaving clear of a snag, or winding in a mass of weed), the contracting of each coil imposes tremendous crushing power on the spool, which may become distorted and bind in the frame, or may be literally crushed to pieces! Plastic spools suffer worst from this, but even metal spools can succumb.

In practical terms, so far as the types of angling covered by this book are concerned, the use of monofil can be almost universal, in all tests up to 30 lb (13·6 kg) class – i.e. about 27 lb (12·2 kg) test. Braided nylon suffers from elasticity, too, and is not only more bulky for its test (thus presenting water resistance problems) but it also wears very quickly.

Braided Dacron (American) or Terylene (British) lines are generally used for big-game fishing in tests over 30 lb (13·6 kg). They are comparatively thin, some being thinner than monofilament nylon for their test, but their biggest attribute is their absence of elasticity. This makes it much easier to strike a hook into a fish and helps avoid damage to the reel spool when winding in line still stressed by a big, strong fish. In British and north-west European waters, however, most fishing techniques for big fish involve fishing a bait on the seabed, and this is where braided Dacron or Terylene lines fail: they do very quickly become weakened by abrasion with sand and rocks etc. In tropical waters, where their use is mainly in trolling for game fish, in the top layers of water, the lines do not come in contact with the seabed and so no abrasion takes place. It is amazing how many British saltwater anglers fail to appreciate that fact.

Braided Dacron or Terylene costs about 2½ times as much as a comparable test of quality nylon monofilament. In 30 lb (13·6 kg) class braid is a justifiable expense for conger, the sharks and common skate. However, with a strong reel spool and careful handling, monofilament nylon will do the job almost as well, and the author has reason to distrust braided lines, having lost several big fish, including salmon in freshwater. These lines do appear to break suddenly for no apparent reason.

Finally there is wire line. This is for use only in boat fishing. Both single strand and braided wire lines are available and their use should be confined to fishing in places where there are very strong tides and fairly deep water and where it is otherwise impossible to use sporting tackle. Being very much thinner for its test than either nylon monofilament or braided lines, wire permits the angler to fish reasonable amounts of lead and hold the tackle on, or close to, the bottom. Using nylon monofilament or braided line of similar test would demand two or even three times as much lead. It is very useful to have a spare spool with a boat

multiplier with monofilament or braided line loaded to within about ¼ in (6 mm) of its lip and about 100 yd (100 m) of wire line wound on top. Wire, especially of the single strand type, which is recommended, takes up very little space on the reel, and it is best wound on over a base so that its coils are kept large to prevent kinks forming too easily. A spool loaded with wire line can make it possible to fish offshore marks at times when tide flow is at peak, when, without wire, the tackle would either just not get to the seabed or would need to be so heavy to do so as to be not worth the effort. Two hours of extra sport is often possible using wire.

Wire, however, is brittle; it can be difficult to control due to its inherent springiness, and it can be dangerous: wire under tension is one of the most efficient cutting devices known to man and it can shear fingers as easily as cheese! Although the best is stainless steel wire (in the author's opinion it is better than monel metal or phosphor-bronze coated material) it does corrode, and it will break very easily if a kink is allowed to form. Also, the rod must have a large roller tip ring and, if possible, rollers throughout, since if wire is wound through even tungsten-carbide normal rings (the tip one where a sharp angle forms in particular), it will work-harden and soon be weakened.

A bite on wire line, even when fishing at great depths, is a revelation, even more so than with braided Dacron or Terylene. Since the wire does not perceptibly stretch it is highly conductive of fishy movements at the business end to the angler's fingers. Wire cannot be knotted and must be joined, using a loop twisted in the wire and a knot made in the other line – of which more in chapter 8.

There are other lines, such as braided man-made fibres with a core of lead, which are used for trolling elsewhere. However, lines other than those already dealt with have no place in sportfishing in the waters of Britain and the neighbouring countries.

The fly lines needed are ordinary weight-forward floating or sinking freshwater lines, although, when using very big flies, it does pay to use a special type of weight-forward line made for casting big, air-resistant lures: saltwater or bug tapers, as they are called.

# Hooks

There is a discussion in later pages about lures to which hooks are already attached or are an integral part; hooks in this chapter are ordinary hooks that are baited.

There are very few major hook-making firms in the world and the sporting sea angler in the waters of Britain and north-west Europe is very well catered for by the world's biggest hook-making concern, Mustad of Oslo in Norway.

From Mustad come the hooks necessary to cope with all the selected sporting species with which this book is concerned, from size 10 (the smallest and for grey mullet) up to 10/0 for sharks or the common skate.

For sharks, common skate, congers, halibut and big tope the Mustad Seamaster hook in sizes 6/0 to 10/0 will be found reliable. It is extremely well made,

strong, with a welded ring and forged bend. The finish is corrosion resistant cadmium.

For general shore fishing for bass, cod and smoothhounds, the Mustad No. 79510 in sizes 1/0 to 5/0 is excellent: round shape, fine wire, forged bend with sharp point and moderate barb. It has many fans and

Hooks: Nos. 1 and 2 are Mustad Seamasters for sharks, conger, halibut etc; 3 and 4 are Mustad No. 79510 – a highly regarded hook for bass; Nos. 5, 6 and 7 are Yorkshire Stronghold hooks, excellent for flatfish, ballan wrasse, black bream etc; Nos. 8 and 9 are O'Shaughnessy types; Nos. 10 and 11 are the nickel-plated strong round bend spade ends from Dons of Edmonton, and the ringed version next to it is a French Cannelle hook; No. 15 shows two sizes of Sundridge Specimen hooks. The two hooks with barbed shanks and incurved (beak) points (Nos. 13 and 14) are not good hookers and should be avoided.

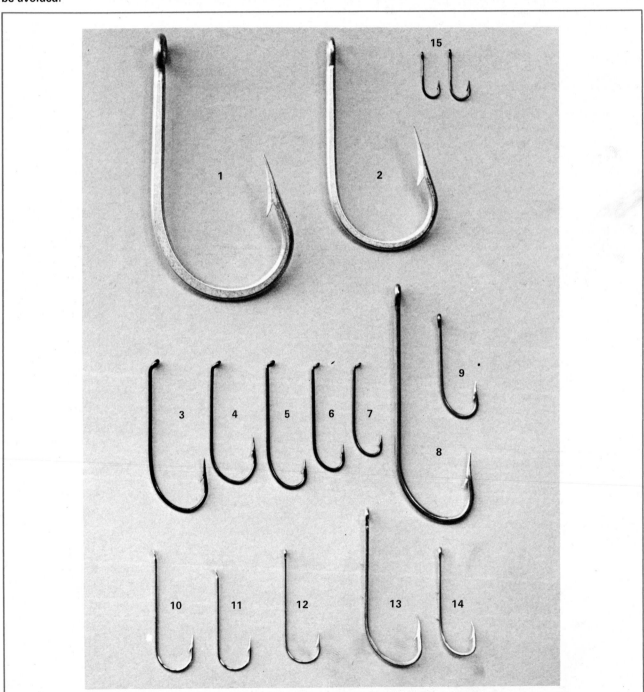

many fine captures to its credit. It is not a massive, rigid hook capable of a performance in the mouth of fish with strong crushing powers, but it is possible to take cod up to 30 lb (13·6 kg) with this hook. It also penetrates easily when light tackle is used to draw the hook home rather than punch it in, as with a heavy rod and strong line.

**The finished edge on the barb – a way in which big hooks can cut their way in with only a minimum strain.**

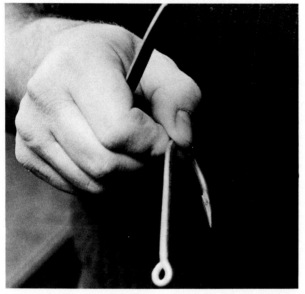

Filing the barb of a Mustad Seamaster hook to a knife edge helps penetration into tough tissue with light rods and lines. The strokes should be made only at this angle to the hook point.

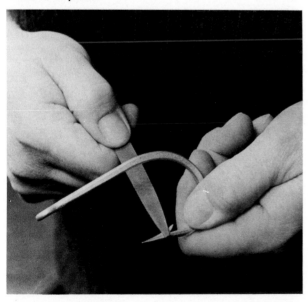

For strength without weight the Mustad O'Shaughnessy hook is excellent. Sizes from 3/0 to 6/0, are recommended for shore tope, conger, pollack, coalfish and big stingray. Use it in the bronzed finish.

Since this is a book about sporting angling, and since it is also about conservation, it is appropriate that an appeal is made for the use of ordinary bronzed hooks whenever possible. If you lose a fish by line breakage, bronzed hooks will soon rust and be rubbed out of the fish's mouth by the fish, or if the hook lodges in throat or stomach it will be 'digested' by stomach acids. The stainless steel, cadmium-plated or tin-plated hooks do not rust and may hamper or kill the fish after a while. Only big game (Seamaster) hooks in the list given so far are plated.

For the breams, flatfish and wrasse a Yorkshire Stronghold hook takes some beating. Intended for dressing lures and big flies for trout and seatrout, it has a long shank and is of high carbon steel with a short, sharp point. Sizes 2 and 4 are most useful, small enough for the fish and the bait, but strong enough – the hook is lightly forged round the bend – to hold a large fish should one happen along.

Do avoid any so-called 'beak' hooks – those with incurved points, and especially those with short shanks. The author's opinion is that they are the very worst shape of all for hooking fish, though once you do get the hook home the design holds very well.

Finally, for using tiny baits for grey mullet, and for garfish and shad, the Sundridge Specimen hook is recommended, sizes 10, 8 and 6.

Hooks are relatively cheap, excepting the Seamasters, which can cost about 30p each in the sizes suggested. So, do not be tempted to use them once they have become rusted or have had the point cut back too much by sharpening.

Always carry in your kit a small stiletto-shaped warding file for sharpening the points and barbs of hooks, especially the heavy boat fishing hooks, and a small, flat Arkansas stone for the smaller, fine-wire hooks. Sharpen from the back of the barb. When sharpening Seamaster and O'Shaughnessy hooks, file the the back of the barb to a knife edge, as they are on Seamasters when bought. This helps the hook penetrate easily in hard-mouthed fish.

# Clothing

Time was when sea anglers went out like gipsies, clad in all manner of war-surplus clothing or tattered sweaters and woollen ski-caps. A few still fish thus attired, but many more take advantage of the purpose-designed clothing and footwear available.

Angling at the coast or out at sea, in winter's cold or summer's heat, can be very uncomfortable without proper gear. The shore fisher in summer needs hard-wearing cool trousers, cotton shirt and a light woollen sweater with a lightweight hip-length parka with attached hood. For spots where fishing or bait collecting has to be done by being in the water, inexpensive thighboots are the answer – not the expensive trout anglers' type with hobs etc, although when slippery, weed-draped rocks are the base, then hobs do help to

## Tackle and accessories

In contrast to the well-wrapped surfcaster of autumn and winter, this summer rock angler is also comfortably attired. Rocks can be hard on the feet without suitable shoes or boots.
Inset: A cold, wet day on the beach can be miserable without adequate protective clothing. Parka with hood covers the tops of thighboots or chest waders.

get a foothold. For fishing from dry rock ledges, from piers, harbour walls and similar dry spots, canvas baseball boots are good, or if the rocks are rugged and have to be scrambled upon, stout boots that come high on the ankle may save a broken bone. Some of the best rock places are really hard climbs.

In winter, on a shingle cod beach, or on a pier or rock platform, thighboots will tend to be uncomfortable, especially when walking a long way across the beach to reach that special spot. Exposed beaches in a north-east wind and rain are not pleasant places to be in winter unless you are well dressed. The special underclothes providing warmth without bulk and weight can be obtained from such companies as Damart Thermawear and Helly-Hansen. They also provide inner boots that are better than two pairs of heavy woollen socks.

Chest-high trousers worn over knee-length boots with a hip-length lined parka (hooded) are comfortable and afford maximum protection from wind and rain. The best type of waterproof gear is, the author feels, made from PVC-coated nylon with a lining of nylon, the gap Terylene filled. Such gear is light, absolutely proof against wind-driven rain, and warm. It is also remarkably hard-wearing. At the present time no clothing tested has reached the standard of the Angler Superjacket, and trousers and one-piece suits made by the Manchester firm of Henri-Lloyd.

Jack Austin shows a surf-caught bass and his protective clothing: the waterproof trousers, worn over thighboots, are snugged in at the ankles with rubber bands to prevent waves surging up inside.

On boats, and whenever there is no need to wade, the best waterproof outfit is the parka and bib-type trousers, the latter coming over calf-length boots so that water is drained off completely – trousers that are too short funnel water into one's boots!

If wading is necessary in winter cold and rain, then the parka will need to be long enough to reach at least four inches below the tops of the thighboots.

In all cases, a parka with a detachable lining is a good idea, since it may be used without the lining in summer and with it in the cold weather.

There are some angling situations that demand the use of chest-high waders – for example surfcasting for bass or tope on Atlantic surf beaches in Ireland or West Wales. Avoid any plastic waders of this type, for they will tear and wear at the slightest provocation. Use proper rubber waders, which will still wear and tear but can be satisfactorily patched with a vulcanizing outfit.

Fishing the whitewater Irish surf beaches can be done in chest waders (or thighboots and overtrousers) to keep out the water . . .

A short (waist-length) jacket is useful with chest waders, and when it is necessary to wade into waves that reach near the top of the waders, a belt tight around it at upper waist level will stop water creeping in. The jacket, waterproof nylon or PVC of course, is worn always over the top of the waders.

So far as short Wellington-type boots are concerned, the best ones the author has yet used are Derriboots. They are made from soft plastic with laces to close the tops, and which are light, very comfortable, warm in winter, cool in summer and have a good sole for grip on many surfaces.

A good waterproof jacket (parka) and trousers will cost about £30; thighboots about £10, chest waders about £28; Derriboots about £7·50. Special, insulated underwear varies a lot in cost but is usually quite expensive.

Finally a word on hand protection. In winter the cold can be so intense on the coast or at sea that ex-posure of the hands, especially when it is snowing or raining as well, can make them useless. They become frozen and senseless. To avoid this it pays to rub some protective cream or grease on and then wear lined leather mittens, leaving the fingers free for baiting up, tying knots etc. Knitted woollen mittens are warm, but they can prove a terrible nuisance since hooks constantly catch in them and are difficult to extricate. A small hand towel can be very useful to wipe the hands dry after baiting up or unhooking a fish. Dry hands never feel so cold nor so painful as wet hands do.

Having now dealt with major items of tackle and the types of clothing suited to the various aspects of sportfishing at sea, it is necessary to discuss how to use the tackle within the many varied situations of shore and boat fishing. The other necessary items of gear, including gaffs, nets, and bits of terminal tackle, will be dealt with as they arise in the following chapters.

**Personal comfort when the water surges waist deep on the wild Atlantic surf beaches of south-west Ireland is the key to enjoyment. Here the angler fights a bass in a gathering storm over Mount Brandon on the Dingle Peninsula.**

# 3

# How to use the tackle: basic techniques

## Shore fishing

Surfcasting in its purest sense involves projecting the baited hook from an open beach into the breaking waves. To do this it is necessary to add sufficient weight to the tackle to carry the bait out and to hold it in position on the seabed.

In other parts of the world, notably on both American seaboards, surfcasting also involves casting heavy artificial lures, then reeling them in again. In the waters of north-western Europe and Britain, however, there are few fish that respond to such technique.

The amount of weight to be cast in surfcasting will vary, with a few exceptions, from as little as 2 oz (56·6 g) to as much as 6 oz (170 g). Rods 1 and 2 will be used; rod 1, it will be remembered, is for casting weights of 4–6 oz (113·3–170 g), the other rod for 2–3 oz (56·6–85 g).

Surfcasting varies considerably in that on the wild Atlantic storm beaches characteristic of South-west Ireland and West Wales one is often wading waist-deep in surf and casting 50–100 yd (45·7–91·4 m) into incoming rollers where the water, over hard sand, is only 2–3 ft (0·6–0·9 m) deep. The quarry will be mainly bass or tope, should the beach be one where they come close into the shoreline. If bass, the lighter rod will be used; the heavier outfit will be used for casting a big bait on a big hook for tope. Or the casting may be done from the dry shingle of a steep beach in Kent, East Anglia, or Dorset where the water is deeper – as deep as 50 ft (15 m) in places – and where the surface

This photograph catches the caster in the phase just as he begins to apply full power. The reel is a Mitchell 602 AP.

of the sea may be quite calm, though a strong tidal current may be travelling along the beach. In winter, the quarry will be cod, big cod running up to 30 lb (13·6 kg) perhaps; in the summer months the species sought may be tope, congers, various rays, flatfish, smooth-hounds, bass, and in a few areas, black bream.

These two different types of beach – the flat, sandy Atlantic storm beach with its lines of white surf rolling in, and the steep shingle beach running down to sandy or muddy ground – need very widely varying approaches from the angling viewpoint. In the first instance, the wild rolling surf is, perhaps paradoxically, very much less of a problem to the angler wishing to hold his baited tackle out there than are the usually less turbulent waves on the steep-to shingle beach. Atlantic storm beaches are generally easy to fish with a lead of 2–3 oz (56·6–85 g) since there is usually little lateral tidal flow to put pressure on the line and thus drag the lead and baited hook in a downtide arc towards dry land. On the other hand, steep beaches in the North Sea and English Channel usually have strong tidal flows and it is sometimes necessary to use 6 oz (170 g) of lead to hold out. The storm beach waves coming straight into the beach, run up the angler's slim line and give no such problems.

To project the baited hook and necessary lead to the chosen fishing position a long flexible rod is used as the prime instrument. When firmly held by the hands and swept through an arc at an accelerating speed, it acts as both a lever and a spring to catapult the tackle up and out. It has been found by trial and error that for all shore angling purposes (sporting angling, that is) the optimum rod length is about 11½ ft (3·5 m).

Although it is not really accurate to discuss the lead and terminal tackle being cast in terms of ballistics, since a bullet, for example, is in free flight while a fishing lead is tailed by the line (and slowed down by having to pull a baited hook, trace etc behind it, adding to air drag) there is some common ground. When a bullet is shot, the less time it spends in flight the less time gravity has to pull on it and drag it towards the ground.

In tournament casting, only a streamlined, bomb-shaped lead is on the end of the line and casters aiming for long distances try to cast the lead as fast as they can: 'tip speed' is a term often heard on the tournament field.

Both the bullet and the fishing lead go farther when projected at high speed but air resistance also acts against both. If two bullets are fired at the same velocity, but one is twice the weight of the other, the heavier bullet will travel farther because the energy it possesses makes it harder to stop. Similarly, if a lead of 3 oz (85 g) and another of 6 oz (170 g) are cast at the same speed and both are cast upwards at the same elevation, the heavier lead will travel much farther. Which is why tournament casting distances for 6 oz leads are considerably farther than for 2 oz (56·6 g) leads.

In actual fishing, however, it is not possible always to cast the streamlined lead at high speed, thus gaining long distances, because its weight and shape are hampered by its having to drag the wind-resistant bait and hook etc behind it. In general terms, a slim, streamlined bait – such as a firm lugworm, big ragworm or a strip of squid – will cast much farther than, for example, the tail half of a 12 oz (22 g) mackerel, a whole Californian squid or a crab 3 in (7·7 cm) across the shell. Also, the angler will find he needs to cast the bulky bait higher, to compensate for its lower speed, to get any reasonable distance.

There are numerous styles of casting and many produce excellent results. Some involve mounting the reel high on the butt of the rod, say 30 or even 40 in (76–101 cm) from the extremity, while others involve the reel being fitted only 10 in (25·3 cm) or so from the extremity. Some right handed casters control the reel with the right (upper) hand while others use the left hand to control the reel at the bottom of the handle. Most casting is done from a position facing the sea, but one or two famous casters on the East Coast of England attain record distances casting with their backs to the sea! The important point is to be able to consistently put the lead and bait where it is required, not only long or short distances out but also accurate laterally. For this reason the writer does not favour the back-to-the-sea style; not forgetting that on a storm beach an incoming wave can hit the caster in the back and tumble him over and into trouble.

For many reasons the free-spool multiplier is the author's recommendation for surfcasting: it is not difficult to use once the basics are understood and a multiplier is a better and more reliable reel on which to play big fish; it also casts farther than a fixed-spool reel for most people. However, some anglers will never be competent with a multiplier and others favour a fixed-spool reel, and, provided a really good, strong model is chosen, such reels will do the job reasonably well.

Casting with the multiplier is done by first putting the spool into the free position by means of a button or lever, then, keeping the thumb of the top hand (with the reel mounted as the author suggests, about 23–30 in (58·4–76 cm) above the butt extremity), the rod is swung to the right side (for a right-handed caster) and back, the tip pointing either immediately behind the caster or even slightly to his left side (when facing the sea). It is then brought forward, round and up, the right hand pushing and the left hand (for a right-handed caster) pulling the butt down. The action is smooth but has an increasing speed as the moment of release comes, at which point the thumb is lifted from the spool and the rod whips over to project the lead and tackle up and out. The light spool of the reel has line pulled from it and if there is any tendency for the spool to revolve faster than line is being pulled off, a light dab with the thumb on the left side of the spool – not on the line, since that will be damaged by friction–

induced heat, as well as burning the ball of the thumb – will slow it down to the correct speed.

Any casting movement that involves both hands being above the head when holding the rod at the start of the cast is wrong and quite useless. Not only the arms but the shoulders, trunk and legs are used to put the correct smooth effort into a casting movement. Short, quick movements are incorrect and can never attain adequate distances for surfcasting.

It is important that the reel spool is loaded to within about $\frac{1}{16}$ in (1·5 mm) with relatively thin line so that the pull of the flying lead is on the periphery of the spool flanges, at which point less pull is needed to make the spool revolve than at a lower point. Also, each turn of the spool yields more line when it is loaded than it does when the coils become smaller as the spool empties. Thin line remains higher on the spool for longer than does thick line, of course, which is another good reason for using thin line.

Some multipliers have devices that wind the line back on to the spool evenly, others do not, and the angler must spread the line across the spool using either the ball of his thumb or by allowing the line to run through his thumb and forefinger. Closely wound coils are a further help in long, smooth casts without over-runs, since each coil that comes off the spool is roughly the same size. Crosswinding produces coils of unequal size and they can cause trouble.

Level-wind mechanisms on the Ambassadeur range work perfectly and there is no advantage in removing them, as some anglers do, in the hope of increasing casting range by reducing a small amount of gear friction. The advantages of having the line rewound in close turns far outweigh any small amount of friction, and when fishing after dark, or in the excitement of playing a big fish, it is nice to be able to forget the line coming onto the reel and concentrate on the fishing.

Multipliers should be kept scrupulously clean and lightly oiled so that they run smoothly. The best of them have spindles ground and polished to a mirror finish that run in well fitted brass or phosphor bronze bearings or in ball races. If the steel spindles on any reel are not really smooth they should be polished with 400 mesh silicon carbide paper, then fine steel wool, revolving the spindle in a folded piece of paper (abrasive) or pad of steel wool. Such treatment often works wonders. Use only fine machine oil on the bearings and a molybdenum disulphide grease on the gear teeth. Protect the reel always after use, washing (freshwater of course) then drying it, followed by a spray of WD40 or similar product.

Fixed-spool reels work quite differently from the multiplier. The drum of the latter revolves to yield line during the cast – and when the line is being rewound – while the drum or spool of the fixed-spool reel remains stationary during the cast and during the recovery: the only time the spool revolves is when a big fish pulls against the pressure of the drag or braking system.

So, line comes off the front of the spool in coils, and as the level of the line falls in the spool, the coils have to climb over the front of the spool, increasingly rubbing harder on the top of the lip. Again, fine line helps to minimise this friction – quite apart from doing the same to the friction through the rings of the rod – by remaining at a higher level for a longer period.

When the tackle has come to rest on the seabed, the pick-up arm is activated on most fixed-spool reels by a forward turn of the handle. In actual fact there is really no need for an automatic full bale pick-up on reels used for surfcasting, and the best American reels have simply a wide roller-bearing in a hook-type affair into which the line is placed by hand after the cast. This set-up is much stronger than a bale arm.

In surf fishing the reel has to take a few knocks and at one time or another some sand is going to get into the works. When this happens wash it out thoroughly in the sea, then wash the whole reel, inside and out, in warm freshwater when you get home. Oil it when all is dry.

Casting with a fixed-spool reel and 2–3 oz (56·6–85 g) of lead is fairly simple: the reel is mounted high up the rod handle, and the reel stand is held between the middle and index fingers of the upper hand, the index hooking the line where it comes off the spool and holding it firmly. In the lighter freshwater situation the forefinger often holds the line against the lip of the spool, but when casting 2 oz (56·6 g) or so, the pressure is too great and the line will slip from under the finger. In fact, there is some difficulty in holding the line under the crooked forefinger when casting with power for long range with leads of 5 oz (141·7 g) or more. Some anglers use a leather finger-stall to help, which also avoids soreness caused by the line whipping off the pad of the finger. There is also a device on the market called a Thumbutton which is whipped tightly to the rod at a point level with the reel spool but on the opposite side of the rod. The line is caught between two faces and held there by thumb pressure on a button. The thumb pressure is eased at the point of maximum velocity in the cast and the line is released perfectly, even being held when punching hard with a lead of 6 oz (170 g).

Playing a fish with a fixed-spool reel is done in the same way as with a multiplier: the clutch is preset to the strain that will bend the rod sufficiently but will slip at a pressure less than the test of the line being used. Any additional strain is put on the fish by pressing the forefinger of the hand holding the rod or the thumb or forefinger of the reeling hand against the lip of the spool's front.

Fixed-spool reels for heavy fishing must have an anti-reverse mechanism which prevents the handle and flyer from being pulled round by a fish taking line from the spool when the drag is hard on. This should always be in operation, even when the rod is being fished in a rest.

Because line is pulled off a fixed-spool reel round the pick-up quite severe friction is in operation at the point of contact with the line. It is therefore of vital importance, as stressed in previous pages, that the line passes over a roller or bollard which turns very freely, working like the pulley on the top of a crane. Keep the bollard lubricated regularly with a little light machine oil or a dry lubricant such as molybdenum disulphide.

While there are many advantages in using fine lines for shore fishing (and boat fishing, of course) the light test lines will not take the shock of a cast with a heavy lead when seeking maximum range. It is possible to cast a 2 oz (56·6 g) lead 80 yd (73·1 m) or so on the bass rod using 12 lb (5·4 kg) test line, but it must be done smoothly. If longer ranges are necessary – and *always* when using 15 lb (6·8 kg) main line with leads of 4 oz (113·3 g) or more on the big casting rod – it is essential to join a casting leader to the main line.

This casting leader is a length of nylon of a stronger test than the main line which is long enough to pass from the reel through the rod rings with about 8 ft (2·4 m) hanging from the tip ring, and make at least three turns round the spool of the reel. Thus the leader takes the shock of casting, and once the leader has passed through the rings the finer line is dragged behind it. Leaders are also useful for protecting the fragile reel line from seabed abrasion and for dragging fish by brute force ashore through heavy surf – in which case the leader should be extended to about 12 yd (10·9 m).

Joining the leader to the reel line demands a smooth knot and many different knots are used. The main problem is that of getting the turns of heavy nylon to snug down with the turns of the lighter, more flexible nylon. For example, in cod or tope shore fishing with line of approximately 15 lb (6·8 kg) test the leader will need to be about 35 lb (15·8 kg) test when casting 5–6 oz (141·7–170 g) leads 130 yd (118 m) or more. Some anglers who can really zip a 6 oz lead 150 yd (137 m) use 50 lb (22·6 kg) leaders! For 12 lb (5·4 kg) test line or thereabouts and 2–3 oz (56·6–85 kg) leads, a 20 lb (9 kg) leader will permit casting to ranges of 100 yd (90 m).

The author has always used a blood knot to join leaders to reel lines and has never had any reason to change. It is, however, very important to make about six turns round the heavy material with the light, and only three turns round the light with the heavy. As always, moisten the turns with saliva before pulling up, and help the coils of the heavy leader to bed down by pulling on the end of the leader nylon as the knot is tightened up, by pulling the main line and leader firmly apart.

Top right: Forming the blood knot to connect a thin reel line to a heavy casting leader. Approximately six turns are made with the reel-line round the leader, and only about three turns round the reel line with the heavy leader. This, when moistened with saliva, may be drawn up into a fairly neat knot . . .

. . . and when the ends have been trimmed off flush with the coils of the knot the junction passes easily through the rod rings. As it is used the ends will snug down and bed the coils even more.

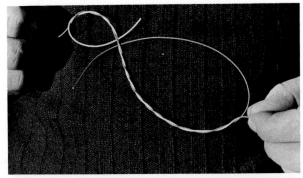

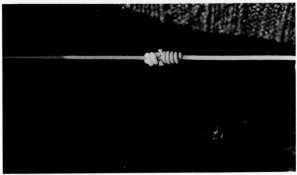

Another reliable knot is as follows. Tie an overhand knot in the end of the leader line, but do not pull it up tight. Now pass the end of the reel line into the front of the overhand knot and make six turns loosely round the leader material with the reel line. Holding the leader line in the right hand (if you are right handed) take the reel line back and form a loop, lying the free end along the leader line. Now, hold all firmly and whip over the free end of the reel line with the reel line loop, and as you do so the turns you originally made will unroll to leave you with a whipping knot of fine line round the leader line. Tighten by pulling on both ends of the reel line, then pull the whipping knot hard up to the overhand knot and tighten the overhand knot in the leader line firmly before trimming all ends flush.

Below (and continued next column): Alternative line-to-leader junction. An overhand knot is tied near the end of the leader material and the reel line passed through before the overhand knot is tightened. Then the reel line is taken about six times round the leader and the end turned back . . .

The end is then made into a circle, the coils made unwound again by forming a whipping knot round the leader with the reel line, and the turns held by the finger of one hand while the whipping is snugged down by pulling alternately on the reel line at both sides. Then the knot is pulled up against the overhand knot.

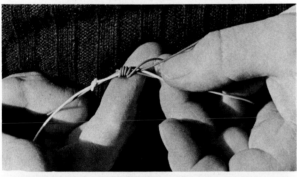

This knot is very popular with tournament casters and is a little less bulky than the bastardised blood knot. They appear to be equally as good and it is a matter of choice as to which of them one uses.

The subject of knots brings us to terminal tackle rigs, of which sea anglers in the UK use scores. However, there is need for only two basic rigs for proper surfcasting and shore fishing on the bottom in general: the fixed nylon paternoster and the running paternoster.

Prime considerations for choice of terminal rigs for

A fixed nylon paternoster for shore casting. Note that the distance between hook and loops is less than it is between loops and the lead. This ensures a clean flight, with the lead leading the air-resistant bait.

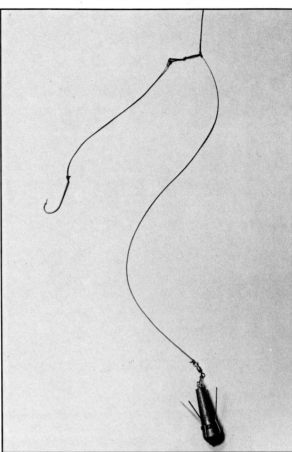

A more refined fixed paternoster. With the swivel running between two stop-knots and the pieces of plastic tube (or small beads) snood twisting is avoided.

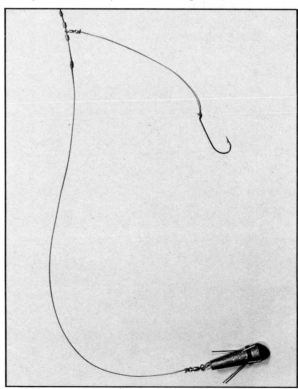

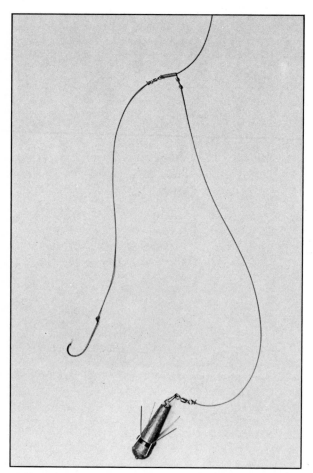

The running paternoster. Note once again that the length of line to the lead is more than the length of the hook trace, which gives a smooth flight and prevents tangling.

shore fishing are that they should cast well and present the bait properly without any tendency to tangle. This means that the lead weight, whenever possible, must be at the end of the line when the tackle is suspended from the rod tip and must lead the tackle in flight.

The fixed nylon paternoster serves perfectly well when it is necessary to have the gear in a state that will cast a long way and remain tangle-free while it is fishing. This applies in situations where fish sought are unlikely to be put off, or are able to drop the baited hook if they do become alarmed by any tension in the nylon linking them to the main line and the anchored lead. This rig is fine for cod, for bass in wild surf, and for some flounder fishing. The running version is excellent for quieter waters where the fish takes the bait, swims away with it and is brought up might have: for bass among the rocks in shallow water or in estuaries, for conger or tope from the shore, and for smooth-hounds. The fixed version can have a short snood or hook link – as little as 4 in (10 cm) – or a long one – as long as 6 ft (1·8 m). If the hook is kept sharp – as all hooks should be – the fish takes the bait, swims away with it and is brought up suddenly by the anchored lead. The point of the hook

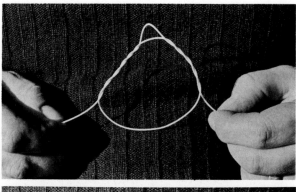

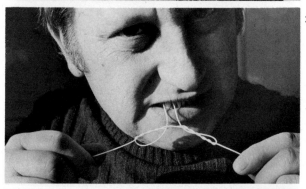

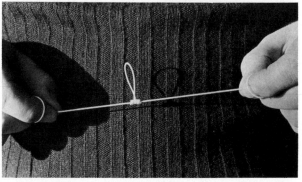

1. Making a blood loop for a paternoster begins with a circle formed by twisting the line around itself (without using an end) or by using an end and tying six overhand knots, one after the other. A gap is then made in the centre of the twists. . . .

2. . . . and the untwisted side of the circle pushed through . . .

3. . . . at which time one's teeth come into play to hold the end of the loop – use the canine inside the loop, do not bite the nylon – while the two ends are pulled to tighten the knot. Keep the loop quite small.

4. A small, neat blood loop for the hook trace loop.

catches in the skin of the mouth, the fish panics, lunges away, and the hook sinks deeper. The angler sees the rod tip movement or feels the pull on the line if he is holding the rod, and pulls home the barb.

However, there are times when fish are not quite so ready to be fooled. A bass hunting at leisure among the weedy rocks for crabs and small fish, for example, will often inspect a bait for a while before gently picking it up and tasting and feeling it. Should the fish at this stage feel any untoward resistance it is likely to drop the bait. But with the running paternoster the hook link may be pulled freely through the eye of the swivel for several feet, depending on the slackness of the line from lead to rod tip, and the fish is likely to swallow the bait as it begins to move away. The signal of the bite is seen or felt and the strike made in the normal way. Not only bass but tope, smooth-hounds, rays and conger are usually best attacked with the running paternoster.

Many anglers no doubt use a normal running leger, the lead on a link-swivel or (worse) on a Clements boom or a Kilmore clip, and are wondering why the running paternoster is being praised while the straight leger, with the lead running directly on the main line and not on a dropper lead link, is being ignored. Well, the reason is that the running paternoster not only casts with the lead in front of the rest of the rig, but it also permits the fish more freedom to take the bait gently. Small swivels are less obvious than Clements

booms and the like; they are also much cheaper!

Simplicity is the key to good terminal tackle. If something does not do a useful job on the rig, then it should not be used.

With the fixed nylon paternoster the length of snood is usually best kept to less than 1 ft (30·48 cm) where the distance between its point of attachment on the standing part of the line is about 2 ft; only rarely is it necessary to change this proportion. And generally speaking, similar proportions of hook link and lead link serve well with the running version.

There are many leads made for surf fishing, and most of them are unnecessary. There is no good reason nowadays to use any shape other than the elongated pear or bomb shape, with free-swinging anchor wires or without. If the water being fished is not too boisterous the ordinary bomb lead will be fine, as it will if you want to allow the tackle slowly to rove about the seabed. If, however, you want to cast far and hold the bait in one position then use an anchored lead known as a breakaway lead.

This lead has been largely instrumental in helping British sea anglers who wish to use lighter tackle to do so, because its adjustable anchor wires collapse at a light pull and trail inoperative behind as the lead is wound in along the bottom. The old type of wired lead has its wires set at a right angle to the lead's axis, moulded in, so that they have to be pulled from the seabed by brute force, and once pulled free often hook in

The final design of the Breakaway lead in the casting position. The swivelling anchor wires clip into slots in the plastic collar. These may be adjusted by bending.

A pull on the line springs the anchors at the predetermined pull and the lead may be recovered without the wires catching on the seabed.

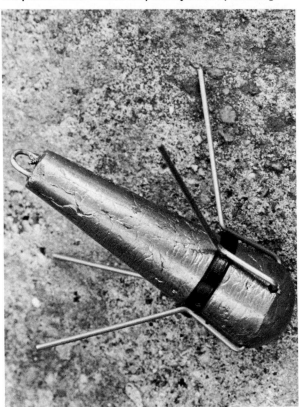

again on the way in. These leads, which, incredibly, many anglers still use, demand heavy lines and strong rods.

The breakaway or break-out lead was perfected by two *Angling* Magazine contributors, Ian Gillespie and Nigel Forrest, following a campaign by that publication for more sporting tackle in the sea. Many weird systems were produced by readers and contributors, including Don Neish, the well known caster and tackle shop owner, finally culminating in two basic types. Both have anchor wires swinging freely through the nose, but on one type the wires are held in the anchoring position by an elastic band; the other has them held by tension in the wires pressing them into slits in a nylon collar fitted round the lead, or by beads on the wire which fit into recesses moulded in the lead.

No sporting shore angler should be without such leads of one type or the other. All work extremely well.

So, on an Atlantic surf beach, for bass or whatever, the fixed nylon paternoster with a 2–3 oz (56·6–85 g) breakaway lead is cast out, the hook carrying lug, razorfish or clam, and the slack line taken up. The light rod is held and bites are felt for by hand, through the rod or through the line.

If it's tope from the shore, or big stingrays, maybe,

A variation of the running paternoster, this time for shore fishing for tope, conger, common skate and other 'toothy critturs'. The hook trace may be quickly detached from the link-swivel and a new one fitted.

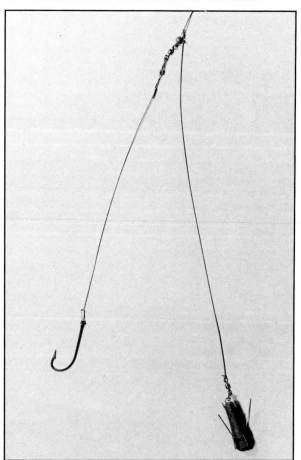

then the heavier rod might be used. For tope or conger the running paternoster rig is made up with a wire trace connecting the hook to the link swivel at the end of the casting leader. The bait, such as mackerel or small pouting is cast way out, the breakaway lead pulled into the bottom, and the rod set up on a rest so that its tip is high. The reel is set so that a taking fish can pull line off against a slight check and so give audible warning as well as the visual one of the rod tip's movements.

Again, when fishing among rocky ground, for bass or conger, the running paternoster is used. For bass the rod is held so that bites of a shy nature may be detected and the correct action taken; for conger the rod is rested, as for tope or rays.

These methods are basic and are at present only being touched upon. They will be dealt with again later.

Another shore fishing situation is the pier, stone breakwater, bridge, rocky promontory or similar seaward projection. Strangely, though it would seem that such places would offer better chances of good fishing than the shoreline itself, such is seldom the case. Such projections are usually in areas of high population or with industry, so that pollution and disturbance weigh against the right habitat for good fish. However, some of the above mentioned spots do produce good fishing for cod, bass, rays, mullet, mackerel, conger, flounders, shads and others on our sporting list. One of the big advantages of a good pier or projection is that not only can legering be tried but float fishing, spinning and driftlining as well.

Before going on to deal briefly with the basics of float fishing, spinning and driftlining, it must be pointed out that no sporting angler should venture on

A rectangular dropnet with a tubular alloy frame and deep, strong net of nylon cord. Rectangular nets do not roll along rocks and breakwaters when a fish is being guided into the rim.

to any projection high off the water without carrying a big dropnet which can be lowered to the water to lift fish up. With fish weighing over 30 lb (13·6 kg) (congers for instance), a gaff on several screw-connected sweep's canes or similar, sufficient to reach the water at the lowest time of the tide, should be carried.

For float-fishing from some form of projection, the fixed-spool reel is generally first choice since casting long distances with reasonably light end tackle is easy. However, should there be no need to cast, just lower the tackle down to the water and allow it to wash around the piles of the pier, by the weedy walls of the breakwater or down the side of the rivermouth shorings, then a centrepin reel will do the job.

Sliding floats will be called for at times to fish at depths much more than the length of the rod, and these may be of balsa wood, plastic moulded, or roughly made from odd pieces of polystyrene to which is tied a small swivel through which the line can run. Sliding floats with holes lengthwise through their centres are favoured, but those with eyes fitted top and bottom are all right too. It is cheaper to make such floats at home from balsa wood of about 1 in (2·54 cm) square. This is cut into suitable lengths and drilled centrally lengthwise to take a plastic tube about $\frac{1}{8}$ in (3 mm) in diameter which is glued in. The float can be roughly shaped by rasp or file, then finished with varying grades of glasspaper. Several coats of paint must be put on to waterproof the body and the top is best painted with fluorescent orange over a white base.

A slim torpedo shape seems to work best and offers less resistance to a taking fish. Make or buy a selection of floats that will support lead bullets or barrel leads of $\frac{1}{4}$–1 oz (7–28 g). There are a number of ways to stop the float on the line at the required depth and yet still permit the stop to travel from the reel and through the rings of the rod without any impediment. But perhaps the best is a length of elastic band about $\frac{3}{8}$ in (1 cm) tied into the line at the selected point with a clove hitch or similar knot that will pull out once the elastic is removed.

Freelining is simply dropping a baited hook into the water from the end of a pier or other projection and letting it waft about in the surges below or be taken away by the tide. A very small lead may be used to help control the bait but it is not sufficient to cause it to sink quickly to the bottom. This can be very effective on a pier for bass and pollack, bites being felt by holding the line below the butt ring of the rod.

Spinning can be practised from open beaches as well as from rocky promontories, piers etc, but it seldom works well in water less than about 5 ft (1·5 m) deep, and 15 ft (4·5 m) is usually better. Species that may be taken this way include bass, mackerel, garfish, shad, pollack, coalfish and big ballan wrasse.

Open steep-to shingle beaches are usually better than sandy shallow beaches, and rocky coasts are better than both. Estuaries also provide good opportunities for spinning.

Sometimes a heavy spoon, such as a 1 oz (28 g)

Toby, 1 oz Koster, big German Sprat (Condor spoon) or an artificial sand-eel (Red Gill) kept down by up to 2 oz (57 g) of lead – the eel, that is – is necessary to get both range and depth. At other times the salmon-type rod and 8–12 lb (3·6–5·4 kg) test line necessary for this work can be changed for the single-handed rod and baits weighing only $\frac{1}{2}$ oz (15 g), which may be cast adequate distances with the fixed-spool reel and line of about 5 lb (2·6 kg) test. Whenever this is possible the real meaning of sportfishing is apparent, especially when a 5 lb (2·6 kg) bass, a $1\frac{1}{2}$ lb (0·6 kg) mackerel or a 6 lb (2·7 kg) pollack grabs the lure.

Last of the shore techniques to be mentioned is fly fishing – which is also very useful when in a small boat, or an uncluttered large one. It will be dealt with in depth in chapter 11. The only point to note at this stage is that fly fishing on this side of the Atlantic is very little done (in saltwater) and it is usually only successful in very clear water conditions and from June to mid-October.

# Boat fishing

Fishing from a boat with sporting tackle may be done in various ways, some of them are very similar to the shore fishing techniques: for example, legering a bait on the bottom from an anchored boat, spinning, fly fishing, driftlining, float fishing. In addition there are some other ways to show the bait or lure to the fish which include trolling a lure or natural bait (fish) behind a moving boat, drifting with the wind or tide (or both, which is not so good) with the baits either being worked on sandy bottoms, jigged over rocks or wrecks (lures etc) or with fish baits on float tackle, usually for sharks and tope.

Boat fishing tactics for the light tackle angler can be extremely interesting and exciting, since there is plenty of opportunity for experiment. Yet the average sea angler, who uses cumbersome tackle, drops a vast hunk of lead and indifferent bait over the side of some evil smelling, unsuitable hulk on a place as barren of fish as the moon's face, leaving it there for crabs to munch while the lazy boatman settles down for a snooze.

The knots used for making up shore tackle are also used for boat fishing, but there are one or two other knots and attachments which must be adopted since the pressures on the sporting gear when fighting big fish from a boat are sustained and the gear must be 100 per cent reliable.

Certainly one of the most reliable knots used by sportfishers (although it is strictly a hitch rather than a knot) is the Bimini hitch, 20-times-around knot, Bimini twist or hangman's jam. It may be used in monofilament nylon or braided Dacron or Terylene lines, being easier to tie in the latter. Not only does the Bimini produce a super-strong end loop, to which many types of terminal rig can be attached, but it also produces the doubled line used when after big fish,

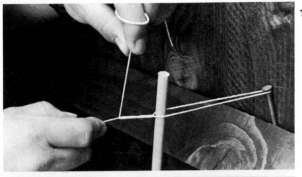

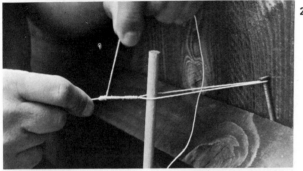

1, 2. One way of forming a Bimini twist, hitch or twenty-times-around knot with a short loop. There should be 20 turns made (1) before the turns are made back to the starting point (2).

3, 4. When the original turns have been covered, always keeping plenty of tension on the whole job, a hitch is taken round one side of the loop which has been formed (photo 4).

5, 6. When the first hitch has been tightened, another one is made round the opposite side of the loop. These lock all the turns, but a final knot is made to prevent the last hitch from coming undone.

7. The completed Bimini. It is not a knot since no part is holding any other in the actual twists, only the twists are locked by the final hitches. This produces almost one hundred per cent of the line's full test. For making a long loop for the doubled line for shark fishing, a helper is needed to take the place of the nail and wooden dowel.

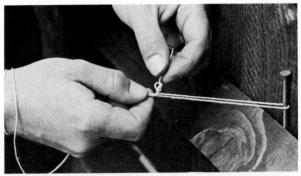

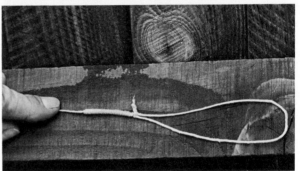

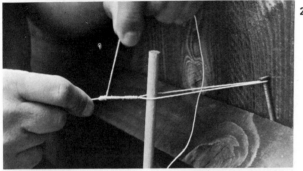

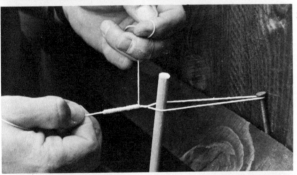

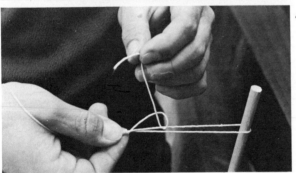

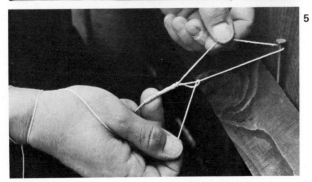

such as sharks. The double portion is usually about 15 ft (4·5 m) long so that it can resist abrasion on the fish better than single line, and it may also be used by the boatman or a fellow angler to haul the beaten fish to the side of the boat for gaffing or tailing.

For producing Biminis with short loops one can make and use an ingenious little tool invented by an angler named Brian Barber and first shown to the angling public in the March 1976 issue of *Angling* magazine. Many anglers have since acclaimed it as a godsend.

Whenever what the Americans call 'toothy critturs' are the quarry, it is necessary to include in the tackle something which prevents the fish biting or wearing through the line above the hook, or, in the case of sharks, prevents the rough hide of the fish rubbing through the line during a prolonged battle.

The usual way of combating fish with sharp, powerful teeth is to use a wire trace to connect the

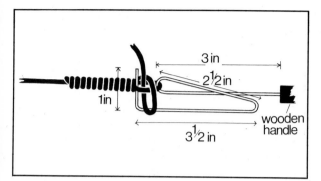

**Bimini tyer.**

hook (or lure) to the rest of the line, usually via a link swivel. There are many types of wire used for traces, including solid stainless steel piano wire, twisted multistrand wire, the same but covered with a nylon jacket, and braided multistrand. While the piano wire is much used in tropical and subtropical waters for trolling for gamefish, it is not much favoured on this side of the Atlantic. Here few species in the cold or temperate waters will react to a trolled bait or lure – species, that is, which demand heavy wire traces.

It is suggested that only twisted multistrand trace wire is used. If nylon-covered wire is used there is a risk of the fish's teeth wearing a cut through the nylon by its teeth continually sawing over one small part of the wire, which will often shear. Without a covering the wire is sufficiently smooth and hard to resist this happening, though once in a while a fish will bite through even 300 lb (136 kg) test wire!

Trace wire for the fish and fishing described in this book from 40 lb (18·1 kg) test to 300 lb (136 kg) test is required (Berkley's is very reliable). The 300 lb material is only used for the last 18 in (45 cm) of shark traces (the hook link) to prevent the big fish from biting through; wire of about 175 lb (79·3 kg) test may be used for the rest of a shark trace. It is not strength with which one is concerned here, simply something bite-proof and wear-proof; and even 300 lb wire is only about 1½ mm thick.

To join the twisted wire securely to hooks, swivels and other rings, and to form loops, it is necessary to have a pair of crimping pliers, some metal sleeves and some wire cutters. Again, Berkley produce excellent crimping pliers and the brass or silvery sleeves in the correct sizes for each diameter of wire.

1. Making a wire trace involves first threading a metal ferrule on, passing the end back to form a loop, then bending the end again and pulling it back into the ferrule . . .

2. . . . crimping pliers crush the ferrule tightly to the wire.

3. Crimp firmly and evenly.

4. The finished loop.

For attaching hook to wire, pass a ferrule up the wire, thread on hook and tie two overhand knots before pushing the wire through the ferrule again. Tuck it back, then crimp firmly.

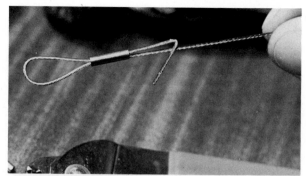
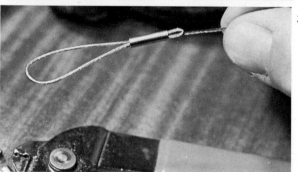

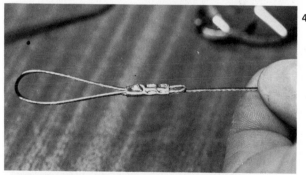

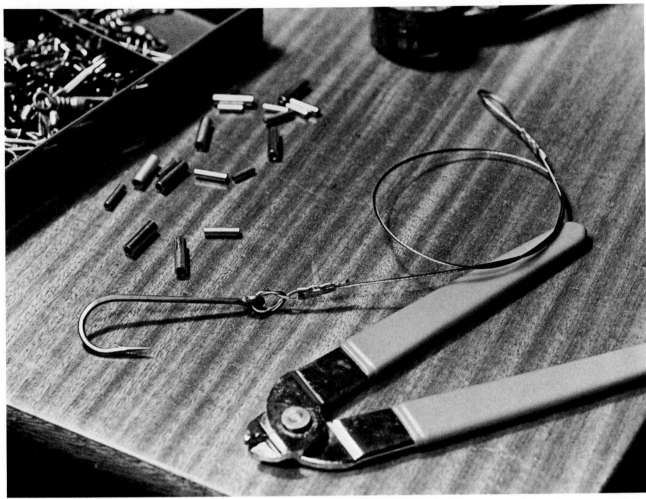

The finished trace with the equipment necessary to make it. Pincers make good wire cutters . . .

Another very useful tool for the light tackle boat angler is a pair of those special pliers that incorporate wire cutter, hook bender and straightener. It is made by the Sargent company of Newhaven, Connecticut, USA and no self-respecting game-boat skipper or mate would be seen dead without one! Built on the powerful double-hinge principle, this tool is rarely found in a tackle shop on this side of the Atlantic.

It will be seen in the photographs that the ends of all wire trace joints are doubled over, then pushed back into the sleeves before crimping so there is no sharp end projecting. This not only stops water-borne debris catching on the trace, but it avoids very nasty cuts on one's hands when the trace is being used to haul a big fish, like a tope or shark, to the waiting tailer or gaff.

. . . but this little tool made by the Sargent company of Newhaven, Connecticut, USA, is even better and can do most of the other work an angler has to do in making up tackle.

# Accessories

On the shore it is not necessary to carry a vast box or bag and a mountain of gear weighing some 20 lb (9 kg), as so many sea anglers do. Of course, if the trip is an extended one and hundreds of miles from home, then a lot of gear may have to be put into the car just in case. However on any actual fishing session ashore, even when fishing part of a tide for (say) tope, and another part for bass, if the two reels and other bits and pieces cannot be carried in a small haversack and weigh less than about 6 lb (2·7 kg), you are taking too much gear!

Apart from a small compartment box containing a few spare link swivels, swivels, hooks, a file or flat stone for sharpening hooks, a reel of elasticated thread (for tying on baits to the hook), one needs a sharp lock-blade knife or sheath knife (no more than a 5 in (12·6 cm) blade), spools of nylon for traces and leaders, spare wire traces, spare leads and, if fishing at night, a small headlamp or torch. A gaff or tailer and a net has sometimes to be considered.

On a boat more gear has to be carried and there is little doubt that a proper box of tough plastic with cantilever trays and drawers helps make life easier by storing everything one is likely to need, even on an extended trip a long way from home. This means, of

Good knives must be of stainless steel and keep a sharp edge. The slim knife is by Normark, the lock-blade by CK and the multi-tool knife is by Victorinox.

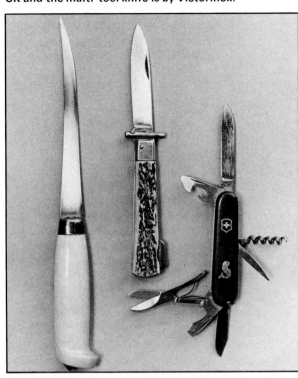

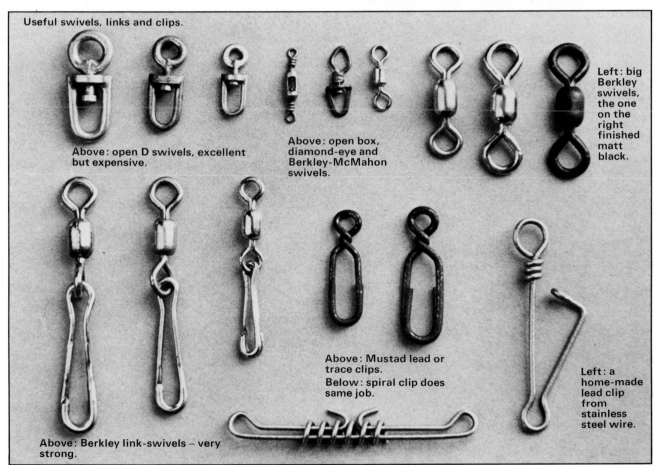

Useful swivels, links and clips.

Above: open D swivels, excellent but expensive.

Above: open box, diamond-eye and Berkley-McMahon swivels.

Left: big Berkley swivels, the one on the right finished matt black.

Above: Berkley link-swivels – very strong.

Above: Mustad lead or trace clips.
Below: spiral clip does same job.

Left: a home-made lead clip from stainless steel wire.

course, carrying one or two tools for making up traces, repairing reels, even spare rings for rods and the thread and quick-drying varnish with which to make a temporary but strong job.

The best of the plastic tackle boxes for boat anglers is the Plano company's range, especially those made from ABS and polypropylene, which are tough enough to withstand the rough and tumble of offshore sea angling. There are others, but many have been found lacking, with weaknesses in the basic material or the locks, hinges and handle attachments – a box that accidentally opens and spills several reels and all a man's gear into the gap between boat and quay is calculated to bring even the mildest person to the point of derangement and is no bargain at all!

Perhaps at this stage the author should state that in mentioning brand names he is not favouring any one company but is stating his personal preferences after many years of using and field-testing a great deal of fishing tackle and accessories. He has no connection, in any financial way, with any maker of tackle or accessories.

So, the following items should go into this big tackle box and always be kept there and any losses made good, so that at all times there are enough items to permit one to go fishing for just about any fish that swims in British waters: swivels and link swivels, sizes 10 to 4/0; hooks, sizes 2 to 10/0; crimping sleeves, crimping pliers, wire cutters; wire; sharp lock-blade or sheath knife; butt pad (for cushioning the rod butt in the stomach when fighting big fish); a set of files and flat sharpening stone; running booms, plastic beads (in case that swivels will not stop a running tackle above the hook); spools of spare lines for making up traces etc; elasticated cotton for tying baits firmly to hooks; mackerel feathers for catching bait for bigger fish, Red Gill eels in several colours, including red, blue and black; a plastic box of bomb-shaped leads from $\frac{1}{2}$–2 oz; a box of heavy spoons (Toby, Koster, Condor); a plastic bottle of reel oil; a coil of commercial longline nylon (about 100 lb (45·3 kg) test); floats and at least two dozen balloons (for shark floats); spare tip rings, intermediate rings; whipping thread and fast-drying varnish; fast-curing epoxy-resin adhesive (all for emergency repairs at sea); spare reel clamps, reel spanners, some reel spares (spools, nuts, washers and screws); polarised spectacles; baiting needles (6 in and 10 in) (15·24 and 25·3 cm) and a small box containing some aspirin or similar, antiseptic plasters, and a tube of sunburn cream.

In addition, you will pack your reels into the main compartment of the box, plus any afterthoughts you may have for any specific trip. Any heavy leads in the range 4 oz–3 lb (113·3 g–1·3 kg) should be carried separately in a small canvas drawstring bag.

One of the author's favourite items, which goes on every fishing trip, freshwater or saltwater, is a Victorinox Swiss anglers' knife with superb stainless steel blades, screwdrivers, scissors, reamer, can opener, corkscrew, bottle opener, tweezers and toothpick. It is invaluable at times.

# 4
# Baits: natural and artificial

Bait collecting is a fascinating and educational pursuit. Here the target is a dozen or so soft and peeler crabs, for bass fishing in the same location when the tide floods in.

Without good, fresh and suitable bait, a very skilled angler with the best tackle, a good boat and a knowledgeable skipper over a good mark can draw a blank; with good bait and indifferent gear another angler could succeed – at least in getting fish to take his baited hook. The skill to beat them is another ball-game, as the Americans say. And it's exactly the same when shore fishing.

Bait may be bought, dug, netted, collected; some is easy to come by, some is only gained by either a great deal of very hard work or paying a lot of money for somebody else, a professional digger or collector, to do the work.

Most of the baits used by boat anglers are fish or fishlike: mackerel, herrings, sand-eels, whiting, pouting, pollack, coalfish, pilchards and the tentacled cephalopods, cuttlefish, squid and octopus. All these may be used whole, as fillets, or cut into strips. If used whole, the most likely fish baits selected would be small pollack, coalfish, whiting, mackerel or herring, weighing between ½–1 lb (226–453 g).

Shore anglers also use fish baits, whole or in strips or chunks, for the larger predators, like conger, tope, pollack, bass, rays and even common skate. But most baits used by shore anglers are either dug or netted or picked up. They include marine worms, shellfish (such as razorfish, piddocks, cockles, clams, and mussels), various kinds of crabs, prawns, shrimps and small fish from among the rock-pools, like blennies, rockling and gunnel (butterfish).

Mackerel used for bait – they are also used minced-up as a smelly, oily attractor when shark fishing – may be caught on traces of feathers; feathers will also produce the big sand-eel (greater launce) at times on off-shore marks. The feathers are usually white cockerel

hackles whipped to the eye or spade end of the shank of a long shanked stainless steel or cadmium plated hook, approximate size 1/0, and set about 15 in (38 cm) apart on short snoods. A lead of suitable weight – 4 oz to 1 lb (113·3–453 g) – is used on the end of the feather trace to search the water with a sink-and-lift motion, from near bottom to just subsurface.

Whiting should be used very fresh. They, too, may sometimes be feathered when the shoals are thick, but any caught on bait can be transferred to the big hook during a mixed fishing session.

Occasionally squid and cuttlefish may be caught on lumps of fish when they follow up the bait to the boat. Sometimes they get hooked, but the best way is to quickly put a net into the water behind them and scoop them up as the bait is lifted out. They will squirt their ink in alarm at this stage, so keep them in the water, trapped against the boat's hull, until the ink has stopped squirting!

**Superb baits: a square of razorfish enclosing some prime lugworms. For cod and bass these are most reliable when fished on to sand.**

Top: A straight, narrow blade with a sharp edge is used for mature lugworms in firm sand or sand/mud mixtures. The spade will cut across the cast and expose the burrow.

The digger has seen the worm's tail, taken a slice of sand from behind it to expose the firm body, and is now feeling for it with his finger. Pulling the worm's sand-filled tail instead of gripping the firm body will cause the tail to break off.

Centre: Success! Up comes a juicy lugworm. The worm is squeezed on to the sand to kill and gut it. This way the worm remains in good condition for several days if wrapped separately in newspaper.

Right: Mature black lugworms like these are a lot of effort to dig and must be carefully treated to remain in firm, fresh condition for several days, if necessary. Place them in newspaper and roll up the paper so each worm is kept separated from any other.

Sand-eels are generally netted in fine seines in estuaries, or raked from the soft sand as the water leaves the shoreline, using a blunt instrument rather like a bill-hook, called a vingler. Sand-eels are very popular as bait in Devon and Cornwall, where they thrive. They are used alive or dead, but must be fresh.

Most fish baits go soft and smelly once they are dead, and quite apart from the fact that most large predatory fish generally prefer fresh fish they become difficult to retain on the hook if not fresh. This is a problem more of the shore angler, who has to cast his bait, while the boat man usually simply lowers his gently over the side.

Close-up of the vingler and the sand-eel it has caught.

Wading in a shallow Cornish estuary Mike Osborne uses a vingler to scrape for sand-eels. The flat, blunt blade has a hooked end in which the sand-eels are caught. Bottom: Considerable skill and speed is needed to grab the sand-eel in the hook of the vingler before it wriggles free and burrows back into the loose sand.

Storms often wash up slipper limpets, which may be collected in a leisurely manner. Good baits in bunches for bass and flounders, as well as wrasse and cod at times.

Gaper clams are dug from muddy estuarine beaches and are fairly plentiful in Ireland. They are excellent bait for big bass in the surf, and outsized flounders are also fond of them.

Filleting the side from a mackerel as a conger or tope bait is accomplished by cutting from behind the gill covers with the blade of the sharp knife held flat against the backbone.

A fish to beware of. It may be caught from the shore on sandy bottoms, or encountered when bait digging or collecting. It is the lesser weaver; its dorsal spines, which are black, inject venom. Weavers are best held down by a booted foot and the head severed before the hook is cut free. Throw the body into the sea, or bury it deeply.

Buying baits from fishmongers can be hazardous, as one is hardly ever able to buy fish that is really fresh; it may be sold for human consumption, but often the tope, conger or bass will turn up its nose! If mackerel look greenish-blue rather than dark blue, they are fresh enough. If herring or sprats or the rarer pilchards have a fair number of scales still adhering to them, they are suitable. Some fishmongers sell squid and octopus; they often have frozen packs of small Californian squids and these make very good baits and may be stored in the freezer at home and used on sudden trips.

Small whiting and pouting may often be caught on bits of worm or herring, from piers, rocky shores or from the boat. They may be kept a few hours in ice and then used as baits for big fish, or used immediately. Some anglers like to fish these small fish alive to lure predators, but it really is not necessary.

So much for the fishy baits, then.

On the sandy/muddy mixture shores, especially near estuaries, lugworms are often found in dense beds, although in recent years professional diggers have reduced some of the more accessible beds by supplying too many worms to anglers who usually have at least half of what they take fishing left over and often wasted at the end of the day.

Lugworms are quite expensive to buy. There are two main types, the big adult worms, either black, darkish brown or maybe reddish, from 6 in (15·2 cm) to 1 ft (0·30 m) long, and the tiny red 'blowers', which may be only 2–3 in (5–7·5 cm) long. Usually the big worms are dug nearer to the low water mark while the 'blowers' can be dug close to the area of beach that is only just exposed on short (neap) tides.

Baits

There are also two ways of digging them. The big lug usually burrow deep into the muddy sand. Sometimes they are in firm sand, in which holes may be dug which do not collapse too quickly. In this case a narrow-bladed lug spade is used, each curly cast on the surface being dug up and the worm's burrow followed down by constantly cutting across it. This can be very hard work and though the rewards are big worms, it may take well over an hour to dig 50 of them.

In other areas the sand may be wetter and looser, with more mud. Here the lug may well be closer together in vast beds and a simple trench is dug in the thickest areas of casts using a flat-tined fork. Usually it will be necessary to dig down about 18 in (45·7 cm).

One or two areas exist, some in Scotland, where vast lugworms 18 in (45·7 cm) long or more may be lifted by hand from soft mud. Such places are rarely found, however, and the finders keep them secret!

Various types of ragworm also make good baits, including the giant king ragworm, often attaining 18 in (46 cm) in length and nearly $\frac{3}{4}$ in (2 cm) in thickness; smaller red ragworms $2\frac{1}{2}$–4 in (6·5–10 cm) long, and white ragworms, 3–5 in (7·8–13 cm). Estuaries, areas of shell-grit, fine shingle mixed with sand, even sandy/stony ground will produce king ragworms, though these areas are limited. Red ragworms are often found in lug-inhabited areas while digging lugworms, as are white ragworms, though the latter prefer coarser sand. Forks are best for rag digging.

The sea mouse, often washed ashore after gales, is a good cod bait, but must be tied to the hook at both ends with shirring elastic, since, if the body is punctured, it deflates into a shapeless mass.

Baiting up with mature lugworms should be done from the tail end after the sand-filled tail has been removed. This way the worm's tail-end holds on to the hook eye well.

64

Short snoods and big black lugworms can be cast a long way to cod without coming adrift. The worms must lie straight on the hook to streamline the tackle in flight.

To keep lugworms there are two main methods: one entails killing the worms first, in the second they are kept alive. Big adult worms are best killed by nipping off the head, then squeezing the entrails out towards the head end. Wash the worms in seawater, dry them in newspaper, then wrap them in dry and preferably old newspaper, each worm being kept separated from the others. The paper should be changed after a few hours and the worms wrapped again. Keep them cool (in a refrigerator, but not frozen) and they will remain in good condition for up to a week.

The smaller, softer 'blowers' must usually be kept alive since they become jelly-like and decompose rapidly after death. This is achieved by first washing them in seawater, then drying and either wrapping them in tens in folds of newspaper, or laying them in damp (not wet) seaweed or in vermiculite chips in a cardboard box. The vermiculite chip method, incidentally, is also used for big ragworms; alternatively, the ragworms are wrapped in newspaper, again kept apart from each other.

All worm baits should be stored in a cool place. Do not try to deep-freeze worms; they become soft and useless when defrosted, although one tackle dealer in East Anglia is reputed to have found a method involving deep-freezing, which keeps the worms in excellent condition when thawed out.

What else can be dug from sandy shores? Razorfish for a start. These are excellent baits for bass, plaice, flounders, cod and they are usually found in beds on sandy banks near the low water mark. They too live in burrows in the sand, usually driving almost vertically. They may be dug with a lug spade or lifted out, once the burrows have been located, by pouring salt down the hole, which makes them surface in a few minutes. Another method involves inserting a metal rod with an arrowhead-shaped tip down the hole. The idea is that the razorfish clamps its shell together as it feels the tip go by and is then lifted out as it becomes wedged by the barbs.

In any method the shellfish has first to be located, and this is done by spotting clean holes in the sand, which are sometimes round and sometimes keyhole shaped. Often there are the marks of a jet of water imprinted in the sand beside the hole. If one stamps about on a razorfish bed the creatures become alarmed by the vibrations and shoot jets of water into the air, thus giving away their positions.

Simply keep razorfish in a plastic bucket after washing them in seawater; covered with a damp bit of sacking and kept cool they will keep alive for nearly a week. Some tackle dealers deep freeze them for stock, but they, like lugworms, also become very soft when defrosted and are not very good baits.

The razorfish's muscular 'foot' anchors itself in its burrow. This one has just been pulled clear after dropping salt down the hole, which caused the razorfish to surface.

In bait-inhabited areas it pays to walk the shore after a big onshore gale because often razorfish, lug, slipper limpets, queen cockles, cockles, whelks, hermit crabs and other useful baits are washed up on the shore, especially by the highest tide.

Hermit crabs live in empty whelk shells and may be caught in a fish-baited dropnet or sometimes picked up in tide-pools at low water. They make very good baits for many fish, including bass, cod, smooth-hounds, rays, plaice and flounders.

The other crabs that make excellent baits are those that grow by changing their old shells for a bigger one every so often – common shore crabs, edible crabs and velvet swimming crabs are among the most used. Immediately a crab has cast its old tight shell it is soft and rubbery, the back and rest of the body gradually hardening into a new shell. It is then a very good bait and known as soft crab or a 'softie'. Before the shell is cast it looks dead and may seem to be loose fitting where it joins the V-shaped underside at the back-end.

**This crab has just crawled clear of its old shell, now lying open. It is as soft as a jelly, and had the angler not found it, the crab would have hidden under a rock or weed until the new shell hardened. Now it will hopefully catch the angler a bass.**

A thumbnail inserted will often lift the whole back shell off: the crab is a 'peeler' and again an excellent bait. Before use, however, it is necessary to peel the dead, hard shell from the claws, legs and underside. Failure to do this will surely result in the hook point being protected by the shell when you strike a bite.

**A peeler crab is prepared for the hook. First the back shell or carapace is lifted clear, then the belly shell and legs are peeled.**

Always keep crabs alive, if possible in a small, damp sack or wooden or plastic box or bucket, since they decompose quickly when dead. It helps to keep them covered with some damp weed. Always keep soft crabs separated from peelers, or else the soft ones will be eaten by the others or become soft and useless from constant nipping.

Sand-eels may be kept alive all day in a cooler-box with ice – this apparent miracle was publicised by a well-known Cornish angler, Mike Osborne.

A small-meshed dropnet baited with some old bits of smelly fish such as kipper and left in deep, weedy rockpools at low water or suspended down by the side of a concrete harbour wall or rocks, will produce prawns. These may be kept alive in damp weed in a cool place for an hour or so and fished alive on float tackle for bass and pollack.

Mussels may be collected from the shore, especially from rocks near the low water area on spring tides, when the bigger ones are revealed. They are good for cod, plaice, flounder and will even catch bass when nothing else is available. Keep them in a small damp sack, again in a cool place.

In some areas where the shore has soft rock, such as chalk, old peat-beds or rotting timbers, the boring bivalve, known as the piddock, may be found. These,

**When a crab is found being carried beneath another (usually larger) crab, the carried crab is certainly either a peeler or a soft crab. Gloves prevent painful scratches from barnacles and mussels.**

like many other forms of shellfish, were hard hit by the big freeze of the 1963 winter, since they often live in colonies high up the beach. Recently, however, there have been signs of a come-back and piddocks of a decent size make excellent baits for plaice, flounders, cod and bass. They may be dug out with a lug spade, a hunk of peat lifted clear and broken up to remove the soft-shelled piddocks, or by levering away lumps of chalk or soft rock. The wood, peat, chalk or even firm clay, in which piddock colonies are found, appear like Gruyère cheese on the surface, and when the holey areas are knocked, jets of water will emerge from the disturbed piddocks.

While searching rocky shores at low water for crabs one often finds small fish and eels in the pools, under rocks. Most of these, alive or dead, will make good baits for bass, congers and rays. Incidentally, in May and June and less frequently later on, one often comes across one crab carrying another beneath. The one being carried will be a hen crab and she will either be a softie or a peeler. Pick up the cock, which will try to pinch you, and sneak the hen away. It's a bit tough on the crabs' love-life, but life on the shore is tough for all creatures, most of which eat others and are in turn eaten.

Although many other creatures of the shore make good baits, there are only two more that really must

not be left out: sea-slaters and harbour ragworms or mudworms. Sea-slaters, which are like big woodlice, live in the splash zone high on the shore, among the cracks of sea defences, in rock crevices, along old, cracked concrete piers. They may often be grabbed as they scuttle around and be put into a plastic baitbox with a perforated lid. They are excellent for float-

Collecting harbour ragworms is a very mucky game. This is a tidal creek in Sussex. Care is necessary to avoid bad cuts from broken glass, tin cans and flints in the mud.

Small harbour ragworms dug from a muddy creek are put to dry out on an old towel. They keep in better condition when dry. The fish is a small, thin-lipped grey mullet.

fishing for bass, and in estuaries seatrout certainly take them when they can.

The little ragworms are found in oozy, evil smelling mud in estuaries, saltwater creeks back in the marshes, or on exposed mudbanks in extensive harbours. They are normally about 1½–2½ in (4–5 cm) long, but sometimes colonies of bigger ones up to 3 in (8 cm) may be discovered. They leave the mud honeycombed with burrows, and a small handfork is a good tool for extracting them. This is a filthy and sometimes dangerous job as it is easy to sink thigh-deep in the ooze. Always take great care when after these worms. Keep them cool in a plastic or wooden box and covered with a seawater damped flannel cloth. They are excellent when floatfished for mullet, bass, flounders and shad, and they sometimes accidentally (!) lure seatrout in estuaries. They will keep well only for about two days. Do not put any green or yellowish worms in with the red ones or else all will perish.

Hook them by the head, and for bass use a bunch of up to a dozen, always on a fine wire hook.

# Cutting bait and baiting up

It is easy to spoil good bait due to bad preparation or bad presentation. There are good and bad, right and wrong ways to bait hooks with various baits.

Always cut fish and squid-type baits on a softwood board, using a *very* sharp knife with a thinnish blade. If you can't shave your forearm with the knife it is too blunt! Such fish as mackerel, whiting and herring should be held by the head, then cut with the blade held flat and against the backbone, sliding the knife towards the tail. Turn the fish over to take off the other fillet.

If the fillets need be cut into strips, lay the fillets skin side down on the board. It is much easier to cut neat pieces that way.

Usually it is best to mount whole fish, tail-first, up the trace, the hook being lodged near the head, as most predators turn their prey to swallow it head-first. One exception is the sand-eel, which is always presented with the hook point facing forward, whether the bait is fished dead or alive. Also, when using small live fish, such as whiting, pouting, various rock-pool fish or elvers (baby eels) they should be lightly hooked through the top lip.

There is seldom need to conceal the hook in the bait, as, generally, fish in the sea – and in freshwater for that matter – do not appear to be aware of hooks, on lures or in a bait. The size of hook should of course match the size of bait. It is also necessary to choose a hook that, when baited, will have its point and barb clear of the bait, to avoid the bait deflecting the hook point from the mouth of the fish on the strike.

A small squid, freely available in some fishmongers or deep-freeze stores. The head has been cut off and the transparent 'pen' removed.

The body has been slit open and spread flat on the wooden board before being cut into strips.

To bait a big hook (for bass or conger, for example) push the point through the complete body at the pointed end and bring it out again.

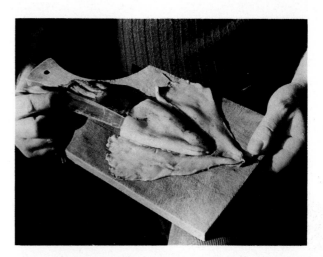

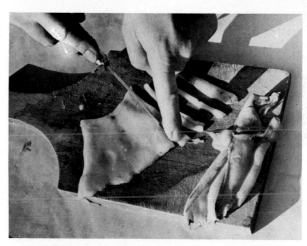

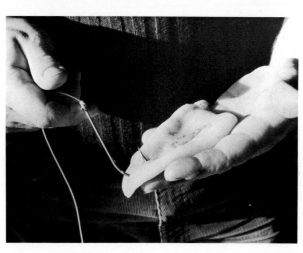

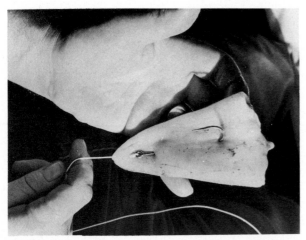

Now push the hook down into the body cavity and bring it out through the side, pulling the point of the body above the eye of the hook.

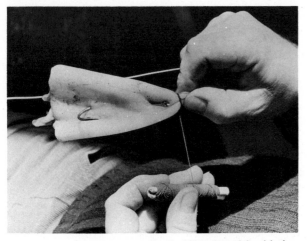

Pinch the body tightly and wind firmly with shirring elastic.

Pull the elastic to break it off. No knot is necessary, the material locks itself. This bait will cast a long way without breaking up, since it is streamlined and supported by the hook eye.

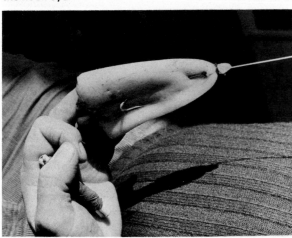

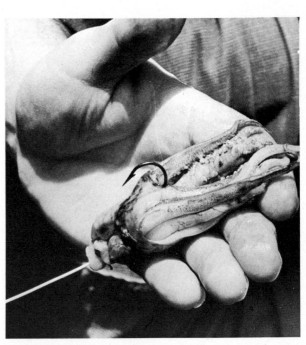

The head of the squid makes a good bait, complete with tentacles, for bass, cod, conger and skate.

Big adult lugworms are best baited head-down: it is at the head end that the scent-laden fluids ooze out, and if the hook point is in that area it is quickly engulfed by the fish. There is also the very important fact that a lugworm's tail end is firm and tends to grip the hook eye and knot more than does the head end, so it casts better, lying straight and streamlined for its passage out to the fish when hurled by the surfcaster. Blower lug, however, are usually so small and so soft that several, up to a dozen for big cod, may be needed on the hook. As these blowers are usually kept alive, they remain soft and are best baited from the head end, the point being carefully inserted into the sucker-like mouth and the worm slid up the hook and onto the trace; this is repeated as often as necessary to achieve the correct bait size. For sole and dab, perhaps, one worm would do on a small hook.

King ragworms are baited from the head, the hook being inserted through the mouth and the worm slid up the hook shank: it should be remembered that the eye of the hook and the knot with which it is attached to the trace should be used whenever possible to hold a bait in a neat position on the hook. For big fish, like bass, a whole big worm will be fine; pieces of worm may be used for smaller fish. Red and white ragworm used singly or in bunches for short casting or float fishing, may be nicked lightly through the head end; when a firmer hooking is required, for surfcasting to 50 yd (45·7 m) or more, then the hook should be inserted into the mouth and the worm pulled up above the eye. Small harbour ragworms (mudworms) are simply nicked through the head, used in bunches on fine wire hooks.

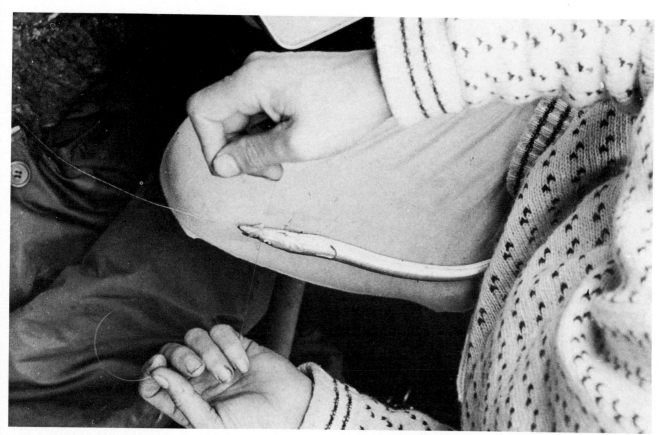

A big sand-eel being mounted on a hook to wire for shore tope. It is secured round the nose with nylon to keep it in position when long distance casting. With a nylon trace, a half hitch may be made in the trace, which is then slipped over the nose and drawn down to the hook. It pulls out when a fish is hooked.

Razorfish are best threaded on the hook from the firm, foot end, the foot holding on to the eye better than the other end. Piddocks, cockles, slipper limpets, mussels and clams need be hooked twice through the hardest part one can find on their body, the soft parts being wrapped round the shank or bend of the hook.

Prawns and shrimps are best fished alive on float tackle, and they are hooked by passing the point once through the second segment up from the tail, from the underside, so that the hook protrudes from the back. Fish usually fold the crustacean in its natural curve to swallow it, perhaps to avoid a stab from the sharp spikes on the head of a prawn.

Fished alive, the sand-eel can be hooked in a number of ways, all of which are aimed at keeping the creature alive for as long as possible. At the same time the hook should be in as good a position as possible to hook the taking fish. However, some of the methods of hooking a live sand-eel are extremely inhumane and unnecessary. Two methods that work well are a simple lip hook job: attached from the inside to the outside of the top lip; and the other by passing the hook carefully into the mouth, out of one gill cover, then nicking it just under the skin a little way back of the gill cover.

Live sand-eels are delicate creatures and the above methods of baiting them will not permit any jerky, long distance casts. Instead, swing out the tackle – be it float, leger or driftline.

Freshly killed sand-eels are a different proposition. (It is best to keep them alive on ice in the cooler-box, then kill them just before baiting up.) One can insert the hook through the mouth and then bring it out halfway along the body. Alternatively two hooks can be used: one some two inches behind the other, so that one is in the bait's mouth, the other somewhere along the body. An excellent way of using a dead sand-eel on a one-hook rig involves inserting the hook into the bait's mouth and then out behind the gills, followed by forming a circle of nylon with a half-hitch ahead of the eel's head, then slipping it over the snout, pulling tight simultaneously. This forms a simple hitch of the nylon on the firm snout and, when a fish takes and is hooked, pulls free so that the trace is unknotted and at full strength. This method permits very long casts without the delicate little fish tearing free.

Large sand-eels may be cut in two equal pieces and used as legering bait as above.

Soft and peeler crabs are sometimes quite a problem when baiting. When long casts are not essential both soft and peeler crabs may be hooked by passing the hook through the back, out at the underside, and out through the back again. Naturally, one needs to choose the right hook size for the size of the crab.

However, often it is necessary to cast 50 to 100 yd (45·7–91·4 m), and crabs baited as above will tear off the hook. So, with a soft crab, bait as above but tie at least two legs up the trace above the hook, using elasticated thread (shirring elastic) from a draper's store. This material can be wound for several turns and tightened, at which point it locks and needs no knot. Do not pull it too tight or it will cut through the soft crab and prove useless. With soft crabs bigger than about 2½ in (6·5 cm) across the shell, it may be best to cut them in half with a sharp knife before use. Then, stick the hook through the shell side, put it back through and bring it out again through the shell, then wind shirring elastic round the whole bait and hook; fish don't care about a 'packaged' crab so long as the juices remain.

Peeler crabs are a somewhat tougher bait than soft crabs, though soft crabs vary in consistency depending on the degree of hardening following the shedding of the old shell: newly shed soft crabs have the consistency of soft jelly; better are those that feel rubbery. The crabs that have hardened to become what anglers term 'cracklebacks' or 'crispies' are useable, but are very second rate baits and do come off the hook easily when cast.

But back to peeler crabs. The shell and the two lobes that are left on each flank just above the legs must be removed; then, the belly segments of shell must be taken off with the thumbnail until the whole crab, including claws and legs has been peeled. Push the hook through from one side of the back, out through the belly, then in again, so that the point protrudes from the back – which is where, normally, a bass tries to grab a crab. Tie two legs up the trace with the shirring elastic.

Much nonsense has been talked in the past about presenting crab bait 'naturally'. A bunch of soft legs is a killing bait, so is a mushy parcel strapped to a hook, made up of bits and pieces of various crabs: it is the succulent smell and taste of the bait, not its appearance, that makes bass (and other fish) go crazy for crab.

**The most famous and most effective of all saltwater lures: Alex Ingram's Red Gill, superb for bass, pollack, coalfish and big ballan wrasse.**

What of hardback crabs? Some anglers have undoubtedly caught bass on them when forced to use them since nothing better was available; but really small hardback crabs are useful only for ballan wrasse in general, though cod will sometimes take them. This is one of sea angling's mysteries: why fish are found to have eaten large numbers of hardback crabs yet consistently refuse to take one on the hook.

All equipment used for digging or other methods of obtaining sea baits must be kept free of rust and corrosion, or else it will become useless. A lug spade or flat-tined fork should be washed in freshwater after use, then dried and wiped with thick oil or grease. A rusty tool makes for hard work as it is difficult to move through sand or mud rather than slicing through. Any net frames used for prawns, hermit crabs or little rockfish should be made from galvanised wire – they need be only enlarged versions of children's toy nets. Both handles and dropnets are easily made at home for less than half the price of shop-bought ones.

# Artificial baits

There are many artificial baits that will catch sea fish in British and north-west European waters, but in the field of sportfishing some of them, the author feels are undesirable, in that they do not necessarily hook fish fairly in the mouth. The heavy lures that will *not* be listed in the following pages are pirks or jigs, some of which weigh as much as 2 lb (900 g).

There are four metal spoon-type lures that have long proved their worth for the sea angler fishing for sport: the ABU Toby, the same company's Koster, the Condor spoon (often called the German sprat) and small bar-spoons such as Mepps, Veltic, Celta, Droppen, Reflex and some others of similar design.

For bass, pollack and mackerel the first three lures are all excellent, from as light as $\frac{5}{8}$ oz (18 g) up to just over an ounce (30 g). The bar-spoons are good for very light tackle fishing for school bass, shad, mackerel, garfish, grey mullet (thick-lipped) and – whisper it– seatrout in estuaries, which sometimes get caught accidentally when after other species.

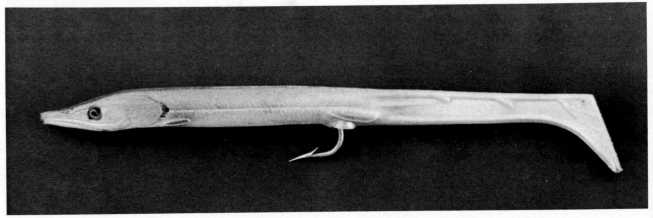

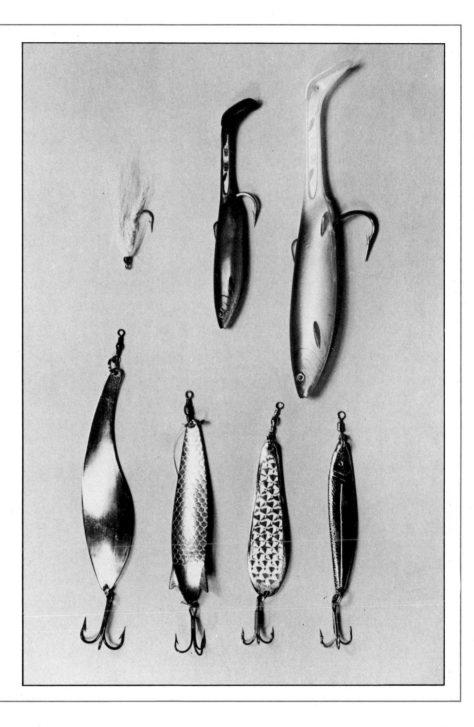

Effective artificial baits:
Top, left to right: a saltwater
fly and two sizes of Wagtail
plastic lures. Bottom, left to
right: Ellips, Toby, Flasha and
a heavy wobbler.

Silver is by far the better colour of the two for most saltwater metal lures.

There are a number of rubber or soft plastic lures available, all of which are eclipsed by the astounding success of Alex Ingram's Red Gill sand-eels. Used in all available sizes, they consistently catch bass, pollack, coalfish, cod and big ballan wrasse. Lures that are made in the same way as the flies of the freshwater angler – from hair and feathers, tinsel etc – are also excellent saltwater lures for the sportfisher, not only for catching mackerel for bait but for bass, pollack, coalfish, garfish, shad, thick-lipped grey mullet – even sharks.

Saltwater flies are generally made to simulate small fish on which predators feed. Various patterns will be dealt with later.

Have no truck with any of the artificial baits that are said to smell or taste 'like the real thing' and which are cast and allowed to fish on the bottom. Such baits as artificial lugworms, crabs and small squid do not catch fish by being so fished and are a waste of money.

# Part II

# The fish
# and the fishing

# 5

# The sport-fisher's sharks

There are four sharks of interest to the sporting angler in British and north-west European waters: blue, porbeagle, thresher and mako and they are caught in the greatest numbers in that order.

Very few anglers specifically fish for mako and thresher sharks in the waters of the British Isles and neighbouring Europe, since the small number of sharks does not justify the effort and cost. Cornwall offers the best chance of a mako, and perhaps the best port to go from is Falmouth where skipper Robin Vinnicombe is the most highly rated mako-hunter in Britain. Looe is also a good bet, and it was from this famous shark-fishing port (where blues are the main catch) that the biggest British mako, a fish of 500 lb (226·7 kg), was taken by Mrs Joyce Yallop in 1971.

Threshers are probably not as rare as the mako in the water, the scimitar-shaped tail of the thresher is sighted at many points round the coast. Unlike the other sharks, which the novice may have difficulty in identifying at a distance while the fish is swimming in the water, the scimitar-shaped tail of the thresher is quite unmistakable and anybody who sees one or more of these tall, sword-like tails thrashing the sea to foam as the fish circle rapidly round a panic-stricken shoal of mackerel, can be sure that the sharks are threshers. The sharks herd the bait-fish into a tight knot and then rush in to feed on them.

There is no particular place one could depend on having a good chance of thresher shark, and it is less easy to advise on than the mako. Perhaps the waters off the Isle of Wight, where porbeagles are fished, would be as good a place as any, though the British record of 280 lb (135·4 kg) was caught, by accident, by an angler fishing on the bottom with a big fish-bait at Dungeness, Kent, in 1933. Since threshers have occasionally been hooked in other places, while bottom fishing near rocky outcrops, reefs and headlands – usually in turbulent water – it is now a commonly held view that the best chance of hooking a thresher shark in Britain and its environs would be to fish a big bait near the bottom in such places. Also some form of groundbait attraction working at that level would help. This method is used mainly for this species of shark; indeed, it is a peculiar way to tackle a fish that, on the few occasions it is seen, is actively herding mackerel on the surface!

More blue sharks are caught than any of the other sharks in British waters. The bulk of the catch comes from the West Country ports of Devon and Cornwall – Mevagissey, Looe, Fowey, Falmouth, Plymouth and Penzance, all having good reputations. The north coast of Cornwall also produces blues, though the charter-boats are in general not as readily available or specialised as the others.

The west and south-west coasts of the Irish Republic are good blue shark waters, too, the best known ports being Kinsale, Dungarvan, Courtmacsherry, Cahirciveen, Dingle, Tralee, Kilkee, and up to Westport, the Clew Bay and Achill areas being particularly good.

Blue sharks do not usually attain big weights in British and north-west European waters, 50 lb (22·6 kg) or so being about average. The rod-caught British record is a fish of 218 lb (98·8 kg). Because the majority are taken on heavy tackle, often hired out by the charter-boats to tourists, the blue shark has a reputation for being a non-fighter. That the blue has not the dash and strength of the porbeagle, size for size, is indisputable, but when taken on lightish tackle the blue can be given the title of sportfish.

The porbeagle is the best of the British and north-west European sharks so far as the sporting angler is concerned. It grows to a good size and it is a strong and tenacious fighter. The British record is a fish of 465 lb (210·9 kg) caught from Padstow, Cornwall, in 1976.

Porbeagles are much more tolerant of cold water than are the blue, mako and thresher sharks and in fact they have figured in late autumn and winter catches of herring in the southern North Sea; Scandinavian boats longline for them in the North Sea, and fish are known to swim in the waters off the Scottish coasts, the area of the Mull of Galloway having produced actual hook-ups.

This Isle of Wight porbeagle, being steadied by the author, was boated in very little time on 10 lb (4·5 kg) test line by Vince Lister, President of the British Light Tackle Club. It weighed 63 lb (28·5 kg) and missed a world 12 lb (5·4 kg) class record by 4 lb (1·8 kg).

Previous page:
**Even modest porbeagle sharks like this can be good sport on light tackle. The author poses with a fish taken in calm conditions off the Isle of Wight by Vince Lister, founder member and first President of the British Light Tackle Club.**

Among the best locations for porbeagle fishing are the Isle of Wight grounds, the West Country ports already listed for blue shark fishing, the north Devon coast between Bude and Ilfracombe, especially the turbulent water off Hartland Point, and Carmarthen Bay across the other side of the outer edge of the Bristol Channel in South Wales. In the Irish Republic porbeagles are taken on the parts of the west coast where boats and skippers have the expertise: the Clare and Galway coasts host many fish, which often come so close inshore where steep cliffs fall to deep water that they are caught from the cliffs. Later in the year, in September and October, the fish appear in large numbers off Achill – although in the past few years the numbers of fish taken has fallen.

Those, then, are the four main quarries for the sportfisher bearing the name shark. However, there are other members of the shark family that are of equal interest, if not more, in spite of the fact that they do not attain such weights. These are the tope, which averages about 25 lb (11·3 kg) but often reaches 40 lb (18 kg), and the two species of smooth-hound: the unspotted variety, *Mustelus mustelus*, and the spotted variety, *Mustelus asterias*. The one without spots certainly reaches weights of over 30 lb (13·6 kg), though a good one is reckoned to weigh 15 lb (6·8 kg), and the spotted one 20 lb (9 kg), though a good one weighs half that.

Both tope and smooth-hounds are, size for size, the equal of any of the true sharks in these waters so far as fighting ability is concerned. When hooked in shallow water, as they often are, they show turns of speed and lengths of run that would make the mako and porbeagle seem tame. Of course, they need to be fished with matching sporting tackle, and these fish are regularly caught at depths of 3–30 ft (0·9–27·4 m). In water that is more than, say, 40 ft (15 m) deep, these mini-sharks do not perform very well as a rule.

Tope are streamlined sharks and capable of terrific speed and long runs. This one is held by angling writer Ian Gillespie.

A large unspotted smooth-hound, *Mustelus mustelus*, taken in Essex.

The beauty of tope and 'smoothies', as anglers describe them, is that they are often taken by casting from the shore – from beaches and from projections over deepish water – and thus they produce excellent sport on the long, light casting rod without having the bother and expense of going afloat.

Tope are distributed all round the British and Irish coasts, being particularly numerous in the bays of extensive estuaries, usually over sandy or gravelly sea-beds. However, there are comparatively few places where shore fishing proves worthwhile. Locations worth trying include the western side of Kent's Dungeness promontory; Selsey Bill; Park and Lepe Beaches in the Solent; Dorset's Chesil Bank; various steep beaches and rocks in Devon and Cornwall, especially the north coast of Cornwall, from St Ives to Trevose Head; the Gower Peninsula and Carmarthen Bay in South Wales; Cardigan Bay and the Lleyn Peninsula up to and including the tope-inhabited waters of Anglesey and the Menai Strait; plus south and south-west coasts of the Irish Republic, especially west Cork and the Dingle Peninsula.

# The sport-fisher's sharks

The smooth-hound is a beautiful fish: this one is the spotted variety, *Mustelus asterias*, just about to be slid back into the sea after unhooking.

Smooth-hounds are strange fish in that they appear to change location for no good reason, turning up in widely different environments. They do have a penchant for very large estuaries – perhaps they favour the less saline water? – and the area from The Wash down to the south side of the Thames Estuary, then again from Selsey through the Solent to Durlston Head, is a regular producer of these fish. Anglesey is also worth a try. In Ireland reports of smooth-hounds are few, but that may be due to the fact that some anglers may not recognise the difference between the unspotted smooth-hound and the tope. The only reliable reports of smooth-hounds in Irish waters have been from Tralee Bay in Co. Kerry.

Seasons for sharks usually begin about the end of May and last until mid-September, both dates being dependent on long-term weather conditions. Although little work has yet been done on the idea, there seems little doubt that porbeagle sharks could be caught right up until Christmas, especially in the southern North Sea (East Anglian herring grounds) – provided the sea conditions at that time of year permitted boats to get out regularly.

For tope and smooth-hounds seasons vary more widely, depending on area. May and June are usually best, especially on shallow water inshore marks, but after the end of June 'smoothies' seem to move to deeper water. Tope can be taken well into October, especially in the south-west of Britain and Ireland. In some of the Welsh estuaries of the Gower, for instance, tope are often taken from the shore in shallow water in April.

# Light tackle and sharks

With light tackle and big sharks it must be remembered that one either spends a lot of money on booking a boat for one or two people, or else, if three or four anglers are required to share the expense to make the trip economical, then before fishing begins, there should be a draw to find out who takes the first fish, who the second and so on, regardless of whose tackle the fish comes to take. Also, it should be decided before booking the boat what tackle will be used – 12, 20 or 30 lb IGFA – and each angler must ensure that the rod, reel and line he takes with him is satisfactory to the other anglers who may have to use it.

The basic shark fishing technique has been so well written about these past few years that it would be mere repetition to go deeply into the matter. However, most of the written lore is based on the use of heavy or comparatively heavy tackle, eg IGFA 50 lb and 80 lb (22·6 and 36·2 kg), and fishing from boats of 30–40 ft (9·1–12·1 m) in groups of three to six anglers. Ideally,

light tackle shark fishing should be carried out, whenever wind and water conditions are favourable, from a fast and manoeuvrable boat of between 20–27 ft (6–8·2 m), so that the angler is given every advantage to play his fish safely on his light tackle. Ideally the skipper of the boat should keep the angler facing his fish over the stern end of the gunwale.

**From shallow, sandy beaches like this one in Ireland big tope may be caught by casting fish baits. Hooked in the shallows, perhaps only a foot or so (30·4 cm) deep, the tope will make runs for the deeper water, taking up to 200 yd (182·8 m) of line – very exciting! The angler must have patience, though, for this is a waiting game, ambushing the few fish that come inshore so far.**

Whether the quarry is a blue or a porbeagle, or even the rarer mako and thresher, the following basic system applies, although suitable variations can be suggested later.

Sharks hunt by scent, even the big-eyed porbeagle being attracted to the boat in the same way as the slit-eyed blue – by chumming, as the Americans and most other English-speaking nations have it, or the use of rubby-dubby in Britain. The basis of the scent trail is oily minced and/or chopped fish, such as mackerel, herrings, anchovies, pilchards, sprats, and even pouting and whiting, which are less oily. The fish need not be fresh; indeed oily fish that have spent a day in the sun and smell quite high make excellent rubby-dubby.

Some charter-boat skippers do the job properly, which is hard work; others simply prepare one onion sack of the evil concoction, then sit back and await results, while having a sleep. There is no doubt that the number of sharks attracted to the boat is in direct proportion to the amount of work put, by both skipper and anglers, into laying a good trail. And obviously, anglers who want a real oil-slick and particle curtain in the water must help the skipper. One onion sack over the gunwale is not enough. Far better to have three sacks, one over the bow, one amidships, the other over the stern. Each bag, which should just be dipping into the water each time the boat rolls, so that oil and particles of fish are washed out continuously, should contain about 8 lb (3·6 kg) of minced fish mixed with about three double handfuls of bran. The

bran helps to release oil slowly, particles drifting away on the surface and fluttering below it. Use strong nylon sash cord to suspend each bag.

In addition, it pays to chop up on a board some 20 bait-fish into tiny cubes – like canned pineapple – and have them going over the side, say, three every five minutes. These pieces sink and will bring up any sharks, porbeagles in particular, that might otherwise miss a scent trail only on the surface. Always beware of putting over too much diced fish or having pieces larger than suggested, otherwise there is a

chance of feeding a following shark, while the plan is to excite the fish's appetite and bring it near the boat.

So, once the boat has been positioned to begin the drift – preferably wind-driven across the tidal flow so as to lay a broad trail, if this can be arranged – the first job should be to put over the three rubby bags and begin to feed over the pieces. Both mincing for the rubby bags and dicing for the deeper attraction should be done on the way out to the mark or, better, before leaving port.

Let us assume an ideal fishing expedition: there are

The head of this spotted smooth-hound, *Mustelus asterias*, is beautifully streamlined and illustrates how the fish can produce such fast, long runs for its relatively small size.

This is the author's favourite boat for light tackle sharking in anything like reasonable sea conditions. This Q22, a twin-hulled glass craft, is very fast yet drifts well to form a stable fishing platform, with excellent handling capabilities when playing fish.

Opposite:
An average size tope taken from a trawler. Fish of this size are excellent sport on 12 and 20 lb (5·4 and 9 kg) outfits, though 30 lb (13·6 kg) may have to be used where tidal streams are strong.

two anglers and a skipper aboard the boat. The boat is a 23-footer, so there is ample room. There has been agreement that both rods will be 30 lb (13·6 kg) IGFA, each lever-drag reel loaded to within $\frac{1}{8}$ in (3 mm) of the lip of the spool with monofilament of about 26–28 lb test or the more expensive IGFA-rated line. As has already been said, the length of line should be in the region of 500–600 yd (457·1–548·6 m) long for this type of fishing.

Traces are 15 ft (4·5 m) long and of plain multi-strand stainless steel wire of about 175 lb (79·3 kg) test, to each end of which is attached a strong link-swivel, preferably of the American Berkley type. Hooks are attached to about 18 in (45 cm) of 300 lb (136 kg) test wire, the free end of which is looped. (Details such as attachment of swivel or hooks to wire are dealt with in chapter 3.)

A Bimini hitch is formed in the end of the reel line, so that the loop forms the last 15 ft (4·5 m) of the line,

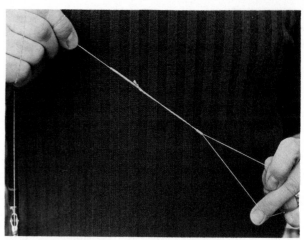

Doubled line is best either whipped for about $\frac{1}{4}$ in (6 mm) every foot (30·4 cm) or, as in this case, held by soft plastic tube.

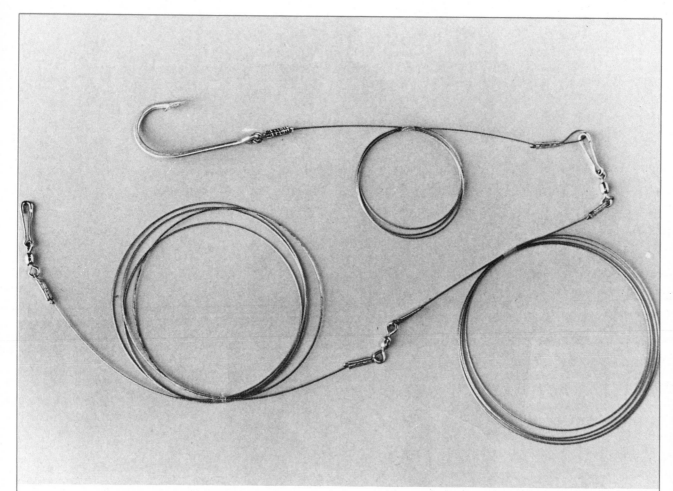

A typical light tackle shark trace: 15 ft (4·5 m) long; this includes the hook trace for IGFA record application purposes. This one is 15 ft long with an additional 18 in (45 cm) hook trace. Both the line/trace and trace/hook link junctions are of the quick release type, formed with Berkley swivels.

this being double the strength of the rest of the line. (The Bimini hitch is also dealt with in chapter 3.) Besides being an insurance factor against any wear to which the last few feet of line might be subjected should the shark's rough skin come in contact with it, it is also an aid to bringing the shark to the gaff once it has been subdued. When a couple of turns of the doubled line – which should be whipped together, or held by plastic tubing every 2 ft (60 cm) – have been got round the spool, it is possible to increase the safe maximum pressure to get the fish within reach.

The main part of the trace is not just to stop the shark's rough hide from rubbing through the reel line, but to give added strength so that once the skipper or a companion can grab hold of the wire below the top swivel, he can afford to pull firmly to bring the shark to the side of the boat and the gaff. The last bit of heavy wire to the hook is to prevent the shark's teeth from severing connection with the angler. Once in a while a shark will manage to bite through even 300 lb test wire! This piece of wire that carries the hook is looped at the free end (see chapter 3).

To the end of the doubled reel line (it is in fact a very long loop) is tied either a plain strong swivel or a strong welded steel ring. A tucked half blood knot is used for this junction. The ring or swivel forms a speedy attachment point for the link-swivel at the top of the trace.

This main part of the trace may be formed of heavy nylon, as used by commercial longline fishermen. This can be bought from chandlers and commercial fishing supply shops in test of about 400 lb (181·4 kg) and is fixed by crimping metal sleeves in the same way as wire. It is said that it is less visible in the water and does not put off a shark from taking the bait. However, the fact remains that a large number of sharks do take baits with wire traces above them, and the visibility aspect is probably a theoretical point that has little bearing on the actual fishing.

The bait used is a large mackerel. A baiting needle is inserted just behind the gill cover and brought out at the extreme root of the tail. The actual tail fin is removed first, with a sharp knife, which stops any tendency for the bait to spin and tangle the trace as it moves through the water behind the boat. The loop in the hook link is now inserted in the hook of the baiting needle and the wire drawn through and out of the tail root. The hook is pulled into the body cavity, so that just the bend and barb lie clear of the bait's flank. Clip the loop of the link to the link-swivel on the trace.

Let the bait overboard now, and measure off by the span between chin and hand a distance of about 15 ft (4·5 m) of the reel line. Hold the line at the selected point and then, bending the line over the tip of a matchstick, push the line and match halfway into a piece of suitable plastic tube about ½ in (1 cm) long. Tie the balloon by its neck to the free end of the tube with thin string. Alternatively, one can make up float links in advance, using a small paper stapler, as shown.

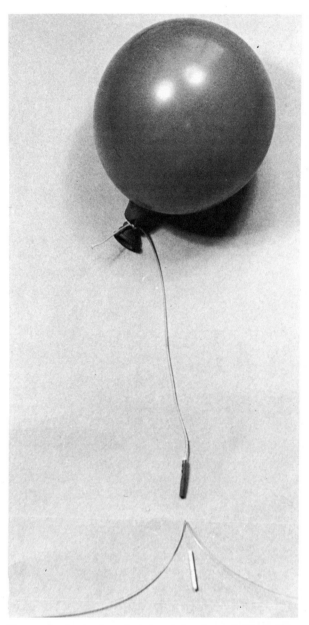

The author's shark and tope quick-release balloon float set-up. The line or cord from the balloon may be tied or stapled to the piece of plastic tube, stripped from electrical wire.

The reel line is bent under tension over the end of a matchstick, which is then pushed into the tube to hold the line in place at the predetermined fishing depth.

This is how the balloon fishes. When a fish takes, the match is pulled out by the tightening line and the balloon released from the line.

When a shark takes, or certainly when the strike is made, the line forces the match from the tube and the balloon is ejected. On light tackle one does not want any 'passengers' on the line when a shark rushes off.

Allow the balloon to float away from the boat some 25 yd (22·8 m) before leaning the rod securely against the gunwale in such a way that the line may run freely from the reel and with the reel in free spool with the audible ratchet engaged. Or else, if the wind or tidal flow is such that the line is not held on the ratchet, leave the reel in gear but with minimum drag that will just hold the line from being pulled off.

The second rod is made up in the same way, except that the fishing depth is increased to about 50 ft (15 m), and a balloon of a different colour to the first one used is attached to the line. This selection of different colours avoids confusion when the baits are fishing. This deeper rig is let out farther from the boat than the first one, about 35–40 yd (32–36 m), so that fish coming up from the deeps towards the trail emanating from the boat may run into it; fish coming closer to the boat nearer the surface are likely to find the bait at a shallower depth.

Once the rods are out keep the diced fish going overboard, and every few minutes give the rubby bags a jerk so that bits of fish flow away. It is essential to retain an unbroken oil-slick on the surface and a rain of tiny pieces of fish sinking through the water. Also, ensure that the area around the rods is free of any junk causing obstruction. Stow all gear securely out of the way, but keep a fighting butt socket (belly pad) within easy reach so that it may be instantly strapped round the angler who takes the rod.

Change the contents of the rubby bags with new minced fish and bran every hour; use the washed-out material to feed over the side in palm-size helpings.

Quite often the fin of a shark will be seen coming up the rubby trail. A pair of binoculars makes the waiting interesting in this respect – although often the first sign of a fish will be the balloon travelling along the surface in jerks, then quickly submerging.

At times a shark, especially porbeagles, will come up to the balloons and bunt them several times; if this happens it is almost certain that the fish will then submerge and take a bait.

As the float goes down and breaks away the check

Vince Lister in action against a porbeagle shark with light tackle.

Some groin protectors (or belly-pads as they are also called) have no crossbar to take the slot of the rod butt. This is an American protector that has proved ideal for the job.

on the reel will begin to sound: the regularity of the clicks is an initial indication of how fast the shark is travelling with the bait held in its mouth. The angler should pick up the rod and knock the lever or button into free-spool (no click), keeping sufficient thumb pressure on the spool of line to prevent any tendency for an over-run to occur. Some fish will take 20 yd (18 m), stop, then rush off again; others will go for 100 yd (91 m), stop, then go off again more slowly; and still others will go off and not stop at all. And, unfortunately, some will move away with the bait, then drop it. Some come back for a second bite, others go

away for good. It is worthwhile, if the bait is dropped, to begin to wind in line fairly slowly – but with a very light drag on the reel. The fish may be tempted to have a bite at a bait moving away as if alive. If the bait is taken on the move, free-spool immediately and let line go against thumb pressure. The other line is quickly reeled in.

If the fish goes a short way, stops, then rushes off again, allow 40 yd (36 m) or so of line to go, then put the reel in gear and let the rod take the strain, pulling the hook into the fish's mouth. Do not, as anglers using heavy gear do, attempt to strike hard several

A small porbeagle is held by the trace close to the boat. It is obviously not a record and is to be released without risking internal damage by lifting . . .
Inset: using long-handled wire cutters to snip the hook off close to the eye.

times. The light rod tip will not sink a hook of shark size properly, but a constant firm pressure will *drag* it in past the barb – provided it is properly sharpened to a knife edge at the back of the barb.

A point here about the drag setting. It should be such that the rod can be pulled into about a quarter-circle before any line is yielded. This is tested with the butt of the rod and the end of the line roughly at right angles. With a lever-drag reel the drag is preset at this tension or, if there is no setting equipment or markings on the drag system – as with a Policansky – stick a piece of tape on the edge of the sideplate. Using this as a guide, the drag can always be returned to the pre-set safe position if it has been moved to allow a fish to run off line, against the ratchet only, while fishing.

Of course, preset drags are a problem on any star-drag reel, since there is no sure way of being able to back off pressure, then return the wheel to its former preset situation. The only safe way is to preset the star-drag and leave it at that position. For a 30 lb (13·6 kg) class outfit the setting should be such that the rod will lift a dead weight of about 6 lb (2·7 kg) bent into a quarter circle when held with the butt horizontal – and the drag will just yield line when the rod is given a jerk. That may seem a very light pull to pit against a shark of 80–200 lb (36·2–90·7 kg), but it is the sustained pressure that weakens the fish, and the rod and reel drag must be allowed to do their work.

Once the fish is hooked – or believed to be hooked, for often the shark will 'come unstuck' after 5–10 minutes, during which the rod was under maximum safe pressure and one felt the fish could not just be holding the bait – get the butt into the belly pad and keep the rod bent into a quarter circle. Usually a shark of over 80 lb (36·2 kg), especially a porbeagle, will more than help in this respect, either by a long run away from the boat, or by sounding, which can be a problem when light tackle is used. It is usual for sharks hooked on 30 lb or less tackle to fight near the surface, perhaps because there is no alarmingly strong pressure being imposed on their movements. The idea is to keep the fish moving, making it swim against sustained light – a safe strain which, it is hoped, will confuse the fish and eventually tire it sufficiently for it to be brought to the boat.

The skipper must keep the engine running during the fight, ensuring the angler is kept facing his fish from the gunwales near the stern. This can mean that the boat will be pivotting from the stern, or moving away from the fish if it tries to run under the boat or go deep. A fish can resist a strong pull from directly above, as anglers who fish with 50–120 lb (22·6–54·4 kg) test lines will know, but when the pull is from a shallow angle, there is a far better chance of the fish being lifted by the water pressure due to its body shape, even if the pressure is very modest.

Beware of temptation to add manual pressure to the line or the sides of the reel spool during the fight; a sudden spurt by the fish is almost sure to result in a break. Patience and that quality anglers (and horsey types) call 'hands' is the name of the game.

Some sharks, particularly male porbeagles, or a mako, will make a very long run or runs away from the boat – perhaps as far as 500 yd (457 m). If this happens the boat should travel towards the fish at a speed sufficient to shorten the line and with which the angler is capable of keeping up by recovering line. A large, fast-swimming fish can easily break a line by taking off several hundred yards, then turning, so as to create a big loop in the line. Water drag on this loop will break the line, even when there is apparently little extra pressure coming through to the rod.

When the fish begins to tire, and comes within a few yards of the boat, the boatman should keep the angler facing the fish as it swims, circling the boat due to the pressure exerted by the tackle. Line is gradually shortened by pumping, which means raising the rod tip slowly and smoothly to the vertical position, then lowering it again more quickly, winding the resulting slack line quickly on to the reel. The angler must always be ready for a sudden lunge by the fish and be prepared to yield line.

Now the skipper, or another experienced angler, must put on a pair of leather, heavy cotton or plastic gloves (industrial type) and prepare to get a firm grip on the top of the trace below the swivel joining reel line to trace. There must never be any attempt to wind the trace round a hand as fingers, or even a hand, could be lost that way, should a fish of even 150 lb (68 kg) make a frantic lunge.

If the fish is not wanted for weighing ashore, ie if it is obviously not a potential line-class record, it is best to let it go. This is best achieved by the trace being held firmly so that the fish is tethered close to the boat, when one person can lean over and cut off the hook as near to the fish's mouth as is possible. Long-handled wire cutters are used for this purpose. A fish will usually survive with a hook in its mouth or throat, provided the point has not pierced any vital organs or blood vessels, and often it will be able to rub out the hook or in some other way get rid of the hook. It is amazing how fish can do this, and proof has several times been obtained when hook-caught sharks have been put into aquaria, and the hook has been found on the floor of the tank next day.

If the fish is to be killed for weighing then it must be gaffed aboard, and if it is a really large fish, it may be necessary to tail-rope it as well.

A proper flying gaff must be used, one that has a head with a ring welded to it and which is a loose fit on the shaft. The hook is held in place by winding the rope that is tied or lashed to the ring in the head several times round the shaft, then, holding the rope firmly against the shaft. The gaff is pulled in firmly, perhaps near the pectoral fins (under the belly) or near the vent area. The rope is allowed to pull free and the gaff head comes off leaving the fish held by the rope. The free end of the rope must be firmly hitched to a stern post or some other strong anchorage in the boat.

The shark is likely to thrash around now. The angler must keep out of the way of whoever is gaffing the fish but must back off his drag just in case the fish comes off the gaff and rushes away again in a frenzy. However, if there is only the angler and his companion to get the fish aboard – the skipper being perhaps occupied with keeping the boat steady against tricky seas – he should quickly unclip the top trace swivel and lay the rod down out of the way before hauling on the gaff rope or putting on a tail rope.

Any fish of great size is best tailed as well as gaffed. The tailer should be made from about 9 ft (2·7 m) of Bowden brake cable or rigging wire with either a ring crimped to the end or a loop formed by crimping. The free end is put through the ring or loop and the other end looped for attachment to several yards of 1000 lb (456 kg) nylon rope. A wire noose can be manipulated under water and over the shark's tail, when the tail may be lifted above the water. At once the fish loses its motive power and is much more manageable.

Once the shark is inboard, beware of its teeth and flailing tail and body. One man must hold the tail while several hard blows with a heavy club or hammer are administered just ahead of the eyes. Beware of

A tope thrashes the surface as it is brought near the boat. These Welsh anglers use a tailer instead of a gaff, so they can return the fish to the water without gaff damage.

missing the fish and crashing the hammer through the deckboards or hull! It has happened. (It is doubtful if a shark, once hauled into a boat, will live if returned to the water since internal organs tend to be ruptured once the water support is absent.)

Immediately the shark is dead, the boat should be sluiced down and scrubbed to get rid of blood and slime, since it is very easy to slip and injure oneself on a slimy deck. In addition, the angler who gets the next fish needs a sure footing to play his fish.

Mention of standing to fight the shark may surprise those anglers who have always thought sharks were fought from a swivel-chair. A swivel-chair can be a great aid to a heavy tackle angler, but the light tackle man, though he may use the chair, will usually find it easier to stand up and fight, since he is not exerting great pressure and can be more active on his feet to deal with sudden moves of the fish.

Never try to remove the hook from a dead shark; 'dead' sharks have a habit of biting off people's fingers! Let the hook remain where it is for at least two hours, if possible. Cut out the hooks back on land, and even then do it carefully.

This may make boating a shark on light tackle sound easy, and indeed it is not very difficult. All that one needs is common sense and an understanding of the tackle and its capabilities. The author knows several

anglers who had never fished shark before and who have subdued fish of up to 182 lb (83·9 kg) on line of 26 lb (11·7 kg) test without too much difficulty, even when using a star-drag reel, which is much less protective of the line than a lever-drag reel.

Beginners have some hair-raising moments when first fighting sharks on light tackle, but usually come out top. Vince Lister holds on to Diane Bellingham as she gleefully bends into a 100 lb (45·3 kg) porbeagle which she eventually boated on 25 lb (11·3 kg) test line.

Chris O'Hara with his first shark, taken on 25 lb (11·3 kg) test line and 30 lb (13·6 kg) class rod on the Isle of Wight grounds. The fish weighed 85 lb (38·5 kg).

One important point to remember is that when a fish has taken a lot of line from the reel, the level of the line having fallen considerably, the amount of resistance from the drag will increase because the line is being pulled from a point nearer to the axis of the spool – in the same way that a big heavy car without power steering is fitted with a big steering wheel while a little wheel handles the requirements of the mini. So, if a fish goes off with 300 yards of line in a rush ease off the drag a little. This is easy on the lever-drag reel, and the lever may be returned to the preset spot when line is being regained, but it has to be a hit and miss affair on the star-drag reel . . . you pays your money and you takes your chance!

Sharks will take a bait well down in the water at times, especially in the areas of reefs and overfalls, and at such times it may be just as effective, or easier, to fish the bait without any float to support it at a pre-determined depth. A bomb lead may be suspended from the line/trace junction swivel with soft copper or brass wire (which will release the lead when a strike is made) if necessary, to get the bait well down, and line is measured off in the same way as when using the float. Always take care when lowering the bait overboard as quite often a shark will grab it immediately, and woe betide anybody whose hands are fouled in the trace.

Fishing depths of up to 60 ft (27·4 m) may be tried in deep water areas, but porbeagle sharks will come inshore into very shallow water – even as little as 20 ft (2·7 m) – and take a bait. Blue sharks and mako sharks, however, are usually encountered over deep water, although threshers turn up in a few feet of water at odd times during hot summers, often to frighten holidaymakers by swimming round the piers of resorts like Newhaven in Sussex or Folkestone in Kent.

Trolling is not a method much used this side of the Atlantic, but it does catch porbeagle sharks, as several anglers proved in an exploratory trip to Ireland's west coast a few years ago. The fact that the fish will follow the bait visibly on the surface for a while before taking it is a big plus in favour of trolling, but for ground coverage it has little advantage, except that when porbeagles are known to be in a very precise small area it is possible to cross and recross the ground continuously, whereas a drifting boat cannot be precisely put over the ground.

The only special tackle needed to troll for the porbeagle is at the hook end. The same type of wire trace is used, of course, to protect the line from the shark's teeth and its rough hide, and the swivels used should be oiled so they turn freely. The bait is usually a dead mackerel with the hook set just behind the head and low down so that it keels the bait in its natural swimming position; the egg-shaped lead is either suspended on the solid wire loop beneath the bait's chin, as in the diagram, or threaded on the wire 6 in (15 cm) ahead of the bait to act as a further stabiliser, as well as to get the bait down a little.

## Mackerel rigged for trolling

A trolled bait must not spin but simply wriggle enticingly on an even keel as it is towed behind the boat. Speeds of 2–3 knots have proved about right and one big advantage of hooking sharks on a trolled bait is that usually the hook is lodged in the corner of the mouth rather than down the throat, which results in a far more lively fight and the chance to put fish back alive and unharmed. With the hook just inside the mouth, it is possible for two or more anglers to hold the fish against the boat while the hook is cut out with a sharp knife and freed with long-handled pliers.

Finally, a thought on trolling baits: a grey mullet makes an excellent tough bait and a 2 lb fish would doubtless prove ideal, though the thought may not be very acceptable to conservationists. A half dozen mullet baits per day, however, would not be unreasonable and they certainly outlast mackerel.

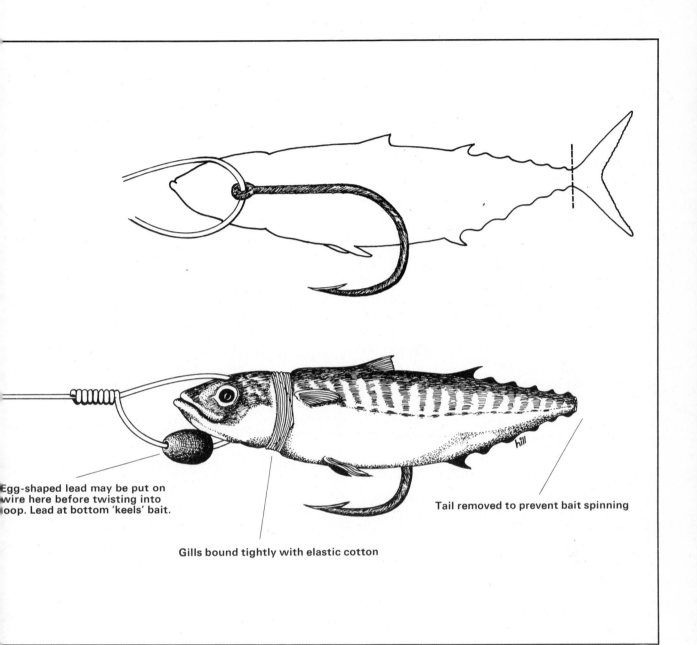

Egg-shaped lead may be put on wire here before twisting into loop. Lead at bottom 'keels' bait.

Gills bound tightly with elastic cotton

Tail removed to prevent bait spinning

hill

The mount is made of single strand stainless steel (piano) wire. The hook is pushed in position first, then the wire is pushed down through mackerel's skull, through eye of hook, out of 'chin' and then twisted to form a loop. This anchors hook to bait and stops damage when trolling.

Porbeagle sharks are catchable from the shore in some places, such as Ireland's rugged West Coast, Kerry and Clare being two notable places where they have been contacted. In parts of West Wales and in North Cornwall porbeagles will undoubtedly be taken from the rocks, once anglers dedicate themselves to the problems involved. Indeed, in Clare a fair number of fish have been taken by the well-known specialist Jack Shine, who has had fish of nearly 100 lb (45·3 kg) on line of 19 lb (8·6 kg) test and over 140 lb (61 kg) on 31 lb (14 kg) test!

The author was present when two anglers, bringing in a mackerel and a pollack on spinning tackle, had them taken by porbeagles on the same day. This happened about six years ago on the Dingle Peninsula in Kerry, and other sharks were seen a few yards from the rocks, too. The sharks that grabbed the hooked fish were well over 100 lb (45·3 kg), and in the same area, in Ventry Bay, only about 12 ft (3·6 m) deep, a massive porbeagle, estimated to weigh well over 400 lb (181·4 kg), was watched for more than an hour by the author and some friends using binoculars. It slowly cruised up and down some 200 yd (180 m) out before it finally went down.

Late July to late September is the period when porbeagles may be expected to be close in to rocky deep shores, and calm sea conditions and an offshore breeze to blow the balloon and bait out is desirable.

Blue shark fishing with light tackle: the fish is gaffed aboard, having regurgitated its stomach during the battle, the angler ready to yield line should the fish struggle free; gloved hands hold the trace preparatory to removing the hook or the trace; and finally the angler shows his fish, which would not have survived had it been returned, due to ejecting its stomach.

A heavy surfcasting rod and the 30 lb (13·6 kg) IGFA reel should suffice, with the usual shark trace and belly pad. Of course, a long-handled gaff to reach the fish and drag it up to the rocks is needed and at least one man got over this by having a set of drain-cleaning rods (like sweep's canes) at hand, which he screwed together to make the necessary length.

The tope is a true shark and is caught in the waters under discussion to weights of 70 lb (31·7 kg) or so. A good fish is over 30 lb (13·6 kg) and anything above 50 lb (22·6 kg) is exceptional.

Tope are sleek, streamlined sharks and they tend to bottom-feed to a greater extent than the other sharks so far discussed. They eat flatfish, crabs, cuttlefish and squids but will also swim near the surface to voraciously attack mackerel or herring shoals. They also swim into water barely deep enough to cover their dorsal fins and quarter the sand for such fish as bass and mullet.

As a light tackle fish the tope is among the best, and the shallower the water in which one can find it, the better the fight. Indeed, tope weighing 30–40 lb (13·6–18·1 kg) are taken in 2–4 ft (60 cm–1·2 m) from shallow, sandy beaches and will frequently dash out towards deeper water and take 300 yd (274·3 m) of fine line, sometimes even leaping clear of the water.

Boat fishing for tope can be done using either the 12 lb class (5·4 kg) or 20 lb class (9 kg) outfits as a rule; only rarely will 30 lb class (13·6 kg) have to be used, such as when fishing for very large tope known to inhabit a strong tidal current.

It is usual to leger a bait for tope, both from boat and shore. However, tope can be caught using the drifting boat and rubby-dubby tactics as for the other larger sharks. First, though, legering from an anchored boat.

The tackle is made up as follows: the 4/0 to 6/0 forged hook (Seamaster by Mustad or O'Shaughnessy by Mustad or Sealey) is attached by ferrule and crimping to about 1 yd (90 cm) of 40–50 lb (18·1–22·6 kg) cabled wire, a loop being crimped to the other end. Then 6 ft of about 60 lb (27·2 kg) nylon monofilament is fitted with a size 1 link-swivel at each end, preferably the strong Berkley type. One swivel clips to the hook link loop, the other to a ring or swivel at the end of the reel line. The heavy nylon is resistant to rubbing by the tope's sandpaper-like hide and is unobtrusive.

On the line (before the trace is clipped to it) goes a small Clements boom or Ashmore's Sea-Boom to take the lead, and if it is preferred, a small plastic bead which will rest on the swivel that connects line to heavy nylon trace, although the swivel or ring will stop it anyway.

Baiting is done in exactly the same way as for the bigger sharks, except that mackerel of 8–10 in (20–25 cm) or other fish, are more suitable. At times when tope are finicky and drop the whole fish after a short run, it often pays to substitute a whole side fillet from a large mackerel. This bait is hooked through the tail end, then once more about halfway along the bait,

after which the tail end is pulled above the hook eye and secured with shirring elastic.

The tackle is let slowly over the side and allowed to touch bottom, streaming downtide. The lead must just hold the bait firmly on the bottom and this can mean leads varying from perhaps 4 oz (113·3 g) up to more than 1 lb (400 g). Some anglers like the bait to be a long way from the lead so that it is wafted freely in the currents. To do this a piece of plastic tube and a matchstick, used as for the shark balloon float release, is used at perhaps 20 ft (6 m) from the swivel joining trace to line. The lead is held above it and then gently let down into the water. A jerk will free it and the lead is pulled up to the usual stop, which will permit fish to be brought close to the boat for tailing aboard.

There is, incidentally, no good reason to gaff and kill a tope, apart from any that may be of record size and wanted for setting up as trophies. A salmon tailer, or a smaller version of the big shark tailer, is fine for both boat and shore use. In fact, from a boat low enough to reach into the water, or from a shelving beach, there is need for neither tailer nor gaff. It is an easy matter to grab the wrist of the tope's tail with one hand and the dorsal fin with the other and lift it gently. Better still, remove the hook or cut the wire trace, while the fish is held by the boat or while in shallow water. The same internal injuries can be caused by hauling them from the water as with big sharks.

But back to the boat fishing.

When a fish takes the bait the rod tip will usually nod once or twice, then will curve over as line is pulled rapidly from the reel, which has been put in free spool with the audible ratchet on, or if the tide is strong, with the drag lightly on to prevent line pulling off, and the ratchet on. While waiting for a run the rod should be held or may be leant against the gunwale so that line can run freely.

A tope will usually run between 30–50 yd (27·4–45·7 m), then stop briefly. Then it will move off again, more slowly. The usual advice is to strike as the fish moves off after that pause, but it does result in a lot of tope being hooked in the throat. It works reasonably well to pull into the fish when the first run has taken 25 yd (22·8 m) of line, though some runs will be missed, which is the price paid for trying to hook the fish in the lip.

Fightwise, a lip-hooked fish performs far better than one that is deeply hooked, plus the fact that lip-hooking permits an almost guaranteed live return of a fish.

As with the bigger sharks, fight the tope by keeping the rod bent into a quarter circle bend. Allow the fish to run against drag pressure; when the run slows or stops, regain line by pumping. A belly pad makes boat fishing for tope more comfortable, since a 40 lb (18·1 kg) fish on the 12 lb (5·4 kg) outfit may take 15 minutes or so to beat, and the rod butt can be very uncomfortable against the lower stomach when the fish makes a sudden dive or rush.

When the anglers can reach the water from a boat with a deck low to the waterline, no gaff is necessary for securing a played-out tope. Here the author lifts one aboard for a friend by gripping the wrist of the tail and the dorsal fin.

Float fishing may be carried out from an anchored boat or, better, from a slowly drifting boat, which covers a lot more ground, in exactly the same way as for the bigger sharks, except that the bait should be just above the seabed, which is arranged by careful siting of the balloon on the line. Also, float fishing may produce better results if a whole side fillet of fish is used rather than a whole fish.

The tope season runs, usually, between mid-May and early October, but when shore fishing, the best chances may come as early as April in some areas and through to the end of May; then will follow a dull period until mid-August and through September, when the fish move inshore again. That is not to say, however, that shore fishing for tope in the intervening months is wasted effort.

Shore tope fishing may usually be divided into two types: casting from an open sand or shingle beach, especially into the deep channel of a wide estuary, to fish the bait in, say 3–20 ft (1–6 m) of water; and casting from a rocky outcrop or a ledge low down a cliff face into deeper and perhaps more flowing water – 15–40 ft (4·5–12 m).

Tackle arrangements must be changed to meet the different conditions, and the main problem to be overcome is that of casting a relatively big and heavy bait a sufficient distance. Distance is not always a problem: in some places a gentle lob of 40 yd (36·4 m) will place the bait where a patrolling tope will find it; but at others, notably the shallow and sandy beach that has little incline, it may be necessary to punch out at least 80 yd (73·1 m), maybe 120 yd (109·7 m).

A long hook trace makes a bad casting set-up, especially when the hook carries about 4 in (10 cm) of the tail end of a mackerel or herring. And more especially when the trace is of wire.

Here is the suggested terminal tackle that has worked very well for a number of keen shore tope hunters. The hook, size 3/0–5/0, is crimped to 18 in (45·7 cm) of the same wire suggested for boat fishing, a loop being formed at the opposite end. To the end of the reel line, which must be at least 250 yd (228 m) of 15 lb (6·8 kg) and better still 400 yd (365·7 m), is knotted a casting leader of about 45 lb (20·4 kg) nylon. The reel line is doubled for a few inches before forming the knot if a blood knot is used. And to the 45 lb casting leader is knotted 6 ft (1·8 m) of 60 lb (27·2 kg) nylon. Moisten the knots with saliva before pulling up tight.

**Left:** Even when the gaff has to be used, it can be so placed that the fish is relatively undamaged. The point can be placed under the jaw or into a pectoral fin, taking care to keep well clear of the delicate gills area.

**Right:** That much-pictured shore-caught Cornish tope again. This shot illustrates the cramped and tricky conditions under which it is often necessary to fish. Here there was little chance to use anything but the gaff.

On to the end of the 60 lb nylon is slid a size 1/0 link-swivel, which can be followed by a plastic bead before a second link-swivel is tied to the end of 60 lb material. The hook trace loop is clipped to the link of the swivel. The lead weight, usually a bomb-shaped or pyramidal model, is clipped to the link-swivel running on the line. If a bomb lead is used it is best not to use one with anchor wires, whether of fixed or breakaway type, since wires can tangle the trace in flight. To hold the tackle out when tidal currents are strong a pyramid lead will be found suitable, provided the seabed is of sand, sand and mud or very fine shingle, and that the leading edges of the lead are sharp. The base of the pyramid lead, an American design, digs into the seabed when pulled by the rod and line.

**The pyramid lead is suitable for most shore tope fishing, as well as conger etc. A pyramid takes a good hold on sandy or sand/mud bottoms by digging in its sharp base edges.**

This is how a 30 lb (13·6 kg) class outfit competes with a big porbeagle shark. Vince Lister contests the issue with a very large fish off Padstow in Cornwall. Although he brought the fish to the boat, it dived under it and cut the line on the keel.

Depending on the location, the bait can be a piece cut from a fresh mackerel, garfish or herring, a whole whiting or pouting, about 4 in (10 cm) long, or a big sand-eel, so far as fish-baits go; many anglers fail to realise that tope, particularly when on their inshore raids, are very partial to soft or peeler crabs.

It is essential to mount the bait so that it permits a long cast to be made, at the same time being retained on the hook without tearing. This is not too difficult and simply means trying to achieve as streamlined a bait as possible.

The tail end of a mackerel is shaped like the nose-cone of a rocket, and provided the narrow end travels first, it will cast surprisingly well. That also goes for a

tail end of herring, but ideally both baits must be fresh and firm, a bit of a problem with herring. One way out with the herring involves first mounting the tail-ends on hooks, complete with wire traces, then freezing them at home in packets, each one individually. The frozen baits may be taken fishing in a wide-necked vacuum flask and, of course, will permit fierce, long casts since they are almost solid ice! The only disadvantage is that the bait will remain frozen in the water for rather a long time.

When mounting a big sand-eel or a small whiting or other whole small fish for shore tope, pass the hook point first through the open mouth, then bring it out about halfway along the body. The mouth should be pulled up above the hook eye and there bound tightly to the trace with elastic cotton. The tail-end baits should also be bound at their slim ends in a similar position.

**This is the cone-shaped mackerel bait for such fish as shore tope. Its shape and shirring elastic support permits long casts to be made with relative ease.**

Sometimes, when maximum distance is called for, and only a sand-eel gives really good range out of the baits so far discussed, it may be necessary to reduce the desirable size of the bait and use a long, slim strip cut from a mackerel or herring or garfish. Then, cut from the tail end of the fish a strip about 5 in (13 cm) long by about 1 in (2·54 cm) and put the hook (this should be reduced to 2/0 or 3/0) in through the centre near the tail end and bring it out about an inch farther on, then put it through once more, pull it above the hook eye and tie it with the usual elastic cotton.

The lead weight is stopped, of course, 18 in (45 cm) from the baited hook when the cast is made, and this fairly short link is a great help to long casts, though it might be imagined that it presents a disadvantage so far as bait presentation is concerned. However, although it is an asset in a boat to have plenty of bait movement in the tide, in practice the short hook link works perfectly well from the shore.

It is usual to rest the rod since shore tope fishing can often involve long waits; in fact, it must be faced that several sessions may pass without any signs of tope being present, which is indeed probably the case. However, when a fish does come across the bait the blank sessions will soon be forgotten, provided that the fish is hooked and is of a reasonable size. On rocks the rod may be rested on a fishing bag or damp hand-cloth to protect the varnish and whippings from damage by abrasion or knocks. The reel must be positioned on top with the free spool lever in the 'free' position and the ratchet on. Again, tidal conditions may make it necessary to leave the reel in gear and have just a very light drag on.

From the open beach a monopod rest is best, the reel again in free spool, ratchet on if possible. Have the monopod angled so that the rod is pointing in the general direction of the bait and at an angle of about 45 degrees from the vertical.

There are several ways in which a shore tope can announce its presence at the bait, the most exciting being a sudden scream from the reel and the rod bending over as yard after yard of line streams out to sea. However, shore tope can be very gentle, and a gentle nodding of the rod tip may be the first indications of a customer. The nods will end soon and line will begin to run out, slowly at first, perhaps, then faster as the fish gains impetus. It is probable that fish rush off like this because they fear another fish might grab their find, though sometimes, if the fish feels heavy resistance from the tackle, it may be due to fear.

When the run is under way, then, pick up the rod, gently, and equally gently thumb the spool to prevent any over-running of line. The fish may be struck in mid-run or after it pauses to move off again. Since shore baits are relatively small, the mid-run strike will often connect.

The word strike should not be interpreted as a full-blooded backward stroke with the rod, perhaps combined with a backward run. Instead it is best to knock the reel into gear (the drag must have been set to pull the rod into its quarter circle before yielding), wait for the rod tip to become heavy as the fish's weight is felt, then simply hold everything firmly for a second or so until the rod takes on its fighting curve and the drag begins to whine.

At this point the fish will probably race off with 80–200 yd (73·1–182·8 m) of line. Make no attempt to do anything about it but keep the rod bent into its quarter circle. In fact, if the fish begins to feel heavier with 150 yd (137 m) of line out, back off drag pressure a little, as explained earlier. When line level on the reel gets low, remember, it takes more pull to turn the spool.

A shore tope, especially from a shallow surf beach of sand, will often run along the beach once its first mad dash out to sea has been thwarted. It then pays to follow the fish, keeping as parallel to it as possible. Use any waves coming onto the beach to bring the fish close in – but be ready for mad rushes once the fish is in a foot or so of water: tope get very alarmed in such a situation and are intent on reaching the far horizon!

From a rocky stand above the water, securing a beaten tope is more difficult than from a flat beach, of course, and is a two-man job. In fact, when fishing from places which involve climbing down cliffs, or walking across mudflats and the like, never, ever, go alone. Tragedies occur that way.

In the shallows it is easy to straddle the fish as it lies on its belly, one knee either side just behind the head, and pull open the mouth by gripping its nose. The hook may then be cut or pulled out and the fish returned to the sea, or if the hook is deep, the wire trace cut as close to the hook as possible. If it is desirable to nick the flesh in the back of the mouth to remove the hook, be sure to use something to gag the fish with first, say a block of wood, bottle etc. A tope can give a nasty bite. On the rocks get the fish back into the water as soon as possible and remember the internal damage that can be caused to sharks once removed from the supporting water; treat the fish gently.

Once in a while, from boat or shore, a tope that has given a good fight will suddenly begin to come in rolling around. This is usually caused by the fish rolling itself up in the trace, which is the reason for the 60 lb, then 45 lb (27·2 and 20·4 kg) nylon links attached to the reel line: a tope's skin is like sandpaper.

Last of the sporting shark species in this chapter, but certainly not the least so far as fighting ability is concerned, are the spotted and the non-spotted smooth-hounds.

The main difference between fishing for smooth-hounds and fishing for tope is that no wire trace is needed. Unlike the other sharks mentioned, the smooth-hound has no razor-sharp teeth for cutting and ripping but has flat, grinding teeth, which marks it as an eater of worms and crustacea rather than a grabber of fish.

The thresher (sometimes called thrasher) shark has an impressive upper lobe to its tail, shaped like a scimitar and used like one to round up shoals of bait-fish.

Other books on sea angling contain very few mentions of smooth-hounds, probably because for so long they had been confused with tope. Apart from the teeth, the smooth-hound can easily be distinguished from the tope since its dorsal fin is set almost directly above the pectoral fins, whereas the tope's dorsal is set well behind the pectorals. Also, the tail of the tope is deeply indented; that of the smooth-hound is far less so and has a very tiny lower lobe, while the tope's lower lobe is almost as long as the upper.

Smooth-hounds of both kinds are found in shallow, wide estuaries, and along open beaches. They seem to like areas of sandbanks, even when the depth is two or three feet (60–91 cm), venturing to the shallows as the tide floods and leaving for the gullies just before the water leaves the banks.

There are two boat fishing methods: one involves using the little freshwater baitcasting rod (when conditions are suitable – shallow, slow-moving water about 20 ft (6 m) deep), or the 12 lb (5·4 kg) boat outfit both fished downtide from the boat; or the bass surfcasting outfit (which is for casting away from the boat) or maybe even the salmon-type spinning rod. The reason for using a casting set-up is that in very shallow and clear water the shadow of a boat and the vibrations caused by water against the hull and by anglers in it can undoubtedly put shy fish off the feed or frighten them from the area.

Using a baitcaster like this to play a fish can be very tiring on the wrist; even modest species, like plaice or black bream, can feel like giants. Some anglers like the agony!

If a large fish is hooked and the fight lasts a long time, this is the best method of using the baitcaster. The right thumb can stop winding to brake the spool if necessary, and the line is wound back level automatically on the Ambassadeur 5000 and 6000 series reels. The butt is supported by the lower abdomen.

Just a final reminder about those shark teeth. This is only a small specimen, a porbeagle, but those teeth can do a lot of damage to a hand or leg!

Below: To make a half blood knot pass end of nylon through hook or swivel ring (eye). Make at least five turns with the end around the standing part . . .

Top right: Now pass the end through the hole between hook or swivel and the beginning of the twisted section of nylon and then through the open hook caused by bridging the gap between the end of the twisted part and the gap between the twists and the eye.

Right: Tighten knot, after moistening turns with saliva or water, by pulling on hook (swivel) and the main part of the nylon. Trim end to $\frac{1}{8}$ in (3·17 mm).

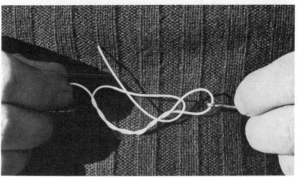

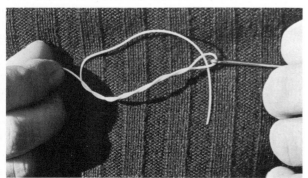

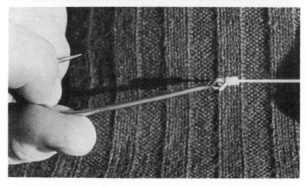

With the baitcaster or 12 lb (5·4 kg) outfit one simply lets the tackle over the side, especially when fishing at low water times in the systems of gullies with which most good smooth-hound grounds are laced. The tackle rig is simple: The trace is approximately 6 ft (1·8 m) of monofilament nylon of about 15–20 lb (6·8–9·0 kg) test to which a forged O'Shaughnessy hook, about 1/0 to 3/0 is tied with a tucked half blood knot. The bait is usually soft or peeler crab or king ragworm, used whole. Smooth-hounds will also accept razorfish and, less frequently, lugworm. But crab and ragworm are by far the best.

The trace is made up as a running leger, as for shore tope fishing, using link-swivels for both lead and trace attachment. The bead stop is again optional.

Nearly all smooth-hound bites are fast and take yards of line from the reel with a rush. So, fish with the reel out of gear and the ratchet on, and be ready to grab the rod should you rest it against the gunwale. In fact, it is best to hold the rod. When using the baitcaster the fight can be very exciting – and punishing on the wrist if you decide to fight single handed, rather than hold the rod ahead of the reel and rest the butt against your body.

To secure smooth-hounds a big landing net is very useful, although the tope tailer will do. The net must be very large (a circular one about a yard across (1 m)) and strong and about 4 ft (1·2 m) deep. The Canadian Stag brand salmon net is absolutely first class, though expensive at about £12.

When using the bass casting rod or the salmon and pike spinning rod to cast away from the boat when anchored on shallow banks, the same terminal tackle is used, except that the running lead is a breakaway type. The cast is made from the side of the boat, uptide and out, and line is permitted to spill from the reel until it forms a big bow in the tide. This bow drags the anchor wires into the seabed and holds the tackle in position well away from the boat, even in strong currents which sometimes run over shallow banks.

The bowed line also affects the way in which the bite is registered. Instead of the reel screaming as line is pulled off by the fish the rod tip is likely to jump back from its tensioned position, and then the line will drop slack and spill downtide. The fish has taken the bait and dislodged the lead's anchor wires, causing it to tumble downtide as the fish moves off with the bait. Pick up the rod, wind in the slack as fast as possible, and wait until the fish is felt as a heavy, moving weight before pulling in the hook. Of course, when fishing with the casting rod in the shallows when there is no tidal flow to worry about, an ordinary bomb-shaped lead may be used to hold bottom; in which case the bite will be a fast, audible check run with the rod bending and nodding.

From the shore the bass rod will usually be found ideal with its matching line and reel. In fact, if the cast does not have to go much more than 40 yd (36 m), then the salmon type rod and reel with its 10 lb test (4·5 kg) line will provide some excitement.

Smooth-hounds fight very hard indeed; in fact they are thought by some light tackle anglers who regularly hunt them to be the hardest fighting saltwater fish of all.

The author's first encounter with a smooth-hound, which just happened to be the spotted variety, occurred while bass fishing in the surf on a Kent shingle/sand beach with peeler crab. The first fish took off on a long run, stripping 60 yd (55 m) of line, out to sea, then ran up and down the beach just behind the surf line for five minutes or so before being beached. The visions of a new name on the record bass spot were destroyed when the mini-shark, at first thought to be a tope, came ashore. It weighed only 9 lb (4 kg) but had fought much harder than its weight, as anglers say.

An unspotted smooth-hound of 35 lb (15·8 kg), or a spotted one of 25 lb (11·3 kg), on the kind of tackle suggested here will prove to be a memorable encounter.

# 6

# The conger eel

The conger is a fish of legends, the malevolent haunter of dark wrecks and reefs, whose bite is terrible to see, a severer of fingers and of thick wire traces. And surely few other fish can look so fierce as they come to the gaff, spinning, lashing the water, mouth snapping, exerting tremendous strength against the tackle.

**The mark of an experienced light tackle angler is confidence. He knows how far he can safely stress his gear and he lets his rod do its job. Here the action is off the West Country on a wreck boat.**

So, how, one might ask, can this monster be taken on light tackle – up to 30 lb class? The answer is, by skill and with sound, good quality matched tackle. And with confidence, of course.

Conger eels no doubt reach incredible weights: 200 lb (over 90 kg) is on the cards and the current British rod-caught record at the time of writing is held by a fish of 109 lb 6 oz (49·6 kg) from a Devon port, though it was taken well out.

However, many big congers are taken, even from the rubble and entanglement of deep water wrecks, on lines of no more than 30 lb test (13·6 kg). One of the clever anglers who has set a standard for light tackle conger fishing – and who has made those who have for years insisted that 80 lb (36·2 kg) test is 'light for conger' look a little silly, is Ray Rush of the British Light Tackle Club. He has taken many big congers on 30 lb class tackle, topped by a fish of 80¼ lb (36·4 kg)!

Once again it is necessary to examine the separate aspects of shore and boat fishing for congers, and to explain how it is that massive, strong eels of the above mentioned sizes may be vanquished on such comparatively light tackle.

Like fishing for sharks, boat fishing for conger usually begins about May, but it ends in late October, not because the fish are not available in our waters at any other times, but mainly because the winter weather conditions make long hauls out to West Country wrecks an impossible or dangerous operation.

Although the Devon and Cornish coastline tends to produce the biggest congers, mainly due to the specialised wreck boats operating with Decca navigational aids and the skill of the skippers, there are also large congers taken from the coasts of Dorset, Hampshire, Sussex and Kent. Excellent congers are also taken in Scottish waters, especially on the west coast.

Boat fishing for conger can be over inshore rocky marks or rough ground, or way out to sea in very deep water into wrecks. Inshore conger fishing can be done from small boats, though anything much less than 14 ft (4·2 m) is a little limited when sharing the space with 6 ft (1·8 m) of lashing eel! Wreck fishing is usually carried out from boats of 40 ft (12 m) or more and the use of Decca is necessary to locate and anchor over far-off wrecks. Often the fishing is limited to neap tides and to the two or three hours or so either side of high and low water, due to the difficulty of fishing in very deep and fast water.

The heaviest outfit listed is the 30 lb (13·6 kg) IGFA rod with matching line and reel, and this is quite capable, in skilled hands, of subduing any amount of 50–60 lb (22·6–27·2 kg) congers, and, as has been proved, much heavier specimens on occasions. It is well to remember, though, that it is a very different matter bringing a big conger to the boat from the bottom in 30–40-odd fathoms (50–70 m) of water, than beating a porbeagle or mako shark twice as heavy on the same outfit. Sharks fight by swimming and can be exhausted by being encouraged to do so; congers do not make long runs when hooked in deep water from a boat; they hang back with powerful, sinuous body undulations, moving backwards in direct combat with the pull of the rod. Usually, once in a cleft in a rock or among the debris of a wreck, the fish will be almost impossible to extricate . . . and so the light tackle tactic is based on not letting the conger ever get into his holt.

Constant heavy pressure will be brought to bear on the tackle in combat with a 50 lb (22·6 kg) plus conger, and for this reason a line of Dacron or Terylene is advisable rather than nylon, which stretches and then recovers, and in so doing can crush very strong metal reel spools. In spite of the fact that many conger-addict wreck anglers do not like to see fellow anglers using braided lines (they reckon that braids are bowed more by tide and drift leads to tangle with other gear) the use of braid for light tackle fishing is advisable for big conger, not just to protect the réel but for other important reasons, sensitivity being one of them.

While fishing in deep flowing water, the signals of a fish at the bait are largely nullified by the stretch in nylon monofilament of 30 lb (13·6 kg) class. It is generally not until the eel has emerged from the wreck or reef, pouched the bait and begun to move back into its lair that the bite is telegraphed up the line to the angler. And that may be too late – at least, too late with light tackle to be able to haul out the fish.

The light tackle man must fish in a different way. His success rate depends on knowing when a conger first touches the bait, so that he can lure the fish from its lair. This is done by slowly recovering line once a bite is felt. The eel will more often than not slide out of its hole or crack to retain the bait, and, if care is taken not to reel too quickly, nor jerk the bait, the eel will come several yards off the bottom with the bait in its mouth.

Then comes the crunch. The eel suddenly feels insecure; something is wrong. Dive it must! Which it does, and then is brought up against the rod tip, and the hook point pierces the soft jaw.

Now is the time for action. The rod is kept at its maximum curve and the eel pumped off the bottom if it will come. If it pulls so hard that there is a risk of line breakage, the drag must be allowed to give a little line; not too much, but just enough at the peak of each lunge to avoid the sudden snatch that spells disaster. For this reason, and the fact that with conger there is no mass of line stripped from the reel, it is best to set the drag a little lighter than for shark, and add any necessary extra pressure by thumb pressure on the spool of line.

Terminal tackle needs no great finesse. Since the braided Dacron or Terylene stretches little a short length of heavy monofil – about 40 lb (18·1 kg) test – is attached to the Dacron by means of a strong Berkley barrel swivel. The Dacron is doubled for about 4 in (10 cm) and the tucked half blood knot tied in the doubled end for added security. The heavy monofil is

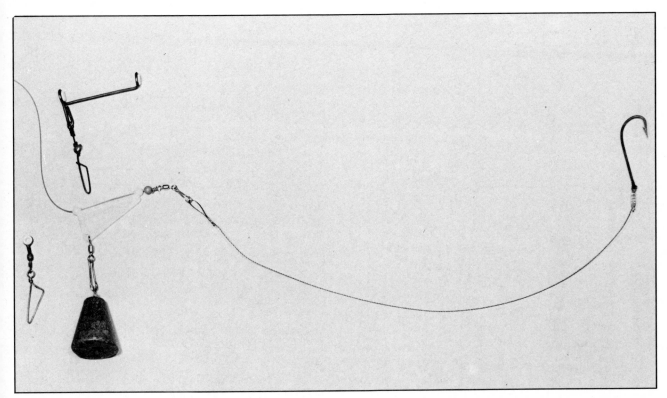

A useful set-up for conger from the boat: a running leger using an Ashmore Sea-boom. Alternative running booms are the double-eyed Clements and the single-eyed Kilmore. Again, the wire trace is ready for quick release via the Berkley link-swivel.

tied with the same knot to the other ring of the swivel. On the nylon runs a Clements boom or a big link swivel to take the lead, with another strong link swivel at the very end to take the hook trace. The hook can be a strong forged type, sizes 6/0 to 10/0, crimped in the usual way to about 2 ft (60 cm) of wire, about 100 lb (45·3 kg) test. The usual loop is formed at the other end to fit to the link swivel.

This rig, with leads between 10 oz (283 g) and 2 lb (900 g) should cope with most offshore conger fishing from a boat. It is appreciated that many anglers will scoff at such comment, but the fact remains that many conger of 50–80 lb (22·6–36·2 kg) have been beaten on such 'fragile' gear. However, in deference to the power of a big conger this is one of the few times in this book that it will be agreed that, at times, a 50 lb (22·6 kg) IGFA outfit may be appropriate. This is not an admission that 30 lb class is insufficient but that many of us lack the skill to use it on such monsters.

Quite apart from these very big congers that live in wrecks and reefs way offshore in deep water, there are many others up to about 50 lb (22·6 kg) or so within half a mile (1·6 km) of most rocky shores and in water no more than 20 ft (6 m) deep. Often the eels of such areas, especially where the rocks are interspersed with patches of sand or mud, can be taken on 12–20 lb (5·4–9 kg) after dark when they leave the rocks to hunt the open patches. Simple leger tackle, made up in the

same way as for offshore congers, is in order, but the wire may be reduced to about 50 lb (22·6 kg) test.

Hooked on this light tackle in open ground the congers on the shallows will often fight harder than the bigger offshore specimens, making long, quite fast runs instead of simply hanging back and undulating.

Of course, to take matters to a logical conclusion, there is great sport in challenging eels that may run between 10–40 lb (4·5–13·6 kg) or so with the bass surfcasting outfit from the shore; or, if the conditions warrant it – such as jagged masses of weed-draped rocks, an old harbour wall laced with conger-inhabited crevices or similar – then the big surfcasting rod and the 20 lb (or even 30 lb) class boat reel – such as Ambassadeurs 9000 or 7000 – will be called into action.

Nylon monofilament lines of 15–18 lb (6·8–8 kg) have been used to land conger of 50 lb (22·6 kg) from rocky shores, and there is no good reason why this should not be a regular occurrence. There is great magic in being out on a warm summer or early autumn night, the water lapping, and hearing the gentle ticking of the ratchet as a conger picks up the bait and slowly moves off with it. The rod may be rested in a monopod on the beach or laid down, reel up, on rocks or a stone pier.

Warm and settled summer weather is the best for conger fishing, especially when it is muggy. Sport

## The conger eel

A really large conger is an awesome creature. This 88¾-pounder (40·2 kg) shown by Bernard Williams came from the West Country. Fish of just over 80 lb (36·2 kg) have been caught on 30 lb (13·6 kg) class tackle!

seldom is good when there is a strong wind blowing, in this case particularly if that wind is onshore.

It is important, when casting into rocky or rough ground, not to drag or allow the tide to drag the tackle across the seabed once it has been cast, otherwise the lead or hook will without doubt become snagged.

Playing shore conger on a bass rod and light line is – or should be – a delicate affair. It is no good merely hanging on like grim death and not yielding any line at all; similarly it is senseless to let the eel have free rein so that it can get into a rocky crevice or hole, there to stay with its tail locking it firmly in position. One keeps that important quarter circle of bend in the rod and takes a turn or two with the reel whenever that curve straightens a little and the eel yields ground.

The rock-hoppers' heaven. The author has just won an encounter with a conger of about 15 lb (6·8 kg) hooked on legered mackerel in this rocky depression. The fish has been gaffed using big hooks on a rope.

Too many British anglers want to see their hooked fish too early in the fight, so they haul hard. And many of them get broken more times than they like to remember. It is not often that a fish breaks an angler's line; it is more often the angler's mistake or a fault in the tackle that does so.

The author's first encounter with conger on bass tackle from the shore occurred one night in a rocky Sussex estuary. Bass were the quarry and the bait was a whole side of fresh mackerel legered in only 3 ft (91 cm) of water with 12 lb (5·4 kg) test line and no wire trace, of course. The two congers caught weighed 18 lb and 22 lb (8·1 and 9·9 kg) and they each fought for about 30 minutes, making runs of 30 yd (27·4 m) or so repeatedly.

Another memorable conger weighed about 25 lb (11·3 kg), but it was beaten on a 7 ft (2·1 m) seatrout spinning rod, fixed-spool reel and 8 lb (3·6 kg) monofil, when the author was fishing for plaice from a dinghy on a sandy patch among the rocks. That fish took only about 15 minutes to bring to the boat, but was a very satisfactory exercise in patience and tackle manipulation!

There is only one practical way of bringing a conger into a boat or onto a beach or rocks, and that is with a sharp, strong gaff. The best type is a simple cadmium plated and tinned lash-on hook (Mustad make good ones) strongly whipped to a broomstick or similar handle about 4 ft (2 m) long. The tang of the gaff shaft is first located in a hole drilled in the wooden handle, the whipping being done with strong nylon or Terylene thread, and well varnished, or with copper or brass wire, which may be carefully covered with solder.

The stroke with the gaff should be made just back of the head and the movement continued in a smooth arc to bring the fish into the boat or onto the beach or rocks. From high rocks, a harbour wall or pier three 12/0 big game hooks brazed back to back to form a triangle and attached to a strong nylon rope with about 1 lb (400 g) of lead pipe on the rope just above it, will bring congers to the platform. The triangle of hooks is lowered in position, the eel held as quietly as possible, and the rope given a sharp jerk to penetrate the fish.

There is no need when boat fishing to go to any lengths to present the bait cleverly. Half a mackerel (cut across the body), a whole one or similar lumps of herring, pouting, whiting, pilchard or squid and cuttlefish are all good baits. In addition, crab is good used from the shore.

On the boat simply hook the bait by putting the hook through one end and bringing it back through the bait so that the point is well clear. When a longish cast must be made from the shore, then baits as for tope fishing from the shore should be used for streamlining and security.

Finally a word of warning: conger have powerful jaws and sharp cutting teeth. Do not be tempted to extricate a deep hook unless either the eel has been still and out of the water for at least an hour or you have long-handled pliers with which to work. Since this is a book on sportfishing and not 'meat fishing', it hardly seems appropriate to advise on quick and humane ways to kill fish. Nevertheless, congers are difficult to unhook and return safely, even fish of under 20 lb (9 kg), because they are so slippery and immensely strong out of water. If it can be done, then do it using pliers. But if the fish must be killed (and conger steaks or fish cakes make good eating) hit the eel hard and several times with a heavy priest across the tail, just behind the vent. The conger's important 'works' are located there and it will soon succumb. A knife with a pointed, sharp and strong rigid blade should be driven through the eel's spine just behind the head, which will irrevocably disconnect the 'sharp end' from the 'works' and make it fairly safe. Even so, anybody who puts his fingers near a conger's jaws, even a 'dead' conger, risks a nasty injury.

A sack should be used to hold congers in a small boat or on shore, the neck being securely tied with strong cord; on a big charter-boat the eels are usually stowed in the fish-hold immediately on being caught.

117

# 7

# Skates and stingray

The skates under discussion here are not the fish so described in the fish-and-chip shops. There are only three true skates swimming in the waters with which this book is concerned: the common skate (*Raja batis*), the white skate (*Raja alba*) and the long-nosed skate (*Raja oxyrinchus*). Of these, the common skate, sometimes called the grey skate, is by far the most common – true to its name. It forms at least 95 per cent of rod-caught skate captures. There has been no true long-nosed skate verified on rod and line to the author's knowledge, although most years some white

skate are caught from Ireland's west coast, especially in the Clew Bay area, in Galway and Tralee Bays.

The so-called fish-and-chip shop 'skate' is in fact a ray, usually the thornback (*Raja clavata*) although other rays are not rejected when they turn up, of course!

So far as the angler, and more particularly the sportfisher, is concerned it is wise to forget the other two skates and concentrate on the common one: the white skate may turn up once in a lifetime, by chance, and the same tackle and techniques will be suitable.

**An 81 lb (36·7 kg) white skate nears the gaff in Ireland. A comparatively rare fish for the angler.**

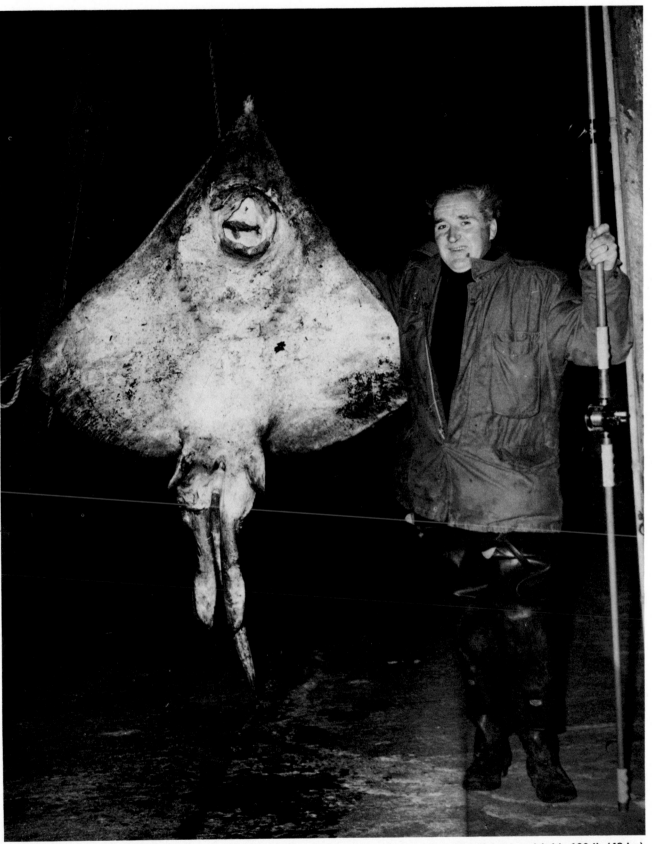

One of the best feats of light tackle angling ever achieved, in the author's opinion: Frank Avery with his 106 lb (48 kg) common skate from Ireland's Fenit Pier. He fought the fish for 4½ hours on line of 19 lb (8·6 kg) test! The reel was a light-weight bass surfcasting model.

It is obvious that many anglers will raise their eyebrows – if they are gentlemen, and utter profanities if they are not – by the very inclusion of common skate in a light-tackle book. However, although many still cling to the idea that skate fishing with anything less than 80 lb (36·2 kg) test line is madness – and that 100 lb (45·3 kg) 'string' is better – one cannot help but defend the sportfishing idea by gleefully pointing out that Robin Macpherson's British record skate of 226½ lb (102·7 kg) was beaten in 55 minutes with 40 lb (18·1 kg) test line on a small Mitchell surfcasting reel and a cheap Japanese rod that a sportfisher would ridicule.

Also, more than a few enthusiasts regularly boat common skate of over 100 lb (45·3 kg) on lines of about 30 lb (13·6 kg) test, and it is a fact that from a few deep-water piers in the country, mainly in Scotland and in south-west Ireland, skate of around this weight are taken on strong casting outfits. In fact, one angler of the author's acquaintance vanquished a common of 106 lb (48 kg) with such tackle, including line of 19 lb (8·6 kg) test from Fenit Pier in County Kerry. The battle took four and a half hours!

The trouble is, most anglers who do seek common skate seek big skate, and that means fish well over 100 lb (45·3 kg). So, they use heavy gear, just in case they do encounter true leviathan, for fish of more than 400 lb (181·4 kg) have been landed by commercial fishing boats. They also tend to fish only in those areas where common skate are known to live but, of necessity, where there are suitable boats and skippers. The small skate they catch are then regarded as tiddlers, whereas the light tackle angler could have some fun with them – fish of 30–70 lb (13·6–31·7 kg) or so.

Where are the skate grounds? They may lie in many as yet undiscovered areas, but the ones that regularly produce fish include the famous Orkney and Shetland grounds, Ullapool, Stornoway, Mull, to name a few of the Scottish ones; the deep water off the Isle of Wight, off the Devon and Cornish coasts (where little angling is done, but where commercials catch them by accident), and the south and south-west coasts of Ireland, the hot-spots being famous names: Ballycotton, Dungarvan, Youghal, Cobh, Kinsale, Baltimore, Kenmare River, Valentia Island and Cahirciveen, Tralee Bay, then right up the west coast (Clew Bay is famous but has been overfished and has declined) as far as Sligo.

As already stated, there may be many more excellent grounds, especially off the north-west and northern coasts of Northern Ireland, the western isles of Scotland and between Shetland and the Faroes.

So far as the light tackle man is concerned, however, the existing skate areas will afford plenty of sport, since the 30 lb (13·6 kg) outfit reaches its lifting limit of skate of about 80 lb (36·2 kg). One has to remember that skate do not usually fight by making long tiring runs and by swimming; they tend to use their vast wings as foils so that tide keeps them 'glued' to the bottom; and even if the tackle will lift

them a few feet they are very capable of regaining the seabed with a few slow, powerful wingbeats. In any really strong tidal stream, the 30 lb (13·6 kg) outfit will be quite incapable of lifting the fish or stopping a dive.

However, since the 226½ lb (102·7 kg) fish was beaten on 40 lb (18·1 kg) line, it is obvious that there are ways to do the apparently impossible.

This is what usually happens: big skate, which favour areas of sand and mud surrounded by rough stretches of marly ground, tend to lie firmly on the seabed when the tide is flowing strongly. When the run eases, at high or low water, the fish heave themselves off the bottom and feed a little before settling in a new position as the tide begins to strengthen in flow from the opposite direction, so that their heads face the flow which keeps them on the seabed. It is therefore at slack water – specially on neap tides – that any light tackle skate fishing should be done. In fact, any skate fishing, whatever the tackle!

Naturally, once a skate is hooked on 30 lb (13·6 kg) tackle, time is of the essence: if the fight extends into the period when the tidal run picks up again there may be little hope of a successful conclusion so far as the angler is concerned. As with the really big conger, it must be admitted here that once the optimum period has passed, or if the fish in the locality do feed into the tidal run period (as is sometimes the case) the 50 lb (22·6 kg) outfit must be brought into use. The actual line test will be in the region of 45–47 lb (20·4–21·3 kg).

One of the main reasons why British anglers do tend to use very heavy tackle, whether for skate, conger, tope or shark, is because few know how to play a big fish and are impatient to see what it is they have hooked. So, they pressure the fish to get it near enough to have a look at it – and that leads to tackle breakages.

The 30 lb (13·6 kg) outfit is used, then, with either Dacron, Terylene or nylon monofilament line, the braids being safer since they stand less chance of crushing the reel when the coils are rewound under high tension. The whole outfit, terminal tackle included, is almost the same as that for conger, except that the hook trace itself must be about 4 ft (1·2 m) to avoid the line being rubbed on the skate's rough leading wing edges, and may be reduced to 60 lb test (27·2 kg).

The first signal of a skate at the bait is often a shiver running up the line – probably caused by the skate settling itself over the bait and moving up to position its mouth to take it, the massive wings rubbing the trace or line as it manoeuvres. Comes a brief pause, then the line will begin to run out in jerks. The rod is usually rested securely against the gunwale with the reel on light drag and with audible ratchet on. The hook is pulled in firmly – in the case of light tackle by simply switching the lever to 'in-gear' and holding on until the rod curves over, then lifting it back into a fighting curve – and an attempt made to keep the fish moving around off the bottom. The light tackle makes this difficult, but not impossible; it means using the

This skate from Scapa Flow in Orkney was taken by the late Terry Brown (left) on 45 lb (20·4 kg) line. It weighed 147 lb (66·6 kg) and the fish had the advantage of an increasing tidal flow.

Dead common skate exhibited on a gantry in Westport, County Mayo, Ireland, make a sorry picture; it would have been far better to set them free at sea, for they weighed 139 lb and 60 lb (63–27·2 kg) — way off record size.

tackle very close to its limit. Smooth pumping is essential.

The belly pad should be worn all the time one is fishing for skate since there is no time to put it on before picking up the rod. The strain must be put on the fish immediately and maintained throughout.

Common skate are not eaten as a rule, although it is said the wings of fish under 50 lb (22·6 kg) are tolerable. Therefore, unless there is a very good reason, the boated fish should be returned to the sea, not killed. To bring the fish aboard two gaffs are usually used, each being inserted through the leading edge of opposing wings about 3 in back and 1 ft out (8 and 30 cm) from the nose. The two gaffers then haul the fish over the gunwale and into the boat. A trophy photograph should now be taken and the fish, still on the gaffs, put back over the side and the gaffs slid free. The small holes are but superficial wounds to a large fish like a skate. Weighing a fish on a boat is seldom very accurate.

Whenever possible, it pays not to allow the tackle to fish too far downtide of the boat: with light tackle especially it is best to try to keep right over the fish, and sometimes a skate will try to swim uptide when hooked, a very helpful move for the angler, who can try to exert only just sufficient pressure to make the fish strive to remain in that position, often fighting slight tidal flow too.

The mouth of the common skate has no sharp cutting teeth but is well equipped with massive crushing pads and muscles, so a strong forged hook, well sharpened as always, is necessary. Baits which commonly succeed include mackerel, herring, small whole coalfish (about 1 ft long – that's 31 cm), pollack of similar size, lumps of dogfish (lesser spotted) and pouting.

Skate fishing is worthwhile from mid-April to early November, with May, June and September providing the best of the sport as a rule.

Having mentioned shore-caught common skate, this aspect had best be dealt with briefly. It must be borne in mind that such fishing can usually only be successful where fairly deep water comes inshore in the form of broad channels; and it should also be remembered that most of the shore-caught skate have come from one place, the deep-water ocean pier at Fenit, Tralee Bay, County Kerry. Good specimens have also been taken from deep-water piers and projections in Scottish sea-lochs on the west coast, however, and anybody given to experimenting could – with perseverance and much patience – discover other places.

Obviously, the heaviest shore outfit in the list in chapter 2 would be used, with the running leger rig as described previously for shore tope. If possible, the 4 ft (1·2 m) of wire trace should be retained, even though it might be a little difficult to cast, since rubbing on the fish is liable to be over a long period, due to the light tackle being used. Casting is made easiest by using an anchor lead and hooking the hook on one of the wires before casting. Air resistance makes it fly free in mid-cast. The reel, Ambassadeur 9000, 9000C, or 7000, or Policansky Monitor 2, should be loaded with 30 lb (13·6 kg) class line.

The Policansky Monitor No. 2 multiplier, made by craftsmen in South Africa, is an ideal reel for battling big congers, common skate and other heavy fish from the shore. It can cast about 100 yd (91·4 m) and has a smooth lever-drag and strong spool machined from aluminium alloy.

Unless there is access down to the water level, when two long gaffs may be used, a special gaff made up from three 12/0 hooks brazed together at their backs and weighted with lead pipe (as for conger fishing from rocky shores) is useful. It is let down on a strong rope in the same way, of course; or else, the long, screw-connected sweep's brush handles in conjunction with a normal big gaff hook (as for shore porbeagle) may be brought into service.

When shore fishing for common skate, and with even a reasonable chance of connecting, it will pay to carry a belly pad, since the fight is bound to last a long time, and stomach and groin injuries could easily be sustained when imposing firm pressure on a skate over a long period. As in the boat, maintain the pressure as firmly as the tackle will stand. The fish is likely to move around the bottom, often stopping to try to hold the bottom. Try to prevent the fish from lying still by pumping, jerking a little perhaps, or bombarding the area with anything handy. It is not only a sulking salmon that can be woken up with a well aimed rock!

The stingray is the only member of the true ray family that warrants inclusion in a book on light tackle sportfishing, as opposed to fishing for the pot. The stingray is a fish of the summer months, moving into inshore waters to lie in the sun-warmed shallows – often only 18 in (45·7 cm) deep – over sand, sandy mud or gravel. Unlike the common skate and other common rays, such as the thornback, blond, undulate and painted varieties, the stingray has a very thick body and is very muscular, swimming fast when hooked and sometimes leaping clear of the water, too, when hooked. Its tail is slender and whip-like, equipped about one third back from the body with a sharp, serrated spine set dorsally. When frightened or otherwise stimulated it tries to bring the tail over and drive the spine into any nearby aggressor, and it often succeeds only in spearing itself. The spine is not only sharp but carries venom-producing tissues in a groove.

Mid-June is a good time to begin hunting the stingray, which certainly reaches weights in excess of 60 lb (27·2 kg) and is regularly caught in the 20–30 lb (9–13·6 kg) class. The fish seem to move to deep water in late summer, around mid-August. They appear to favour extensive estuaries and shallow water interspersed with banks of mud or gravel, especially when the area is protected from prevailing winds.

Although stingrays occur fairly widely in the southern North Sea, the favoured areas extend south from The Wash, the coast between Felixstowe and North Foreland being famous. Stingrays also occur on shallow sandy areas on the Sussex coast, especially along the shore between Hove and Selsey Bill, Lancing and Rustington being hot-spots. The Solent is also well worth visiting, although Solent fishing has deteriorated somewhat during the seventies, mainly due to industrial and domestic pollution plus some excessive commercial fishing. South Wales' Gower Peninsula also produces, as does Tralee Bay in Kerry.

Stingrays, like the other skates and rays, are bottom feeders: they avidly take baits of king ragworm, crab (soft, peeler or hermit), sometimes lugworm or herring strip.

Since this ray is such an active fighter, much lighter tackle may be used than for common skate. It can be fairly said that a 40 lb (18·1 kg) stingray fights about three times as hard as a common skate of at least double that weight. The fight, however, is more like that of a round fish, like the tope, and so it is possible to make the fish run and tire itself, even with, say, 10 lb (4·5 kg) test line.

Warm and settled weather with a calm sea are the optimum conditions for stingray fishing. From a boat it is wise to begin fishing, when possible, about half-way up the flood tide on the edges of shallow sandbanks leading to deep-water channels. As the tide approaches the hour before high water the boat should be quietly moved on to the sandbank or flat, where the fish may be expected in water little more than knee-deep, though often the depth in which fish will be taken may be 4–8 ft (1·2–2·4 m). As the ebb gets under weigh it helps to move the boat to the downtide edge of the shallows to ambush the fish as they move into the deeper channels, for often the best flats and banks for stingrays – and other sporting fish – dry out completely on many a low water period.

It is possible to fish with the 12 lb or 20 lb class boat outfits. However, since both the shadow of the boat or noise can frighten or put off the feed fish that are in very shallow water, it is often a good idea to cast well away from the anchored boat, as little as 20 or as far as 50 yd (18·2 or 45·7 m).

A light boat rod of the two standards mentioned will permit the bait to be lobbed the shorter of the two distances, but for anything more ambitious a casting rod is called for such as the boatcaster mentioned in chapter 2. This, as we know is 8½–9 ft (2·5–2·7 m) long and casts 3–5 oz (85–141·7 g). It is also possible to use the bass rod. In either case, the reel may be an Ambassadeur 6000 series or 7000 model and should be filled with 10–15 lb (4·5–6·8 kg) line, depending on the average size of the stingrays in the area.

The most useful tackle is a straight running leger, a link-swivel (about size 4) being slid up the line before another ordinary swivel of about the same size is tied to the end of the line (which is doubled first) with a tucked half blood knot. The hook trace should be about 4 ft (1·2 m) of nylon of about 30 lb (13·6 kg) test, to which a strong forged hook is tied. This should be from size 3/0 for ragworm and smallish baits, up to 5/0 for a big crab or any big bait. Stingrays do not have cutting teeth, only grinding, crushing pads, so wire traces are unnecessary while sharp hooks are, of course, as always.

When using king ragworm for stingrays use a big one whole, do not cut it in short lengths. Pass the hook into the worm's mouth and thread it well round the hook so that the worm's head ends up well above the hook eye.

125

The sveldt appearance of this fish belies his dangerous character. An Essex stingray is pictured before return to the sea.

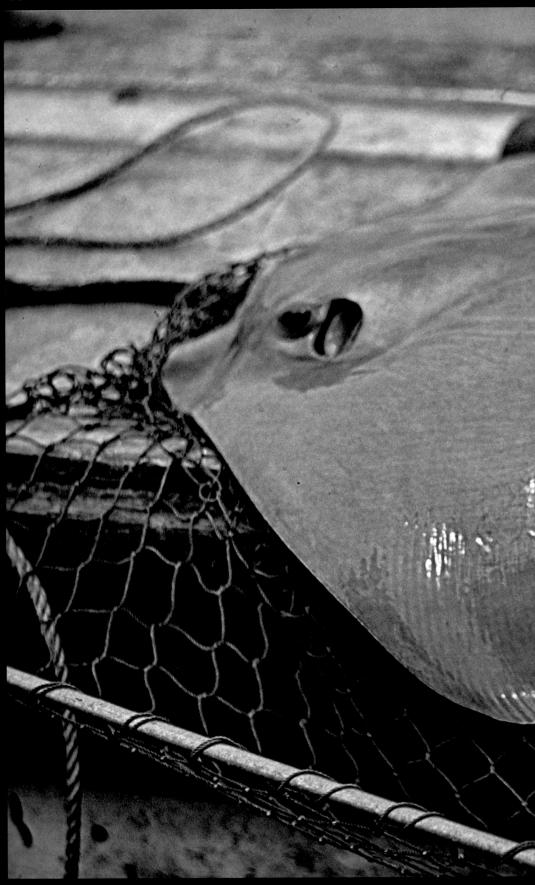

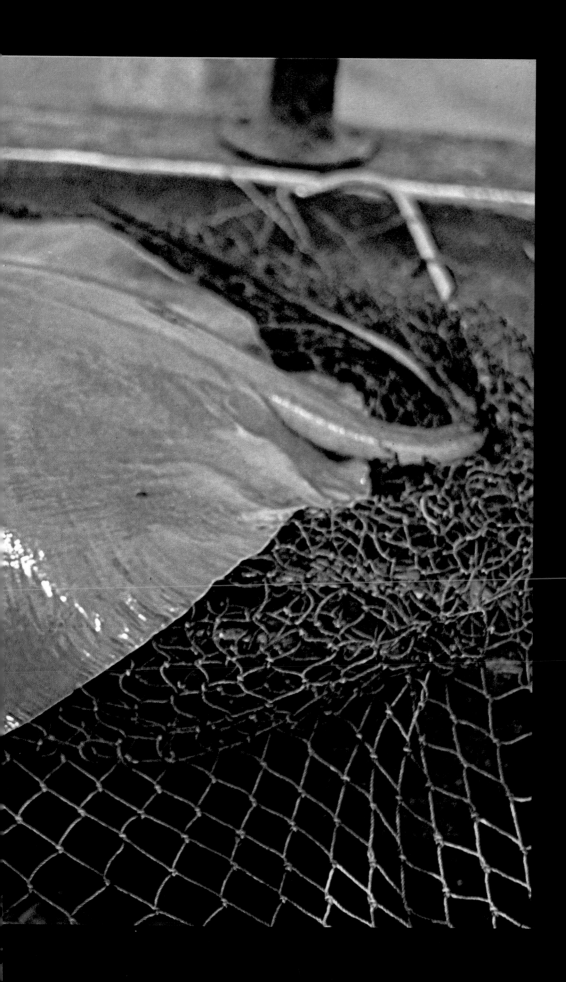

Mark of an experienced stingray man. Hold the fish well away from the legs. This is an Essex specimen, the Essex and Thames Estuary areas being well populated by large stingrays.

The bite of a stingray can be sudden and savage, stripping yards of line from the reel. Sometimes, if the angler is paying attention, advance warning in the shape of little twitches will be seen or felt. The fish should be struck firmly when it has taken a yard or so of line, which in most cases means as quickly as one can pick up the rod, put the reel in gear and lift the tip back.

The first move of the ray is normally a fast run away from the boat, and it is essential that the drag on the reel has been previously adjusted to yield line safely below the strain the line will stand. Any extra pressure can be put on the fish by pressing a thumb on to the line or the edge of the spool. When the fish comes in close to the boat, apparently beaten, always be ready for it to suddenly dive under the boat. It must be countered by thrusting the tip of the rod far under the water, pushing the line down so that it cannot rub on the keel and be broken.

For stingrays up to 20 lb (9·0 kg) or so a big landing net, such as the Stag model, or a home-made one of rugged construction, is a good idea. For anything bigger use the gaff, clipping it just inside the leading edge of the wing to one side of the mouth.

It is useful to have a wet sack to throw over the ray once it is aboard to forestall its tail lashing; keep a foot on the tail while the hook is removed with strong, long-nosed pliers. If the fish has been netted, put it back by holding the net over the side and inverting it quickly. If a gaff is used, keep the fish on the gaff while unhooking, then put it back still on the gaff, which is disengaged with a quick push.

Shore fishing is very similar to the casting system from the boat. Expect the fish to be in range from about halfway up the flood tide as it comes over the sandy or muddy flats. The rod can be rested in a suitable monopod with the reel out of gear and on check, if this is possible in the tidal conditions prevailing. To hold bottom it may sometimes be necessary to use a breakaway lead, though it will usually be found that a straight bomb will hold position since most stingray shore grounds are out of the main run of the tide.

Although stingrays, big ones especially, will leap clear of the water, even when boat fishing, this occurs much more regularly when shore fishing, since the bait will frequently be picked up in little over a foot of water. The spectacle of a bat-like shape kiting out of the water on being struck is quite exciting.

A long-handled gaff is best for securing a ray from a flat beach, and keep a foot on the tail when unhooking the fish, as before. Anglers are not often spiked, but once is likely to be enough!

Finally, once in a while when stingray fishing a strange-looking 'sting' will come along. This specimen is the eagle ray, which has a tail spike but also has a small dorsal fin just in front of it. The stingray has of course no dorsal fin. The eagle ray also has a pronounced Concorde-like nose, distinctly separated from the actual body disc, and rising in a steep line to thicken out when joining the disc. The author once saw an eagle ray of about 30 lb (13·6 kg) taken on lugworm by an angler fishing for soles on a Kent beach in late summer. Everybody thought it was a stingray, and that's how it was reported in the newspapers.

An easy quick check is to look at the tips of the ray's wings: if they are round it is an ordinary stingray; if they are pointed (plus the other features mentioned) a comparatively rare eagle ray has been caught.

# 8

# Cod

The cod is a fish sought in autumn and winter in the southern part of England, to which shores the shoals migrate, usually in late September/early October. In the North Sea, however, from Yorkshire to beyond Caithness and back down the western coast of Scotland as far as the Firth of Clyde, fish are present throughout most of the year.

That statement needs clarification, since it is an oversimplification of the picture, a rough generalisation.

In brief, from the Norfolk bulge down to Hampshire the inshore cod fishing is done during the October to January season, with the odd fish being taken before and after those dates by as much as a

month or so. The Essex/East Anglian coast gets a run of small cod in March. But some cod, usually big ones, are taken during the summer months as well, from boats fishing deep water, miles offshore in that area – and right down to the Atlantic coast of Cornwall and North Devon.

In Scotland spring and summer cod fishing from the shore can be good, especially in some of the west coast sea-lochs. Irish cod fishing is virtually all boat fishing on deep-water reefs and wrecks, though a few fish are taken by shore casting on steep to rocky shores.

Although the cod does not figure high in the 'best fighter' tables, it earned itself a great reputation in the

Evening flood-tide, an ideal time for shore cod. Anglers wait for action – hot drinks, warm clothes and lamps at the ready.

sixties when modern tackle and long-casting techniques, pioneered largely in the south-east of England by an angler whose name became a much revered one for his huge successes, Leslie Moncrieff, produced one-man catches on the beach for a day of 100 lb (45·3 kg) or so. Since then, alas, cod fishing has declined alarmingly, especially in the areas where sport depends on the autumn and winter migration. The cause has been argued from many aspects. Some of the cause – pollution and weather pattern changes, for example – may have a certain effect, but the author has no doubt at all that callous short term exploitation by commercial trawlers, both in distant waters and along the beaches, has been responsible. The fishery scientists at Lowestoft have been stressing that over-fishing has severely reduced what was once considered to be an almost inexhaustible stock. However, it appears that neither the other European, British nor Irish governments have taken heed: our own link-up with the continent has had its dark side.

To be interesting to the shore angler, especially the sportfisher with his light tackle (much of it developed in a very short while to take those great cod of the sixties) cod must be available in good numbers and in a variety of sizes. The run in late September/early October usually has a vanguard of 4–10 lb (1·8–4·5 kg) cod, (cod weighing 2–6 lb (900 g–2·7 kg) are commonly called codling), and by mid-November there should be fair chances of catching 20-pounders (9·0 kg) or even 30-pounders (13·6 kg) from some beaches and piers.

Most of the good cod beaches (shingle/sand or just sand) lie along the coasts of south Yorkshire, Lincolnshire, Norfolk, Suffolk, Essex, Kent, Sussex and Hampshire and Dorset (Chesil Bank). In these areas there is good pier and harbour wall fishing, as well as inshore and offshore boat fishing.

In North Yorkshire the shore cod scene is different. There are sand beaches, often hemmed in by rocky cliffs and rock outcrops, but much cod fishing is done from the cliffs themselves, casting over beds of tough kelp to fish the bait right among the rocks. Yorkshire rock anglers once used 50 lb (22·6 kg) line and more for this fishing, with massive rods and special wide diameter 'Scarborough' reels, the single action spools being made either of walnut or a tough mixture of linen cloth and resin called Tufnel. Some still do, but a more modern and light tackle approach is now asserting itself there – while catching plenty of good fish.

When fishing from a shingle or sand beach the cod are usually found at a certain point from the fishing stance: on a shingle beach giving way to sand, that is usually a few yards beyond the junction of stone and sand and normally when the tide is sufficiently high to give a depth of water of 15–50 ft (4·5–15·2 m); on a flatter sandy beach it is often necessary to place the bait well beyond the breaking waves.

Thus, when cod fishing from beaches, either the steeply shelving shingle banks, like those at Orford Island in Suffolk, Dungeness in Kent or Chesil Bank in Dorset, or from sandy beaches like those in the Spurn Head area north to around Bridlington, in Yorkshire, for example, there are two criteria for consistently successful cod fishing. They are good fresh bait and the ability to cast it to where the cod may be at any point in the tidal situation: distances of 120–140 yd (109·7–128 m) with a lead weight of 4–6 oz (56–170 g). Not only that, either: cod beaches are crowded places and it is essential to be able to fish out beyond most of the other men on the beach, yet not tangle their gear when your own is wound in, either to be rebaited or when playing a fish.

The tackle to choose for shore fishing in the sporting context should be similar to rod 1 in chapter 2, the reel to match, the range of multipliers preferably, or the suggested fixed-spool reel, loaded with nylon monofilament of 12–18 lb (5·4–8·2 kg) test – and loaded in either case to within about $\frac{1}{16}$ in (1·5 mm) of the lip of the spool.

The business end is a simple nylon paternoster. There are two good ways of making it. Either tie a blood-loop into the casting leader about 18 in (45·7 cm) from the end, to which is looped the hook snood, or tie the blood-loop in the same position, leaving 2 ft (60 cm) of end, thread a size 8 barrel swivel on, then tie another blood-loop 6 in (15·5 cm) or less below it. Trim off the loops closely and you are left with the swivel running freely between two stop-knots. The hook snood is tied to the free eye of the swivel with the tucked half blood knot. This second system is very useful when pouting and whiting are numerous and prevents tangled snoods when constantly reeling in these 'nuisance' fish, since they spin on the way in and can ruin a blood-loop snood quickly.

The tackle is completed by a forged ringed or eyed hook, bronzed for preference, or a spade-end hook. Sizes 2/0 up to 5/0 will cope with small codling or a 30-pounder (13·6 kg).

Avoid all wire booms, running or fixed, big swivels and clips. They are unnecessary, expensive, hamper casting and are just old hat. The only metal on the terminal tackle should be the hook, the tiny snood swivel (if that system is used) and a small link-swivel at the end of the gear to take the wire loop of the lead, a breakaway type.

Bait the hook as recommended in chapter 4. The number one bait for successful shore codding is lugworm, perhaps several big ones threaded up the snood. Razorfish is also excellent but more likely to be jerked off when casting for distance. Crab, too, is a fine bait but is very difficult to cast a long way; it is best for piers etc, where range is not so important. Mussels are useful and need to be tied on the hook in a big bunch with fine elastic thread. After a big onshore storm, many baits will be left on the high water mark. They will probably include whelks, hermit crabs, sea mice and other types of shellfish. All of them can be excellent.

It is necessary to realise that the reason for using

A typical winter scene at Dungeness, Kent's famous cod beach. Casts of well over 100 yd (91·4 m) are usually required to catch good fish, and such distances are best achieved with light reel lines and heavy leaders. Light lines also hold out better than thick lines.

thin line is to be able to cast a long way, keep the tackle out there without the tide getting a grip on the line and dragging it shorewards in a bow, as well as that of having to exercise some skill in bringing the cod, if it is a big one, to the beach. Line of 12 lb test (5·4 kg) is not ridiculous, although some of the old guard who still use 25 lb (11·3 kg) test and upwards, plus massive rods and wired leads, think so.

Thin line is an advantage in many ways, as outlined in chapter 3.

With anglers lining the beach it may be a problem to find a gap: 15 yd (13 m) between two other anglers is the absolute minimum needed, and even then one should ask permission of the other bordering anglers. Most cod anglers use two rods, the very keenest having matched pairs, identical in all respects, with matching reels. With care, two outfits may be used, even on a crowded beach.

Modern shore cod gear: matched Conolon blanks with Ambassadeur 7000s loaded with 15 lb (6·8 kg) test line – not a ring out of place!

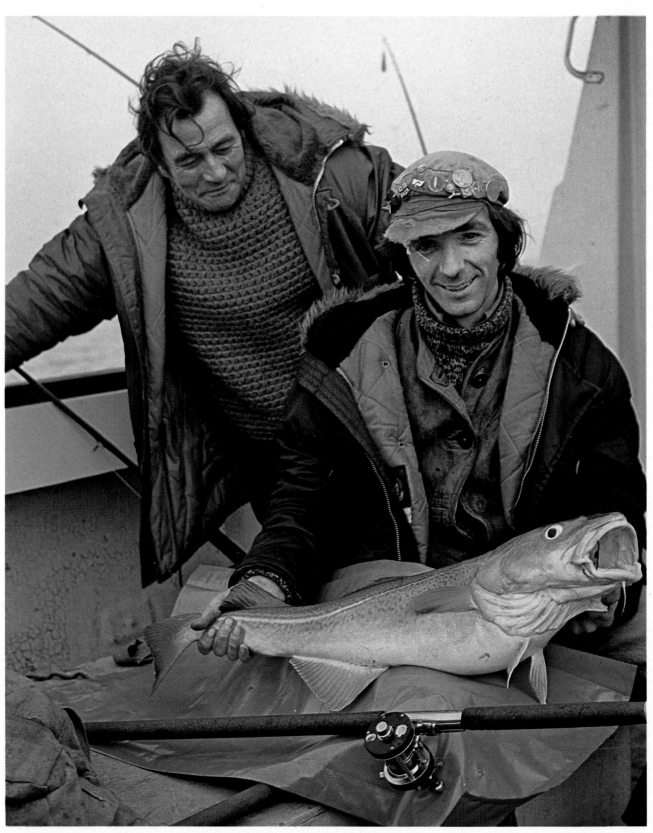

Cod of this size are quite big enough for good sport on 10–15 lb (4·5–6·8 kg) test line and matching rod and reel. The angler Alan Cotter, caught using the boat-casting technique mentioned in the text.

'Told you I wouldn't lose it for you, didn't I?' Skipper John Rawle shows a light tackle angler his fish.

Some years cod begin to come onto the beaches in September. Here are typical 'matched pairs' of rods and reels set up together in monopods.

Watch the anglers on either side. They probably cast straight out, or slightly at an angle. If you can cast farther, then the following system is almost foolproof. Again, explain to neighbours first.

Walk uptide of your selected position, say about 20 yd (18·2 m), behind the other anglers, then make your long cast from a gap in the ranks, so that when you take your high-held rod back over the rods of your neighbours to your spot, the tackle comes to rest a little uptide of your fishing position. Do it with both rods if you fish two. Place the rods in monopods, preferably made from alloy angle, as shown, about a yard (1 m) apart and at an angle of about 20 degrees from the vertical pointing towards the sea.

Friction can occur between anglers on a crowded beach, and if it is possible for several friends to fish together in a line, this system of walking up to cast works well when adopted by all the anglers. Often anglers who cannot cast far will cast over the lines of those who can, dragging them in whenever a rebaiting is carried out. And naturally, if the long caster simply casts straight out from his position, by the time his tackle has sunk and the lead taken a grip of the seabed, it will be 20–30 yd (18·2–27·4 m) downtide of his pitch. When he reels in he is likely to hook up 50 yd (45·7 m) downtide the lines of his downtide neighbours. It is necessary to have patience, for unpleasantness never makes angling enjoyable. Watching to see if one's line is underneath or over the top of that of a neighbour can help to bring the gear in without affecting the neighbour's, by passing one's rod over or under the other line.

It is important to spill line when the lead hits the water on completion of the cast, else tide will drag it as it sinks. It is impossible, no matter what other anglers may say to you, to fish with a line straight from rod tip to lead. Everybody's line will form a downtide bow, the greatest bows being in the lines that are out farthest, of course.

Once the lead has taken a grip, wind the line in until the tip of the rod takes on a curve and the line is as taut as it can be short of springing the anchor wires on the breakaway lead. By the way, the wires can be adjusted to break at a wide range of strains by bending them to clip more firmly or more loosely into the recesses or collars, depending on the type used, or, in the case of elastic band types, on the size of or number of turns given to the elastic band.

Most cod bites will move the angle of pull on the lead and free it, so that the rod will spring back as line slackens downtide. At other times the rod tip will shudder, then be pulled over hard, nodding away as the fish swims off downtide. The rod is picked up and the line reeled taut before striking firmly as one walks back up the beach in the second case; in the event of a slack-line bite, grab the rod from the rest and run up the beach until the line goes taut and you feel resistance, then strike hard. Nylon stretches and absorbs attempts to move the lead and the hook and sink its point.

Gaffed! Not the best place to set the point, but sometimes with a strong tide, light tackle and a skin hook-
hold, there is no second chance should the fish suddenly
go berserk.

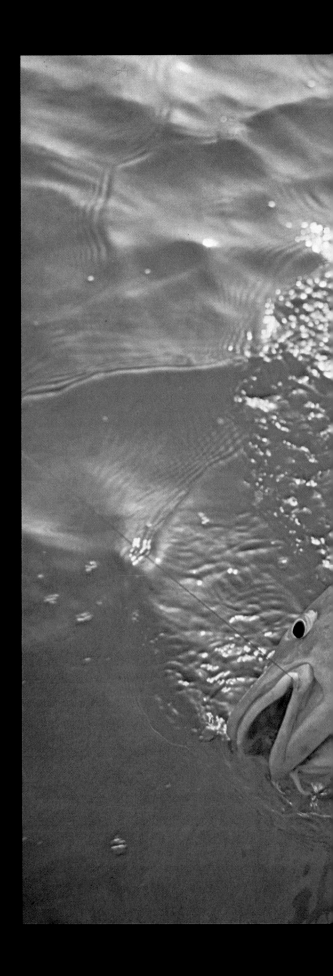

When a cod of this size is brought into the last waves, even as small as these, it is wise to have a companion gaff the fish to be sure, just in case the line is overstrained or has become nicked on the seabed or by the shingle.

Hooked at long range, cod usually come towards the angler, swinging downtide, and seldom is there any real battle at first, although there are exceptions, and a cod of 15 lb (6·8 kg) or so will sometimes hare off with 20 yd (18·2 m) of line against the reel drag immediately the hook goes home. With the fish within 30 yd (27·4 m) or so from the beach it is likely to liven up, not liking the shallowing water and the noise of the breaking surf. Be ready to yield line if a run along the surf or out to sea comes suddenly. Such runs are seldom longer than about 10 yd (9 m). With levelwind

multiplier reels the thumb of the rod hand can apply pressure to the line on the spool, the hand being positioned behind the reel; with open multipliers, the rod hand is in front of the reel to lay the line in close coils across the spool (which is immensely important to good, backlash-free casts) so the drag has to do all braking. It is necessary to adjust the brake (star-drag) to work when the fish is way out and when it is close in, although extra pressure can be imposed with the thumb of the reeling hand if a long run develops.

Cod of up to about 6 lb (2·7 kg) can be beached, as

When the surf is rough and there is a strong undertow there is no room for a mistake with the gaff. Here the author brings out a 10-pounder (4·5 kg) for a companion. Many fish are lost by inexperienced 'helpers' grabbing the line between rod and fish and hauling.

they are rolled up the shore by any incoming breakers, but anything bigger requires the angler to call for assistance with the gaff.

Never must any attempt be made to haul a decent size cod through a surf when a backtow (receding wave) is occurring: the pressure imposed on the line will break even 30 lb (13·6 kg) test if the fish is 10 lb (4·5 kg) or so; in fact, a fish of that size must not be held against a receding wave. Time an incoming wave to bring the fish in, when the line is rapidly recovered until a turn or two of the leader is round the spool.

At this point the man with the gaff, who ought to be in thighboots, nips into the swash and plants the gaff just behind the fish's head and brings it ashore. The fish is immediately killed with a blow over the eyes with a pebble or a priest.

If a very large cod, 20 lb (9 kg) plus, runs off down-tide in a rough sea – which is the best of all conditions for daylight codding – the angler with light gear must follow, passing his rod under or over the lines of other anglers to avoid tangles. It is an unwritten law among surf anglers on a crowded beach to make way for a man playing a big fish – anybody who doesn't can be sure of getting well cursed by all and sundry!

Good daylight fishing conditions usually come after an onshore blow when the sea is crumping on to the beach in slow 'walls' and is turbid with disturbed sand and mud. A hazard then is weed drifting into the line and dragging the lead out of the sand. There is no cure for this, except to keep bringing in the gear and recasting after clearing any heavy collections of weed. But if the weed is only present in the inshore breakers, as it often is, a move to the highest part of the back of the beach and keeping the rod tip almost vertical, will help keep the line out of trouble.

It is surprising just how rough the sea has to be to make fishing impossible, and with a thin line and skill such conditions can be effectively mastered and some terrific catches of cod made. In fact, very rough seas produce the memorable cod hauls, both in overall weight and in size of fish.

Quite apart from keeping line clear of the big waves crashing on to the beach, it is necessary to combat increased tidal run (strong winds and big tides usually coincide) and maybe debris in the water. An extension of the walking-up-and casting technique is the way to achieve success, but it may be necessary to walk up 50 yd (45·7 m) to get the lead to hold, pushed into the seabed by the tidal stream instead of being swept away by it. The lead must come to rest uptide of the fishing position to permit the method to work – and this may have to be achieved with the lead only 70–80 yd (64–70 m) from the beach. Casting into an onshore wind is not easy!

Fishing at night is very popular with some cod anglers – in fact, some will not fish in daylight. Certainly, in anything less than rough seas and with clear water the cod tend to feed inshore best after dark. There is no great change necessary from daylight tactics, save that a few anglers who are able to use a multiplier in daylight find they have to use a fixed-spool reel at night. That is strange because an angler's headlamp enables the line leaving the multiplier to be seen just as well as in daylight; it also permits levelling line on the open reel spool when recovering line.

A paraffin pressure lantern is essential. It is placed behind the rod or rods and leaning backwards up the beach at an angle (a pile of sand or shingle can be put under the lantern's base) to shine up the rods to the tips, making the rings gleam and the rod tip(s) easy to see without straining the eyes. Anglers who habitually fish at night either paint about a foot (30 cm) of their rod tip white or they apply reflective tape to show up in the light glow. Avoid clip-on rod lights such as Beta; they do not work as well as expected and strain the eyes.

Cod fishing on a winter beach with a north-east gale blowing can be extremely painful. Some anglers use portable canvas-covered shelters or windbreaks, but they need to be moved up and down with the tide. Good clothing is the answer for comfort and mobility, and lying down in a shallow trench scooped from the shingle will avoid excessive exposure to the elements.

Fishing from piers, breakwaters, and rocky projections giving access to deep, clean-bottomed water is carried on in the same basic way as from the beach. Of course, a big rectangular dropnet is needed to bring up the fish once it has been played close to the base of the pier, but otherwise there is little need to say anything further. The fact that some anglers advise the use of rods 8–9 ft (2·4–2·7 m) in length for piers etc, holds no water; the long rod not only casts farther, absorbs sudden strains quicker, but it also helps to push a fish out when it tries to gain sanctuary of rough piles, concrete supports and the like.

Boat fishing for cod can be done in two ways: bottom fishing with bait, as for shore situations, and lure fishing. Boat fishing with the bait legered can also be subdivided into fishing shallowish water where the tidal stream is not vicious, and fishing deep fast water well offshore. And the boat may be a 12 ft (3·6 m) dinghy used up to maybe 2 miles (3·2 km) from shore with two anglers aboard or a 40 ft (12·1 m) charter boat with eight or more anglers.

Lure fishing can be dealt with quite summarily. It is mostly done over deep water and over a wreck or reef where cod are known to gather. The lure can be a pirk, usually a chrome-plated banana-shaped or elongated, faceted, diamond-shaped piece of metal, weighing from as little as 6 oz to as much as 2 lb (170 g to almost 1 kg), or a king-size version of mackerel feathers, usually white.

The lure is fished on a 12, 20 or 30 lb class boat rod (5·4, 9 or 13·6 kg), depending on the water depth and weight of lure, and allowed to tap the bottom before being lifted about 1 yd (1 m) and being jigged sharply up and down with short rod movements. Long lifts are both unnecessarily exhausting and less effective. A trace of 3 feather lures with the lead at the bottom of the trace is fished in the same way.

However, so far as the sportfisher and his light tackle is concerned, the use of more than one hook or lure is not advised, since shoaling fish can be hooked two or more at a time, which does not, as might be thought, add to the fight but simply allows one fish to pull against the other, thus causing tackle breakage. Also, sporting anglers eschew the pirk or jig because its use results in a high proportion of foulhooked cod, fish that may try to grab the lure but are instead hooked outside the mouth, in the eye, or many other parts of the body by the upward jerk of the rod.

Lure fishing is only really useful in clear water.

On the other hand, cod fishing with legered gear from a boat can be excellent sport. Using one of the conventional boat rods in the 12–30 lb (5·4–13·6 kg) range the bait, which may be a big bunch of lugworms, crab, whelks, sprats (single or a bunch), half a fresh herring, a whole small squid, or a strip of a large squid or cuttlefish, is dropped overboard and allowed to touch bottom. It may be left with a suitable weight to hold it there, or lifted and bounced downtide to

Anything you can do I can do . . . well, maybe not better, but how about this for the lady's first cod! The author's editorial assistant Anne Lewington beat this 14-pounder (6·3 kg) on 15 lb (6·8 kg) line in a strong tide.

cover some 50 yd (45·7 m) behind the boat. Weights for such boat work may be simple cones with the loop at the apex. The trace is the same as that for stingray, as is the running lead on a link swivel.

Usually 12 lb (5·4 kg) or 20 lb (9 kg) class rods and lines will be adequate, but in very deep water well off-shore where up to 2 lb (1 kg) of lead might have to be used to reach bottom, it may be necessary to increase the gear to 30 lb (13·6 kg) class. That condition is met in very few places.

Up to this point no mention has been made of the use of the wire line outfit for boat fishing. The reason is that, although wire is used for conger and ling fishing in very deep, fast-flowing water, it is not a good idea for a number of reasons.

For example, should a big fish break the wire line, or should a bad snag be encountered which makes a deliberate break-off necessary, not only is the second action dangerous, due to the cutting power of thin steel wire under great tension, but when it does break the slack wire off the reel will undoubtedly form a terrible tangle and will have to be cut from beyond the rod tip.

So, wire should ideally not be used on rough ground for big fish, but it does permit good fishing to continue at periods of strong tidal flow that make normal lines either unusable or distasteful, due to the great amount of lead that has to be used to keep the tackle down.

It is as well to keep a reel loaded with 30 lb (13·6 kg) stainless steel single strand wire in the boat kit, or a spare spool for a reel such as the 9000 series, or Penns and Mitchells with quick take-down systems – not for level-line reels. The spool should have been filled as described in chapter 2. Always keep the end of the wire taped tight round the spool in some way; an elastic band serves the same purpose. Failure to do this results on the line springing off to form a terrible coil which is not easily untangled.

Any terminal tackle has to be attached to the wire line on a separate length of nylon monofilament as this will permit a running leger set-up without creating angles in the wire, which can kink and break and work-harden and break. The nylon is also a useful buffer when a big fish is hooked as the wire is to all intents and purposes non-stretch.

Six to 10 ft (1·8–3 m) of nylon is about right, and the attachment can be made by forming a loop in the end of the wire line by first twisting for 4 turns, the thumb and forefinger holding both strands of wire, then turning the tag-end at a right angle to the standing part of the wire and wrapping it around the standing part in close, touching turns (like whipping) 10 times. This loop is permanently left on the line, as well as the length of nylon, which may be attached using the Albright knot.

The running swivel or boom is put on to the nylon terminal piece, after which the trace is added in the normal way via a barrel or box swivel.

It is important when using wire always to keep in mind how potentially dangerous it is. Keep fingers clear of it when it is under any degree of tension and never try to free it from a snag using fingers, gloved hand or by wrapping it round a length of wood etc, as is usual with other lines. Always keep wire cutters handy for such jobs!

Also remember that roller rings at tip and butt, preferably all through, are necessary to fish wire successfully, else the wire will kink and snap or work-harden and snap.

So, wire is not often used in sportfishing but when it is needed, nothing else will do the job half as well.

The cod is the only species in this book for which wire line is fully recommended in special circumstances.

If there are only six friends sharing a big boat, then casting away from the boat with the boatcaster rods and matching tackle will be useful for, say, half the party: the casting covers the seabed at the sides of the boat while the dropped-down conventional gear gets the cod that come up the tide from behind the boat or drop down in line with the bows.

Casting uptide and from the sides of a dinghy, especially in shallow water, is a deadly way of fishing and will, of course, permit the bottom to be held with lighter leads than otherwise, as is the case with beach fishing. Great care must be taken when casting from a crowded boat as serious injuries will result if the lead or hook hits a fellow angler as the power stroke is made.

When fishing downtide from the boat the bite is likely to be a sudden heavy drag, in which case a firm lift of the rod is all that is necessary to sink the hook; however, the casting system mostly results in a nod or two of the rod tip, following by fast slackening of the line and further trembles as the lead is lifted from its anchorage and trundles round on the seabed. The fish is often only skin-hooked and it is necessary to wind rapidly until the weight of the fish is felt before striking firmly. Failure to follow this advice will result in many lost fish.

In strong currents a big cod can impose a terrific pull on the tackle by simply opening its mouth and increasing water resistance; whether it does this deliberately or whether it is due to exhaustion after battle is immaterial. What is important is that the light tackle angler recognises this fact and does not try to force the fish to the surface or haul it uptide to the boat 'just to have a look'. In the words of the proverb . . . 'softly, softly catchee monkey'.

There are times when vast shoals of whiting and pouting prove a nuisance to the cod fisher, either from the shore or boat. From a boat the answer is either to move thus trying to avoid them, or to use a large dead one of their number mounted on a 6/0 hook and legered.

From the shore the problem is made worse. The favourite cod bait in this situation, the lugworm, is torn to pieces and pulled off the hook quickly by the hordes; and even if one wishes to kill one of them and

# The Albright Knot
for joining wire to nylon monofilament

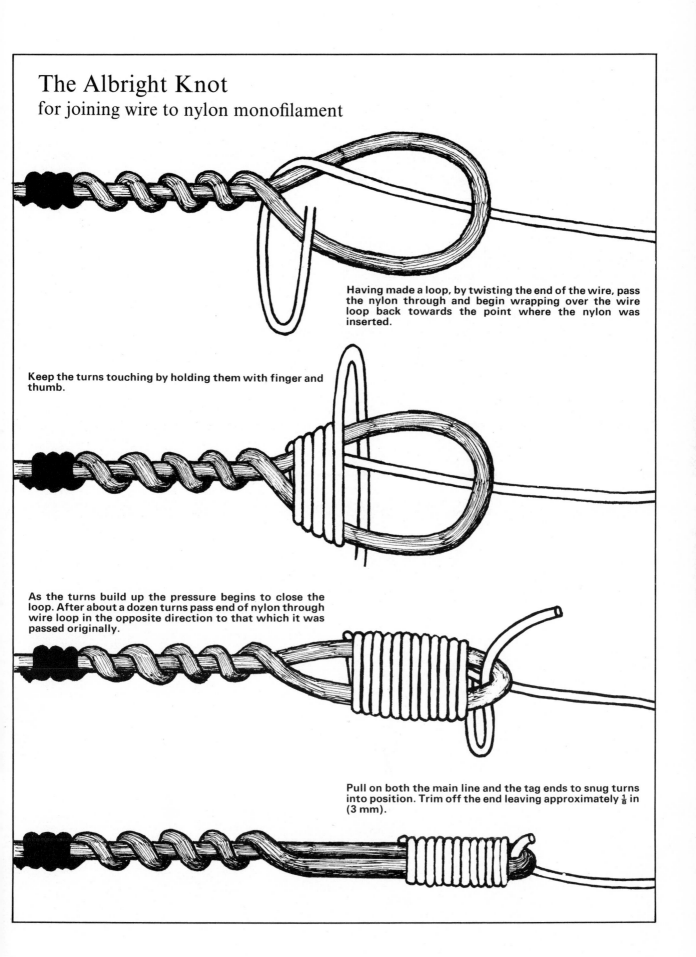

Having made a loop, by twisting the end of the wire, pass the nylon through and begin wrapping over the wire loop back towards the point where the nylon was inserted.

Keep the turns touching by holding them with finger and thumb.

As the turns build up the pressure begins to close the loop. After about a dozen turns pass end of nylon through wire loop in the opposite direction to that which it was passed originally.

Pull on both the main line and the tag ends to snug turns into position. Trim off the end leaving approximately $\frac{1}{8}$ in (3 mm).

A beaten cod rolls belly up at the side of the boat. Note that the hook is only just inside the bottom lip. Any strong hauling might have ripped it free, but gentle yet firm handling made sure of some tasty fillets.

cast it out for a big cod, the size, weight and shape of a dead whiting or pouting makes adequate distances remote. There is a way, though, to fish a big fish way out, and a live one at that!

The ordinary snood is used, but having knotted on the 5/0 hook, a tag-end of about six inches of nylon is left. To this is tied a size 1 hook which is positioned about two inches from the big hook. The little hook is baited with an inch or so (3 cm) of lug.

The rig for fishing a live whiting at long range. The large hook is a salmon-fly hook whipped with Terylene to the nylon snood, the turns afterwards being well varnished.

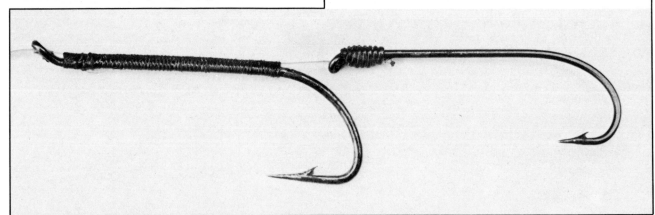

In summer West Country anglers catch heavy cod while fishing the wrecks that lie in deep water 12–20 miles (19–32 km) offshore. This one weighed just under 27 lb (12·2 kg).

The long-distance cast is made and the line tightened up. Soon a whiting or pouting will rattle the rod tip: leave it well alone. After a minute or so your livebait has swallowed the lug and the little hook and is struggling to get free from the restricting lead. As its struggles cause vibrations and scale flashes a large cod will home in and grab it – the vast mouth engulfing it – and thus swallow the big hook which by now, as the fish is swallowed head-first, is lying alongside the whiting's gills.

The rod tip goes heeling over and the strike is made, the big hook getting the cod in the throat or mouth. . . . Very big fish are caught this way, but often this is a waiting game since there are many other live fishes out there apart from the one on the hook.

Some areas of coastline seldom get runs of cod proper, only codling of up to about 4 lb (1·8 kg). However, the use of the salmon spinning rod with 7 lb (3·1 kg) line and 1 oz (28 g) of lead, where tidal conditions are gentle, will provide some shore sport. In a boat the baitcasting rod, light lead and 7 lb line will do likewise.

Finally, although the cod is certainly not among the top fighting species in British waters, it can sometimes be surprising. There was the time when, having taken half a dozen cod up to double figures from a Kent beach, the author was thinking of packing up, the tide being on the ebb and well down the beach. He was 20 yd (18·2 m) away from his rod and gutting his catch when a noise caused him to look up, just in time to see his rod pulled out of the rest and set off down the shingle at a rapid rate. He had to sprint and do a rugger tackle on the extreme end of the butt as it was disappearing into the waves. The cod that resulted from the ensuing five-minute fight weighed only 12 lb (5·3 kg) but was short and thick and extremely beautiful.

This indicates that if the rod is left to fish for itself it is essential that the drag is light and the check on, so that if a large fish does grab and rush off, the rod and reel will not be lost – it happens every season, many times.

Below: Leaving rods to 'fish for themselves' like this can result in the loss of the whole outfit if a lively cod grabs the bait and drags the rod from its rest.

Left: When the sea is calm, cod from the shore will generally be found well out in the daylight hours. Here the author punches out about 150 yd (137 m) with a single hook paternoster baited with lug. Note how the glass rod is compressed.

149

# 9

# Coalfish and pollack

These two members of the cod family share many similarities of body shape and fin conformation. The coalfish, *Pollachius virens*, is silvery-grey with a dark green, almost black back, the flanks being rounded and marked by a white straight lateral line. This fish grows to more than 30 lb (13·6 kg), but the bigger specimens, over about 6 lb (2·7 kg) are found only in deep water over offshore wrecks and reefs. A good coalfish weighs 15 lb (6·8 kg) or so and the chance of catching heavyweights is best in winter when the hens are carrying big roes.

Small coalfish of about 1 lb (450 g) form huge shoals and roam inshore rocky waters for small fish. They are of little interest to sportfishers, except perhaps as bait for other species.

The coalfish swims on both sides of the Atlantic, but in American and Canadian waters, where it has been caught to over 40 lb (18·1 kg), it is called 'pollock', just to add to the general confusion on fish names.

The pollack, *Pollachius pollachius*, does not swim on the American side of the Atlantic. It is a less rounded fish than the coalfish, softer allround, with a beautiful green back and olive and gold flanks. The pollack also swims in much shallower water than the coalfish; fish up to about 12 lb (5·4 kg) being caught from rocky shores where there is 15–40 ft (4·5–12·1 m) of water.

In sportfishing terms, the worthwhile coalfish can normally be caught only from a boat, usually in depths of over 20 fathoms (36·5 m) while the pollack, which reaches weights of 25 lb (11·3 kg) or more in deep water, does provide excellent shore and inshore boat fishing. Devon, Cornwall, the Isle of Man, Scotland and its islands and also Ireland's west coast are good coalfish areas. Iceland is superb in this respect.

First, then, coalfish from a boat way offshore. Winter weather conditions sometimes make the distant wrecks and reefs unreachable and summer and autumn fishing is more reliable.

Ideally for sportfishing the big trawler-type boat that specialises in deep-water wreck and reef fishing should be chartered by only six like-minded anglers, although one or two such enthusiasts can sometimes persuade those fishing for bottom fish on a wreck to allow them places in the stern to fish with light gear.

As has been stressed earlier, light tackle fishing from a crowded boat is the way to frayed tempers.

The boat will either mark the wreck or reef with a small buoy or buoys, called dans, then anchor uptide so that the baits may be fished down into the rough ground, or the skipper may make repeated slow drifts over the ground, slowing his drift with engine power.

For summer fishing the 12–20 lb outfits will be fine, and once the run of fish has been established one set may be discarded, ie for big fish keep the 20 lb outfit in action; for small fish under 10 lb (4·5 kg) keep the 12 lb outfit, or drop down to use the double-handed spinning rod and 7–8 lb (3·1–3·6 kg) line.

Some regular wreck anglers will scoff at such comments since they regularly use 40 lb (18·1 kg) line and get broken by fish. However, they mostly fish several baits or lures on snoods and when two or more large coalfish can pull against each other the heavy line or trace will not stand the strain.

Light tackle work means one bait or lure and one hook. The best way to fish is with a 10 in (25·3 cm) long stainless steel wire boom, fixed by its lower eye to the wire loop of the lead with a split ring and attached to the main line via a link swivel tied to the end of the line. The free eye of the boom takes another link swivel, about size 4, to which is tied the hook trace, 15–20 ft (4·5–6 m) of nylon monofilament. Coalfish do not bite through traces but they have hard mouths and fight with such speed and energy that they can quickly wear through thin, soft nylon. Choose a hard nylon for the trace. For 12 lb (5·4 kg) class or thereabouts the trace should be 25 lb (11·3 kg) test; for 20 lb (9 kg) class tackle the trace should be about 30 lb (13·6 kg) test. Even when using the spinning rod and 7–8 lb (3·1–3·6 kg) line, keep the trace at 20 lb (9 kg) test.

The hook, when bait fishing, can be about size 4/0 and should be strong and forged, the O'Shaughnessy pattern being very suitable. The bait should be cut in a long, slim strip, whether it be mackerel, squid or

A big pollack is a handsome creature and a worthy opponent on light tackle.

A famous light tackle angler, Rita Barrett, shows a 22 lb (9·9 kg) wreck pollack taken on a 28 oz (794 g) pirk. Rita holds world line-class records for Britain.

whatever; a whole big sand-eel is a very fine coalfish bait.

Coalfish tend to increase in size as the depth increases, the bigger specimens of 20 lb (9 kg) or so being taken in 40 fathoms (73 m) or more. So, by asking the skipper the depth on the echo-sounder as the mark is passed over, it is often possible to select the tackle outfit that will suit the size of fish.

The use of the wire boom in this instance serves a very useful purpose: it prevents the long trace tangling round the main line as the gear is let down over the side of the boat.

When the lead, which may need to be 6 oz–1 lb (170–600 g) taps bottom, the reel is put in gear – making sure the drag is properly set to the line test – and a slow, steady retrieve is begun. Often the fish will take soon after the bait begins to lift from the wreck or reef; at other times the fish will follow into midwater, then take with a bang that continues in a crash-dive of almost frightening speed and power. The fish must be given line, but not too much or it will make the wreck and cut the line. Frequently the bait is taken on the way down, as it nears the bottom, and in this instance the tackle must be tested to the utmost to prevent snagging.

Coalfish do not suffer as much from decompression as other fish do and will fight from the depths to the surface. A big strong net is a good way of bringing coalfish aboard and if this can be arranged the fish may be returned and will be able to get down to the depths again.

The famous Red Gill sand-eel is the best of the artificials, and it is fished on the same tackle as the moving bait, and in the same way. Also good is a pirk, especially on snaggy wrecks, and it helps to tip the big treble or single hook with a strip of fresh mackerel or squid.

In winter, when the very heavy females are about, fishing a wreck is best done with either a pirk or just one Red Gill fished on a snood about 1 ft (30·4 cm) long and about 3 ft (91 cm) above the lead. Such gear will often be taken as the lure goes down and the short snood or single pirk tends to tangle less with the wreck than a long snood. If fish do repeatedly break 20 lb (9 kg) tackle, increase to 30 lb (13·6 kg) with 30 lb trace.

Reefs usually hold smaller coalfish than do the wrecks, and it is on the reefs that the long spinning rod and lighter line comes into its own. A very subtle touch is necessary to hold the fighting fish just within the margin of strain the tackle will stand, and the longer rod is well able to cushion the sharp dives and directional changes of the fish.

# Pollack

Much of the boat technique for coalfish also holds for deep-water pollack of the wrecks and reefs. However,

Members of the British Light Tackle Club are pioneering sporting saltwater fishing in the United Kingdom. Here a good pollack is exhibited by the 'gaffer' sporting a flamboyant hat.

there is seldom – if ever – any need to use tackle heavier than the 20 lb (9 kg) class outfit for pollack, and usually the 12 lb (5·4 kg) outfit or the long spinning rod with line around 8 lb (3·6 kg) test will be found suitable.

The long trace with the Red Gill is perhaps the most deadly of all methods for pollack from the boat, be it in very deep water or shallower water on a reef. However, the baits worked as for coalfish also do well.

Reef pollack run about 4–8 lb (1·8–3·6 kg) on average with the occasional double-figure specimen. On a newly found wreck the average can be more than 12 lb (5·4 kg).

Pollack usually take the moving natural or artificial bait more gently than a coalfish does. The lead touches, the reel is engaged and winding begins. Perhaps after a few turns a tap will be felt. Do nothing. Just wind on. There comes another light tap. Wind on. This can continue to mid-water or even to within a few feet of the boat, then the rod tip is felt to become heavy and a firm lift will set the hook.

Spinning and float-fishing from the rocks for pollack. The author (nearer the water) and Irishman Kevin Linnane work a well-known Irish hot-spot, near Clogher Head, Dingle Peninsula.

Like the coalfish, the pollack is a crash-dive artist *par excellence*, and trying to slow and stop the fish before it reaches sanctuary is great fun and extremely testing to the tackle and 'hands'.

In some areas there are vast ranges of reefs quite close inshore – such as in Devon, Cornwall, Scotland and particularly west and south-west Ireland – where the water depth is about 30–40 ft (9·1–12·1 m) and dinghy fishing for pollack is fun, especially with the spinning outfit. With the small multiplier with 10 lb (4·5 kg) line or fixed-spool reel carrying line of about 7 lb (3·1 kg) test, casts are made from a slowly drifting or anchored boat. Use either a Red Gill with about 1½ oz (42·5 g) of lead in the form of a bomb on a nylon link about 4 in (10 cm) long and suspended from the top eye of the swivel, which joins reel line to 3 ft (91 cm) trace, or a 4 in (10 cm) goat hair fly on a 3/0 O'Shaughnessy hook. White and orange or white and blue hair is good, whipped tightly round the shank of the hook beside the eye with strong thread and varnished. An alternative lure is a heavyweight wobbling spoon, 1 oz (28 g) or so in weight, such as Koster, Toby, Condor and Ellips. No additional weight is used on the spoons.

The first cast must be counted down and the seconds memorised once the lead or lure taps the rock. Each cast must reach the same depth, the recovery being started just before the last number is reached, so that snagging is kept to a minimum. It is essential, however, to 'live dangerously', for a lure that swims too high over the kelp-covered rocks will often be left alone by pollack.

Even when chasing the spun lure the take of the pollack is initially gentle, the rod tip just becoming heavy, followed by the judder and crash-dive as the fish feels the hook and panics.

It is essential to keep the rod tip high when striving to prevent the pollack reaching sanctuary. It is amazing what elasticity there is in a long spinning rod.

Shore fishing for pollack may be the best of all pollack fishing situations so far as sportfishing is concerned. The atmosphere is different when one is perched, perhaps somewhat precariously, on a rocky ledge above the surging green and white-laced water as it sucks and gurgles below, the rocks' dark patches on a sandy ground, maybe, the weed waving like a massive mermaid's hair.

Spinning is the most used and most productive method and it is carried out like that done from the dinghy. However, it is easier to see the rocky outcrops, the deep gullies between them shown by darker water, and to make long searching casts, testing depths, maybe bringing the lure along a rock face deep under water and only a yard out. Besides the high perches one is usually forced to use facilitating seeing into the water, they also enable the angler to see much of the fight of the pollack, its golden flanks flashing deep down as it dives and struggles.

Usually one has only to beat the pollack's initial dive to land it, since the subsequent struggles are seldom so severe, though some fish fight harder than others.

It is best to fish rocks where pollack swim in the company of one other experienced angler at least, both to permit the landing of the fish by dropnet and

for safety's sake: clambering down cliffs and over slippery rocks to reach the best pollack grounds is a calculated risk; alone it is asking for trouble. Always be watchful of the occasional bigger-than-usual wave for they can come from nowhere and sweep the unwary to death. Venture with extra care on to rocks that are wet with spray; try to remain at least 6 ft (2 m) above the water's highest surges.

**Not just sheer cliffs but an overhang – yet the angler got down to fish. This is Brandon Creek in Kerry where congers, pollack, ballan wrasse, mullet, mackerel, garfish and other species may be caught at one time.**

Coalfish are superb. This one weighed 26 lb (11.7 kg) and was taken in the West Country by Tony Allan.

**Left:**
**Obviously, Scottish angler David Wilson thought the terrible climb he has just completed was worthwhile. A nice shore pollack is brought back to the hotel. They are very tasty when filleted and smoked.**

Another excellent light-tackle method is float-fishing. The long spinning rod will serve well, used with fixed-spool reel and 7–8 lb (3·1–3·6 kg) test monofilament. The float should be a balsa-wood or modern plastic type, cigar-shaped with a central hole, lined with plastic tube in the case of the balsa type. A bead larger than the tube through the float is threaded on the line before the float, and a stop-knot of nylon or elastic, or a linen thread is tied on the line at the depth at which the bait is to be fished. It should drift about 5 ft (1·5 m) above the rocks.

The hook should be forged, about 1/0, and on a yard (91 cm) of nylon. The trace is joined to the main line by a number 8 swivel, above which a barrel, pierced ball, Hillman or other lead of about ½ oz (14 g) is fitted.

The bait should be a 4 × 1 in (10 × 2·5 cm) fillet of fresh mackerel, garfish, herring, squid, or king rag-worm, perhaps even live prawn, although the latter seems a little wasteful when much more easily come by and easily kept baits are satisfactory. A live sand-eel, of course, is the absolute ultimate pollack bait for float-fishing, and if they are available and can be kept alive (or freshly killed) on ice, they will be worth the work of collection and carriage. The good fresh mackerel strip, though, will seldom be ignored.

A final point about pollack fished from the shallower waters along the shore is that, even though they may not often reach double figures like the fish of the deeps offshore, it is possible to catch them and put them back unharmed, with a good chance of survival. Fish from deep water, however, suffer greatly from decompression and most come to the boat with their 'innards' protruding from their mouths, and they cannot swim back down if they are returned to the sea.

Seeing that reduces the pleasure of offshore pollack fishing: every gallant fighting fish a dead fish.

# 10

# Halibut

A few years ago the halibut was given the big public relations treatment by tourist agencies in Scotland, the northern isles and in Iceland. Until about the past seven years little was heard about halibut in angling circles. In fact, it appeared that very few had been caught at all on rod and line in British and European waters, the most publicised being an 84-pounder (38·1 kg) by Leslie Moncrieff, the famous English sea angler, who caught it in deep water on rough ground south of Valentia on Ireland's south-west coast. The Irish record halibut of 152 lb (68·9 kg) was also taken there.

Within the past few years, however, the PR work has produced good results. First Orkney, then Shetland, and finally Iceland hit the headlines by producing fine halibut for the adventurous few, who were prepared to break new ground and could afford the expense. And more recently, the rugged ground off Caithness has rewarded those who kept faith and fished consistently. Other grounds are considered to hold this giant flatfish that bears the superb scientific name *Hippoglossus hippoglossus*.

Perhaps most halibut taken by anglers in the past four years or so have come from Iceland's Breidfjordur during late summer. This recently discovered fishery has not only produced more fish – including many 20–50 lb fish (9–11·3 kg) that are ideal for the light-tackle angler – but it has done so in depths of only 15–20 fathoms (27·4–36·5 m) as opposed to the more usual halibut haunts of twice that depth. Lots of modest halibut in shallow water not affected by savage tides – truly ideal for sportfishing!

However, Iceland is a long journey for a tilt at a halibut if you live in Southern England. . . .

Not one angler in a thousand who fishes British saltwater has caught a halibut, and most of those who have, have done so on heavy tackle – 80–100 lb (36·2–45·3 kg) line. A few pioneers have used 30 lb (13·6 kg) class outfits with success, but there is little evidence that captures on such gear have included the 100 lb plus (45·3 kg) specimens.

However, since the author is among those who have not actually boated a halibut – though he did hook and lose one in Orkney – it is difficult to assess the true picture of the halibut as a fighter. But experienced longliners, who regularly catch fish over 100 lb (45·3 kg) or more, have said that if the fish is coaxed gently but firmly to the surface immediately on hooking, without jerking, it will hardly struggle, and a quick stroke with the gaff will secure it. They also add that the fish will begin to fight in the boat and it is so strong that serious damage can be done by a fish boated 'green'.

Many anglers agree with this generalisation, but if the fish does become alarmed at the upward move and dives, to try to stop it reaching bottom is to risk breakage of even heavy gear. Yet the experienced anglers also say that if the fish is allowed to make the dives to the bottom against safe drag pressure, it can be coaxed to the top again, perhaps to come to gaff then, or make more dives before doing so. Thus, it appears that the usual game of give and take and patience works on the halibut as it does on most fish. But it will not work with 30 lb (13·6 kg) gear in 40 fathoms (73 m) or more of fast-flowing water! Not when the vast flattie weighs well over 100 lb (45·3 kg).

The halibut is a fish-eater, and in the Icelandic fishery inshore is thought to feed largely on lumpsuckers and sea scorpions. Baits of herring, mackerel, coalfish, whiting, codling and squid will be taken.

Halibut reach enormous weights – a fish which weighed over 600 lb (272 kg) after being gutted was taken off Massachusetts, and specimens of over 500 lb (226 kg) have been caught by the longliners off Iceland. In spite of the fact that such monsters are beyond the scope of this book, since they are usually taken in extremely deep water where vicious tides also occur, it is well to remember that British anglers have taken fish of over 200 lb (90·7 kg) on lines testing 50 lb (22·6 kg) or under.

Only the 30 lb (13·6 kg) class outfit detailed in chapter 2 can be matched to the halibut in any sensible way and even then the reel must play a very important part. Top choice should be a lever-drag model – Policansky Monitor number 4, Penn International, Roddy Dominator, ABU's 9000 and 9000C, a Penn Super Mariner or Senator 4/0. The exception to this advice can occur when, in places like the Breidafjordur, there are lots of small halibut in shallow and

Leslie Moncrieff (right) with the 84 lb (38·1 kg) halibut which he caught off Valentia Island in Southern Ireland. This fish, unlike so many others caught by anglers, fought very vigorously.

The flasher spoon can be seen just outside this 105½ lb (47·8 kg) halibut's mouth as it is gaffed aboard an Icelandic boat.

comparatively slow-moving water, in which case a 20 lb (9 kg) class outfit might be used.

Terminal tackle is usually made up with fishing on the drift in mind since halibut, like many predatory fish, have a penchant for a moving bait. A small Clements boom, or a big link-swivel is first run up the line and a swivel big enough to stop the weight-carrying link-swivel or boom from running down the trace is tied to the end. A trace of 80–100 lb (36·2–45·3 kg) test commercial monofilament, 4–6 ft (1·2–1·8 m) long, is connected to the free eye of the stop swivel, and another strong barrel swivel tied to the end. This swivel is linked to about 10 in (23 cm) of cabled trace wire by crimping, and onto its free end is slid a silver spoon with a split ring through the hole in the narrow end. A bead and about 2 in (5 cm) of brass or hard plastic tubing keeps the spoon away from the eye of a strong forged 6/0 hook, an O'Shaughnessy or Seamaster for preference.

The spoon flashes as the tackle drags along on or bumping the seabed and is an additional attraction to the fish. Reg Quest, famed kingpin of the British Conger Club, brought back this spoon idea from Iceland following an exploratory trip for *Angling* magazine, reporting that it did better than traces without a spoon and was at its best with the angler working the tackle to keep bait and flasher lifting and dropping as the drift proceeded. Ivor Kilbourn, another keen British angler, gave Reg the tip-off.

To quote Reg: 'I would have no hesitation in using the same tackle on a future visit (50 lb IGFA) but the 30 lb (13·6 kg) tackle, although adequate over the inshore areas where the depths were not great and the tides very small, might be overstrained on a really big fish when the sheer dead weight might have to be pumped up to the surface, for although such tackle could handle the running fish, the accumulated weight might be too heavy to lift.'

The author's only comment here is that since other free-swimming species of the size reached by halibut are beaten on 30 lb (13·6 kg) gear, there is reason to expect some success with the giant flatties, although the deep, strong water is the main opponent of that success, not the halibut itself, since coaxing will persuade almost any fish to come to the surface, provided it is a live fish and not a dead or dying one. . . .

Overleaf:
**Peter Peck of ABU, the tackle company, is a confirmed light tackle angler. He is illustrated holding an Icelandic halibut.**

# 11

# Bass

The bass is one of Britain's most beautiful saltwater fish. Green or blue backed, silvery or brassy flanks, a stark white belly and large, strong fins, the head bony and ending in a vast mouth; it is a real anglers' fish. It reaches an ultimate size of over 20 lb (9 kg), but many anglers go to the grave not having caught a double-figure specimen. A good bass weighs 8 lb (3·6 kg) and fish of 2–3 lb (1–1·3 kg) are called school-bass because they tend to form big schools or shoals.

Bass are slow growing and long-lived: fish of 10 lb (4·5 kg) may be 15 years old in southern England, more than that in western Ireland. Bass over about

**One cannot fish bass in the surf with tackle much lighter than this. John Darling shows a thick fish taken on a carp rod, tiny ABU 2100 reel and 10 lb (4·5 kg) line.**

4 lb (1·8 kg) or so are nearly all hens, though some cock fish of 7 lb (3·1 kg) or so have been taken, mainly in south-eastern England. Any 10-pounder (4·5 kg) can be relied on to be a hen.

In spite of all this, it was common until about eight years ago to find most anglers using big, stiff rods, heavy leads, and lines of at least 20 lb (9 kg) test for bass fishing from the shore. In fact, some still use that outmoded gear. But since the bass attracts such angling pressure, it – like the cod – has been responsible for much of the trend towards lighter, more sporting tackle.

Winter bass fishing in the white water of Derrynane Strand in Kerry. In the off season for tourists, the country is peaceful and the scenery breathtaking. Besides good bass, excellent flounders may be caught, too.

Bass offer great opportunities for varied angling techniques. They will pick up a legered bait in the wild combers of a clear-water Atlantic surf beach, like those in south-west Ireland, west Wales and the West Country of England, coming into a foot of water to do so; they will swim among rocky, weed-draped gullies searching for crabs, prawns and small fish, where legering or spinning or float-fishing may work; they move into estuaries and swim far up tidal rivers, where spinning, legering and float-fishing will catch them, and in rivermouths with extensive banks or rock outcrops; they will also come to the skilful fly fisher, as they will when the whitebait or sand-eel shoals are herded in the waves of steep shingle beaches during calm settled weather in late summer and autumn, or when the bass shoal up in thousands over offshore reefs. And on the reefs spinning, trolling, driftlining may all be expected to work on their day.

Bass can be sensitive and difficult to catch, but at times they can become almost suicidal, being caught in multiple hook-ups on mackerel feathers fished from boats. They will sometimes fight extremely hard, especially in clear water, but at other times they can be

extremely sluggish opponents, hardly resisting rod pressure, indeed sometimes swimming into the angler and almost beaching themselves.

Bass fishing takes the angler to superb scenery, and since the best of this is the wild surf-pounded strands of south-west Ireland with the Kerry mountains as a backdrop, it is surfcasting on these storm beaches that will be dealt with first.

Rod 2 in the list in chapter 2, $10\frac{1}{2}$–$11\frac{1}{2}$ ft (3·2–3·5 m) and to cast 2–3 oz (56–85 g) using 10–15 lb (4–5–6·8 kg) lines, is the one to choose, with the small multiplier, or, alternatively the fixed-spool reel. With surf bass averaging 4 lb (1·8 kg) or thereabouts, 10–15 lb test might at first appear to be stronger than necessary, but the gear has to be cast 100 yd (91·4 m) at times, and it has perhaps to cope with heavy rafts of weed and the abrasion of sand.

Top bait on surf beaches is lugworm, with clam, razorfish and sand-eel close followers. In autumn squid will catch the larger fish at the cost to the angler obtaining fewer bites from modest fish.

The terminal tackle is simple: a single-hook fixed nylon paternoster made up in exactly the same way as for cod from the beach, except that the hook should be from 1/0–4/0, depending on the bait size used, and made of fine wire: Mustad's number 79510 is a favourite with most bass addicts, though a spade-end pattern in nickel finish, sold by Don Neish's Edmonton (London) specialist tackle shop, is excellent too.

Some anglers make up running paternosters for surf bass, but experience has proved them to be unnecessary: such well-known bass anglers as Des Brennan, Kevin Linnane (both of Ireland's Inland Fisheries Trust), Clive Gammon, John Darling, among others, use the fixed paternoster. It does not tangle, gives immediate signal of a bite, and, used with a breakaway lead and a very sharp hook can result in many fish just skin-hooking themselves as they turn away with the bait, whereas a running line can give a fish warning by *slowly* increasing tension, at which the bait can be ejected in a flash. The fixed line brings the fish up *sharply*.

Casts of 40–100 odd yd (36·5–91·4 m) are the usual range, and chest waders are best when it is found necessary to wade well out into a rough surf to cast beyond the worst turbulence. In fact they are best at all times for true surfcasting since one can stand out in the troughs waist-deep when awaiting a bite; this shortens the line to the lead and bait, which means a faster strike and less line stretch. Failing chest waders,

When a bass is brought into the swash on a surf beach and it feels sand beneath its belly, it is likely to make a last fast run out to the deeper water. Here Kevin Linnane, Sea Angling Officer of Ireland's Inland Fisheries Trust, enjoys the experience.

Fishing from a rocky ledge at the base of a sheer cliff in Sussex, Ian Gillespie caught this 6½ lb (2·9 kg) bass on peeler crab legered in the boulders. The rod is made from a freshwater carp rod blank.

which are very expensive, thighboots will do, but wear oilskin or PVC overtrousers over them and put strong elastic bands over the lot at ankle level to prevent waves seeping up. Bib-type trousers with shoulder straps are best.

Since most of the bass will be unhooked and returned to the sea alive immediately, it is best to carry all the gear you need on you, because the need for a new hook, lead, swivel or bait often entails a walk of more than 300 yd (274 m) over wet sand to the dry base or the car in the dunes; and farther if you've walked *along* the beach, too! Breast pockets on a waterproof parka or anorak will keep things fairly dry; if it's too warm to wear any form of jacket, then both the bait and the end-tackle spares may be carried in a small canvas or plastic bag round the neck.

Although most surf beaches fish well on the flooding tide, particularly during the first two hours following low water, there is no hard and fast rule of thumb on timing. Bass roam surf beaches and can turn up at any time during the tide, and sometimes the best fishing will come after high water and right down the ebb. The high water period – lasting about an hour – is usually a slack period for bites, but even then there are exceptions. For daylight fishing plenty of surf rolling in from about 200 yd (182·8 m) out is desirable, conditions which can follow a local onshore blow or a vast storm way out in the Atlantic. At night surf is still needed, but bass will come very close inshore after dark when there is little in the way of white water. Dull days can be better than sunny days, but again radiant sunshine, blue sky and a roaring surf have produced superb fishing.

One hears advice about 'casting to the third breaker where the bass lie' – as if the fish were glued to the seabed at that point. It helps to cast about 50 yd (45·7 m) for a start in a moderate surf and extend casts seaward from there until fish are contacted. Failing that, try shorter casts: bass will often take in the swash of the last comber as it runs up and down the clean sand, the water calf-deep. Good spots to try are where freshwater streams cross the beach, or where there are gullies or banks of sand – made visible by the pattern of the breaking waves seen from a distance, preferably above on the mountainside.

On these surf beaches there is very rarely any trouble from lateral tidal currents, the breakers running in straight up the line from the position of the lead. In such cases, for maximum comfort and sensitivity, it may be found best to cradle the rod along the forearm, butt under the arm, the tip pointing down, either straight at the lead or, as the author prefers, at an angle of about 60 degrees from the lead pointing slightly out to sea and along the line of the surf.

This latter stance gives quick response to a rapid pull or pluck or a rapidly occurring slack line, the body and arm simply swinging away from the direction of the lead and bait. The rod must be held always when surf fishing for bass, else many fish will be missed. Sometimes even the most comfortable stance will impose strain on arm or back, in which case try a suitable alternative for a few minutes, such as back to the sea and the rod 'at the slope' over the shoulder. A strike can be quickly made from that position, too, and it is particularly useful when holding the rod tip high to keep the line clear of drifting weed inshore, which can be a big problem after a prolonged onshore gale.

Bass bites in the surf vary from slack lines, a few fast taps followed by a firm pull, a mind-bending lunge, the savagery of which can take the rod from the hand of the unwary, or a gentle sucking sensation. All must be struck, all must be recognised. To be able to do this consistently takes time and persistence.

Bass in the surf usually make short, jagging runs immediately on being hooked. Then they either race inshore, the angler running back to help the reel take up the slack line, or they kite along the crests of the rollers. The occasional fish, not always a monster, will rush out to sea, the clutch on the reel whining, for maybe 30 yd (27·4 m) or so. In the swash of the final wave that shoots up the beach and rushes back like a torrential river, a bass can rush around and put a lot of strain on the line. Keep the rod tip up and the drag light, thumb or finger pressure on the spool to provide sensitive control of any lunges.

A damp piece of towel or similar, kept in a pocket or the little bag, is useful for handling fish while unhooking without leaving the water. The fish is held in the cloth under the arm and cradled along the forearm while the hook is disengaged. One has only to stoop and let the fish slide from the cloth into the water. For those who don't know, beware of the sharp spines on the dorsal fins of the bass, also the razor-sharp anterior edges of its gills. Very bad gashes can be sustained from these.

When wading out to cast – and when returning to the shallower swash – always watch out for the incoming combers. Time the cast between them: to be hit by a big wave in mid-cast can roll even a heavy man over and up the beach. It is seldom very dangerous, but it can be very uncomfortable and embarrassing!

The slimmer the line used, the less lead it is necessary to use, and the more the bass will be able to fight without the encumbrance of a lead 'necklace'. The 10 lb (4·5 kg) test line is usually ample, but when casting farther than 40 yd (36·5 m) the line will break from the sudden shock, even with 2 oz (56·6 g) leads. A leader of 15 lb (6·8 kg) will prevent this happening. If breakaway leads are used it will not be necessary, 99 times out of 100, to use a lead of more than 3 oz (85 g) in any surf beach conditions, and most fishing will be comfortable with 2 oz (56·6 g).

Bass in the surf of Kerry and west Cork can be caught all the year round due to the relative consistency of the water temperature. April and May are usually very good months, late September to the end of November excellent, especially for big fish. In the depths of winter bass of 3–6 lb (1·3–2·7 kg) can provide some hectic sport, and although it is likely to be wet and windy, Irish west coast weather is seldom bitterly cold. The winter surfs can be quite magnificent, the power of the waves never to be forgotten.

Bottom fishing for bass in other places, like the steep-to shingle beaches of the southern Irish, Welsh and west, east and south-east of England coastlines can be covered by the same casting outfit in general. The difference lies in the behaviour of the bass and the depth and character of the water.

There will usually be lateral tidal currents with which to contend, and the bass tend not to be so numerous as on surf beaches, where one good angler can catch 20 fish on a good tide. The bass can average 6 lb (2·7 kg) or so, however, and bigger baits of crab, squid or cuttle, half a mackerel (side fillet) or herring, a sand-eel, small pouting or rockling, bunch of slipper limpets, king ragworm and so on will tend to work.

Bass will work very close in on such beaches with their often turbid water and little wave action, and a running paternoster allows the fish to get the big bait into its mouth and move off without feeling untoward resistance, provided a slack line is fished, thus permitting the angler to set the hook – as big as 5/0 at times – even when awaiting bites over long periods with the rod in a monopod and the reel out of gear but with the audible ratchet on.

Such beaches usually fish best when there is some turbulence after an onshore blow, although at night calm seas can produce fish. In England, and most of Wales, the surf beaches of the extreme west apart, the bass season begins in late April or mid-May and ends about the end of October, only occasional fish being taken in winter. There are some exceptions, warm water outfalls for instance; but even at some atomic power stations the fish have mostly quit by mid-November.

Estuary bass fishing is conducted in a very similar way to that of steep-to beaches, but estuaries vary widely in character and some are confined by man-made structures, deep and fast flowing on flood and ebb; others are wide and natural, with sandbanks, gullies, rocky outcrops *ad infinitum*. On both these steep, deep water beaches – 10 ft (3 m) or more – and in most estuaries the flood tide fishes best, from just after low water for two hours, then there follows a lull until the last two hours. On some estuaries, though, the ebb fishes best, and some beaches can produce at such times. It pays to know that the estuary of any river fed by acid water draining from moorland can be extremely unpleasant to bass in times of flash floods: the fish will usually move away to pure saltwater until the floodwater is dispersed, and this can even occur when small streams crossing Irish surf beaches run vinegar-hued with peat drainage.

John Darling again, a very successful bass angler and a light tackle fanatic. Here the scene is Sussex rocks at the base of high chalk cliffs, where casting crab baits into the gullies produces exciting tussles with bass like this brace.

One of England's most famous bass fishing locations, beneath the towering chalk cliffs of Beachy Head in Sussex. The

Estuaries sometimes provide very short periods of activity, perhaps only for three hours at the top of the tide, due to very fast currents in their constricted channels on flood and ebb. Also, estuary bass have to be understood, because they move in and out of the rivermouth and up the main channel along very closely defined routes. Never be put off by shallow water when bass fishing, either on open beaches, in estuaries or among rocky foreshores. Depth matters little to the bass; the fish is a wanderer and goes where the food is. The author knows two rivermouths where bass are taken on the ebb in 2 ft (60 cm) of swift water over gravel, whereas a bait placed a short distance away goes unnoticed.

With light lines estuary bass sometimes need careful playing when they get into the full flow of the river's ebb-tide current. Often concrete groynes, wooden breakwaters etc are good vantage points, both on estuaries and open beaches, but a dropnet is needed to secure the beaten fish.

In many estuaries, especially the more natural ones, and those in which bass run several miles upstream on the flood, the surfcasting rod is unnecessary and the double-handed spinning rod with as light a lead as possible and 6–8 lb (2·7–3·6 kg) line makes a great combination. A good bass, even a six-pounder (2·7 kg) will go well on this outfit.

When wading in rivermouths with sandbanks and channels, always fish with a friend and keep an eye on the incoming tide. It is easy to become engrossed in the fishing and be cut off by the flooding tide.

Various piers and breakwaters at seaside resorts can provide good fishing for bass, by legering any of the deep-water beach baits mentioned, by float-fishing with live prawns, bunters in bunches (they are small, brackish-water shrimps), soft or peeler crab, king ragworm, bunches of white or red ragworms, small live fish, such as pouting, blennies, butterfish, preferably live or else freshly deep-frozen sand-eels, or slim strips cut from mackerel, herring or squid. The tackle is rigged as for float-fishing for pollack from the shore and the bait fished from mid-water to just clear of the bottom.

Bass, like most predators, like to hang in the shadow cast by a pier, bridge or groyne, to dash out at food that comes by. Float-fished baits should be held near such places and even encouraged by the use of currents and wave action to drift under the pier structure. Bass hooked thus need to be held firmly and 10 lb (4·5 kg) line may be necessary, whereas without obstructions – with smooth concrete walls going down into the sea – 6 lb (2·7 kg) line on the double-handed spinning rod will provide some exciting battles.

Fish strips, live small mackerel called joeys, live pouting and so on may be driftlined from the ends of piers and breakwaters where there is sufficient tidal current to take the bait away. Just the baited hook is needed for much of the time, although a small amount of lead may be necessary to get the bait down in stronger flows. A live fish may be guided to swim where the angler wants it to go by judicious gentle twitches in the opposite direction. A single 3/0–5/0 hook nicked through the back of the pouting or mackerel just behind the front dorsal fin works well. When the bass takes a strong pull is felt, at which line must be allowed to run off in free spool – or the pick-up arm must be open with a fixed-spool reel – for several seconds. The bass will usually go for about 10 yd (9 m) and slow down, then move away in jerks. That is the time to pull the hook into the fish's jaw. But make sure the line is taut first.

Spinning can be good active sport from some piers and seaward projections, provided the water is fairly clear – visibility from above should be for a distance of at least 8 ft (2·4 m) down into the water. Spinning in murky water seldom works for saltwater fish.

The Red Gill sand-eels, the soleskin lure about 3 in long (7·6 cm) with a small mackerel spinner at its head, Toby, Condor, Koster and Ellips heavyweight wobbling spoons, even a silver Devon minnow about 2 in (5 cm) long with a willow-leaf shaped piece of chamois leather about the same length on one hook of the tail treble, will work at times. Carry a selection. Make casts far out where tide-races form, along weed-covered walls; fish deep and fish shallow, fast and slow. Usually the artificial sand-eel recovered at a modest pace around midwater will find the fish. The wobbling spoons in 1 oz (28 g) or heavier will usually cast far enough and fish deeply enough without additional lead.

For the rubber sand-eel and soleskin lure a bomb-shaped lead suspended from the top eye of a size 8 swivel which links a 4 ft (1·2 m) trace of matching nylon to the main line by a few inches of nylon will serve as sinker, anti-kink device and it will cast much farther than the more usual Wye or spiral spinning leads used.

In a boat, a dinghy close to the shore or a bigger boat way out over reefs or wreckage, shoaling bass may be tackled with trolled Red Gills or spoons, strips of mackerel and squid, or by casting and spinning such lures and baits from an anchored position. When tackling bass from a boat it is usual to first find the shoal by looking for birds working, especially terns. The bass may be feeding on sand-eels, whitebait or shoals of mackerel, even whiting and pouting that are tumbled around in the turbulence of the water flowing at speed over the obstruction. Then it is essential not to motor into the shoal but to keep to the edges, casting along the shoal's edge. A lure right in among the shoal may be ignored; a lone lure wriggling or twinkling along the edge in open water stands a better chance of being taken.

Spinning for bass is usually best in the period from late June to mid-October when there are shoals of either mackerel or of sand-eels, whitebait and sprats.

When fishing from a small boat which forms a stable platform or from steep-to beaches, rocks or wide-open estuaries, this period also produces excellent sport with the fly rod, a technique which has been de-

veloped to a high art in saltwater in warmer parts of the world but is yet in its infancy in Britain and Europe. The prerequisite is visible activity near the surface by bass, not necessarily a vast shoal but reasonable numbers of fish showing. Again, as in spinning, clear water is essential to success, as is a quiet approach with the engine turned off and casting along the fringes of the shoal, not into its middle. Dawn and dusk are favourite periods.

Spinning and bottom fishing around old towers in the Thames estuary produces plenty of action with shoaling bass.

Another boat-caught bass from the towers in the Thames estuary. Holding it is Martin Ashby, famous rod builder of Southend-on-Sea.

Bass

The coast of Essex, especially the Blackwater, Crouch and Thames estuaries, is famous for the many large bass taken, both inshore, and many miles out on the various banks. This fish held by John Rawle weighed 10½ lb (4·7 kg).

**White water rolls around the angler's legs as he points his rod down the line, out to the spot where his lug-baited hook lies in wait for the bass in the surf: Inch strand in County Kerry.**

The reservoir fly rod and reel suggested in chapter 2 are the backbone of the outfit, and since casts of at least 25 yd (22·8 m) should be easily attainable, even into a stiff breeze at times, with well over 30 yd (27·4 m) when necessary, the obvious choice of fly line is either a weight-forward saltwater or bug taper, or a shooting head backed up with monofilament shooting line. And since the bass may be near the surface or several feet below it, both a floating and a fast-sinking line should be carried – one on a spare spool for the reel.

If shooting heads rather than weight-forward lines are used, then they should be joined to the mono-filament either with a nail-knot or stuck into the end of the fly line with a cyanoacrylate adhesive, such as Loctite I.S.-12. This adhesive sticks anything to any-thing in seconds, including finger to finger, so care is needed when using it, else surgery will be necessary. It will secure about $\frac{1}{4}$ in (6 mm) of shooting monofila-ment in a hole formed in the hollow end of the flyline and take all the strain necessary.

Dave Collyer, the famous fly dresser, explained the method of joining with the adhesive in *Angling* magazine, August 1976 issue. He pushes a needle into the fly line for about $\frac{1}{2}$ in (1·2 cm) and heats the eye until red. When cool the needle is withdrawn, leaving the plastic-covered line with a hole inside. This is widened slightly with a thicker needle and the end of the monofilament pointed with a sharp knife, razor or scalpel, by slicing it when held flat on a piece of old wood, and the last $\frac{1}{4}$ in (6 mm) roughened with abrasive paper. The nylon is given a thin coat of the adhesive and quickly pushed into the flyline. Adhe-sion is almost immediate, but the joint is best left over-night for maximum security.

Cyanoacrylate adhesive is said to break down in water, but Collyer and others found it did not occur in practice, though the joints made were so tight the water probably could not seep in. Loctite do make a solution which makes the adhesive waterproof, although building up a smooth junction with liquid PVC does the job as well.

For those who do not know how to make a nail-knot the following diagram explains all.

**Instructions for attaching monofilament to fly line.**

1. Make a hole through the end of the fly line with a pin or needle, passing this out on the side of the line. While the pin is still in the hole, heat its head with a match flame to redness, then let it cool before removing the pin. Pass the end of the monofilament in at the end of the fly line and out at the side.

2. Wind the monofilament three times round the end of the fly line and lay the end of the monofilament parallel to where it leaves the hole in the side of the fly line.

3. By winding the turns of monofilament backwards over the end, and carefully pulling on the ends and ad-justing the turns, snug down the resulting knot. With a good pull applied between the end of the monofilament and the part emerging from the end of the fly line, squeeze the turns of the knot down into the fly line dressing.
   Remove some of the dressing from the end of the fly line so as to expose the braided fly line core. In doing this, be careful not to cut or nick the monofilament. Fray out the end of the braided core and apply varnish.

4. Whip over the frayed core with fly tying silk or, prefer-ably, very fine nylon thread, building up to a taper shaped by successive layers of turns, to form a smooth transition between the diameters of the monofilament and the fly line respectively. Thoroughly cover this bind-ing and the turns of the knot with Vycote.

(Reproduced from *Angling Magazine*, by kind permission of Richard Walker)

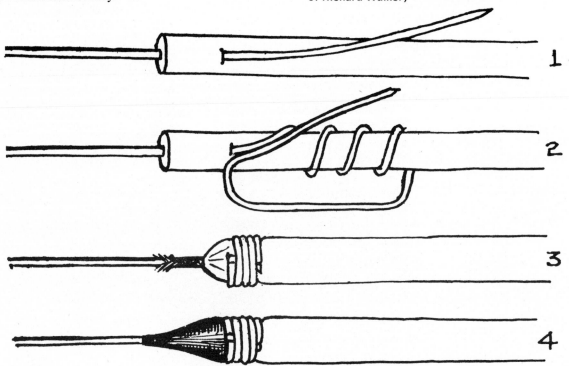

1

2

3

4

A little dinghy can be ideal when sea conditions are right, for bass fishing just offshore, trolling or spinning, especially at dawn and dusk.

Spinning from the rocks for bass makes for some interesting fishing, locating ledges and gullies through which to work the lure. This angler is fishing at Rame Head, Cornwall.

Derrynane is one of Ireland's most beautiful surf beaches. It provides superb surfcasting for bass — and big flounders — and fishing from the rocks at high water at the mouth of this little river.

Bass Blond.

Since long lengths of fly line and shooting monofilament are going to be draped all over the place in a boat, or underfoot on the beach or rocks, as a shoal of feeding bass are followed and cast to, a line basket worn low on the left hip (for a right-handed caster) is an essential item of equipment. It not only helps shoot line for long casts, but prevents damage to the line by treading on it or the line tangling with weeds when wading.

Leaders need only be 6–8 ft (1·8–2·4 m) long and of level nylon – about 7–9 lb (3·1–4 kg) test. The strength is not important with regard to the fight or weight of the fish, only to the stiffness of the nylon which must be sufficient to turn over a comparatively big, heavy fly.

Flies should be dressed on strong hooks, such as the Yorkshire Stronghold or similar, even on O'Shaughnessy bends when fishing deep from a boat. It is important that the fly takes a streamlined and mobile aspect in the water and that it should have some white hair and silver tinsel in its make-up. The author dresses a fly which he calls the Bass Blond, modelled on the Blond series of flies invented and popularised by the great American sportfisher, the late Joe Brooks. The author added colours suggested by the English writer John Bickerdyke, who fished fly for bass in the middle 1800s.

The Bass Blond is dressed with white tying nylon and has a carrot-shaped body of white Orlon baby wool ribbed with wide silver Lurex. An underwing of pale blue bucktail is put on halfway between eye and beginning of bend, the body being then continued forward and fattened. The wing is built up of, from top to bottom, white, red and yellow bucktail and the head is built up big and thickly covered with white varnish before black eyes are painted on.

The fly is made on hooks 1–2/0 and besides being attractive to bass satisfies the fly dresser's whim for artistry. Much plainer bucktails and streamers, white or black, especially with deer-hair Muddler heads, have been effective in recent summers.

The fly is cast ahead of or near visible signs of bass chasing fry, from open beach or rocks, and is then fished back in smooth pulls, not at a fast pace, but so that it darts and stops, like a little fish. When fishing across an estuary with a flow coming from the side, the line may be allowed to swing round with the current, as in wet fly trouting or seatrouting, before being brought back with smooth pulls. If the fly furrows the surface this will often trigger a smashing take.

There is much to be learned in saltwater fly fishing in the waters of the United Kingdom and neighbouring countries. Because it is a difficult technique to master in the sea and not so numerically rewarding with fish, progress will be fairly slow due to so few anglers having the mental attitude to persist in the face of many failures. Success, when it comes, however, is extremely sweet.

# 12
# Grey mullets: thick-lipped and thin-lipped

The mullet family, of which the two above named species are members, inhabits nearly all the warm and temperate coastal waters of the world. They favour brackish water and during the angling season – in British waters from May to October in general, although in some western harbours mullet are taken in winter as well – are seen in great shoals. They move up and down with the tides in estuaries, penetrating

This thick-lipped grey mullet was taken on float-fished bread in Christchurch Harbour, Hampshire. Note how the hook is near the edge of the mouth.

Grey mullets

tidal creeks, lagoons and drains, and mooning in harbours to mop up the dross and offal of human habitation.

The thick-lipped grey mullet, which is the more plentiful and more widely distributed of the two, runs the rivers only to the limit of the tide, but the thin-lipped grey mullet presses on into pure freshwater where it may spend the whole summer sojourning with coarse fish.

*Chelon labrosus* is the scientific name for the thick-lipped mullet; *Liza ramada* is the thin-lipped mullet. Thick-lipped mullet reach weights of 10 lb (4·5 kg) and more, the thin-lipped probably weighing almost as much, but because fewer are caught by anglers, and some not recognised for what they are anyway, positive records are scanty. A third species of grey mullet, the golden grey mullet, inhabits our coastal waters, but because it attains weights of 1 lb (450 g) only, it is not of great interest to sportfishers.

Both thick- and thin-lipped mullet are superb fighters. They can make long fast runs, they bore doggedly for the bottom, and just when the angler is reaching for the net they will make another run, and maybe circle under the rod for up to 5 more minutes. Many anglers hold the view that, size for size, mullet are the hardest fighters of all British saltwater fish.

Grey mullet are a very successful family of fish because they can tolerate living conditions that kill other fish, both sea- and freshwater fish, such as pollution and low oxygen content and a diet that most other fish do not touch. These two species of grey mullet eat a basic diet of diatoms, plant detritus and algae which they skim with their lower scoop-shaped lips from mudbanks, boat hulls and harbour walls. In freshwater and water only slightly brackish, the fish have been found to contain a small proportion of midge larvae (bloodworms).

However, in areas where human waste gets into the water, such as harbours with plenty of boats, fishing ports, seaside resort piers with cafés and marinas, the mullet, more so the thick-lipped species, happily waxes fat on a diet of pulpy bread, plate scrapings of meat, fat and vegetable matter, fish guts and filleted carcases and many other unpleasant items that are washed in from sewage outfalls and drains. In Ireland mullet swarm round pipes carrying creamery waste to the sea or tidal inlets.

A mullet of over 4 lb (1·8 kg) taken float-fishing bread in 2 ft (60 cm) of water in an estuary. On this day a number of good fish were caught on 3 lb (1·3 kg) test line and roach tackle.

In muddy harbours and in tidal reaches of muddy-bottomed rivers and creeks, the mullet do sometimes happen across free-swimming tiny harbour ragworms, usually 1½–2½ in (4–6·5 cm) long which live in millions of tiny burrows in the bottom and banks. Periodically the ragworms emerge to migrate.

Although similar tactics may be used for both species when they are either in the sea or in harbours, estuaries and creeks, a separate system must be adopted for catching thin-lipped mullet once they have entered freshwater or are moving up and down a river between freshwater and the brackish water lower down.

In this situation the thin-lipped mullet will accept only one bait for 95 per cent of the time and that is harbour ragworm. Once in a while a coarse fisher will catch one on a maggot, or even a piece of bread flake, but anybody who wishes to catch thin-lipped mullet up the rivers with any regularity should use harbour ragworm. Details of obtaining these are given in chapter 4, but always keep an eye open for Water Authority men or harbour staff when digging. They seem to think anglers damage the banks by digging ragworm, although how they justify such thinking when they use draglines and dredgers in the same places leaves most anglers wondering – and they dig regardless. In truth, it is best to fill in any holes made, just to keep the peace!

The tackle for upriver thin-lipped mullet consists of the Avon-type rod (rod 5) in chapter 2 and line of 3–4 lb (1·3–1·8 kg) test, which on wide rivers or other upriver waters can be on a fixed-spool reel and in narrow rivers, up to 15 yd (14 m) in width, a centre-pin, for sheer pleasure and control of the fish from the direct drive.

Nearly all the fishing will be with a float, with many rubber rings to prevent slippage, and best of all is a long slim one, either a peacock tail quill, gull quill or hard balsa-wood. The length needs to be about a foot (30·4 cm) and when it is supporting a swan shot, or equivalent load, about 2 in (5 cm) at least should remain above the surface of the water. Even though the ragworms to be used as bait, singly or as many as three at once, are tiny, the hook must not be too small. Long experience by anglers of thin-lipped mullet has shown that size 8 is most useful, sizes 10 and 6 being carried for special circumstances.

The author nets a good harbour mullet for his son, who has caught fair numbers of these so-called difficult fish on light tackle, proving the point that even boys can succeed when properly guided.

Inset: A typical float rig used by the author for bread or ragworm fishing for mullet in harbours, creeks and tidal rivers. The float is cane and elder-pith and held firmly by several long lengths of cycle valve rubber. The shot is pinched on over a piece of balloon rubber, again to keep it in position when rapid striking is necessary.

Thick-lipped grey mullet vee the surface of this quiet Essex creek, beguiling an angler who has the place to himself and cannot accept that they are uncatchable.

The shot is usually fixed about 6 in (15·5 cm) above the hook, first slipping on a sliver of balloon rubber so that the squeezed shot does not damage the line and is prevented from slipping to the hook when hard, fast strikes are made.

Warm and settled weather in June is a good time to begin looking for thin-lipped mullet. Travel light with either a small haversack, landing net and lightweight waterproof or fly-fisher's waistcoat. Always carry polarising glasses, both for searching for shoals of fish and for freedom from dazzle when float watching.

Unless the local mullet anglers can, or will, tell where the shoals of thin-lips are to be found, one must do the work oneself. On many occasions mullet can be spotted by watching for swirls and Vees on the surface as the shoals move up or down the river. The swirls are usually large, an oily upwelling of water from a sudden movement by a powerful body deep down. Mullet men call them *whelms*. Once the direction of the shoal, which may be half a dozen fish or several hundreds, has been pinpointed, head it off and cast the tackle with two ragworms, head-hooked, in front of it, the fishing depth initially at about 1½ ft (45 cm), regardless of the depth of water.

Feeding mullet will usually indicate interest quickly, the float suddenly disappearing in a flash, or dithering over several seconds before shooting down; often the tip of the float will tip one way, then the other, before going down. It is essential that any strike is delayed until the whole of the 2 in (5 cm) of float above water has disappeared, since mullet will pull the float half-way without having the hook in a sinkable spot.

However, once the float has gone the strike must be made like lightning. It takes lots of practice to be able to connect with thin-lipped mullet bites regularly, and unless plenty of bites are being obtained, it is a problem to get keyed up to the right pitch anyway! The float tackle, being set so shallow, will be whipped from the water at great speed when a bite is missed and can do some damage to anybody standing on the bank beside or behind the angler. One spectator had a porcupine quill float embedded in his forehead by one mullet angler who was getting on the ball!

If the initial depth setting gets no attention from the fish, but they are obviously still in the area, try 2 ft (60 cm) and then down from there. Rarely are thin-lips found to take red ragworm at much more than 3 ft (91 cm), or more than half the total depth of the water, as a rule.

If the fish are not visible on the surface, one has to fish up the river, trying every 10 yd (9 m) or so, until a bite or bites are forthcoming. It is obviously a far quicker operation if a number of mullet enthusiasts do this together, leap-frogging to cover the water quickly. Once mullet bites or fish are forthcoming, it is recognised practice that the anglers cast their floats into the taking area, even a foot or so from each other. The effect of a number of baits being close together is that more scent is given off and the fish home-in – a form of mutual groundbaiting.

To make a big catch of thin-lips in freshwater, or in places where there is little salinity, it is essential that the fish are feeding, or are prepared to feed once stimulated, and that they will either remain in a small length of river, dyke or similar or can be tempted to do so. Many shoals of mullet in a river system may be uncatchable because they are not feeding when the bait is cast to them or will not begin to do so when a number of baits are put in. Another method that will sometimes work and hold a shoal together involves throwing in an evil smelling mixture of mud in which ragworms have been kept and where some of them have died, plus a little soaked bread mixed in with the mud. This does not work, however, if the river flow is such that the odour is carried away. The best conditions for thin-lips are no current or a slight current and a wind against it to keep surface water in a state of near balance.

One's first mullet, if it is much over 1½ lb (600 g), will be a revelation. It is likely to streak away with the reel clutch whining, swirl savagely on the surface and run up and down the channel, all at great speed and with such power that a fish many pounds heavier is suspected. When you think it safe to reach for the net, the fish will begin boring round and round under the rod tip, in spite of maximum pressure. A 4 lb (1·8 kg) thin-lipped mullet may take 10 minutes to bring to net on the kind of gear mentioned, sometimes even longer. The occasional fish of 5 lb (2·6 kg) upwards will be contacted that will whip 50 yd (45·7 m) of line from the reel with one run, and then keep pulling.

To strike both quickly yet avoid the impact breaking the tackle is tricky: a low, sidewise strike can help, trying to cushion the line near the float in the surface of the water. Unless there is a troublesome surface drift or wind that will drag the float out of position, always keep the line well greased and floating. This helps make striking fast. If a sunken line is the sole way of being able to fish, the chances of connecting with fast bites are narrowed a lot.

On occasions the thin-lip will relent and one gets a slow sinking of the float, in a sidewise direction. Such bites are fairly easy to hit, but are rare. Occasionally winding in *slowly* produces better bites.

Thick-lipped grey mullet are another matter. In tidal reaches of rivers, in creeks, in harbours, lagoons, from breakwaters and piers, they may be fished with almost the same tackle, except that when fishing in water 25 ft (7·6 m) deep or more a sliding float will be needed – one with a central plastic tube through a cigar-shaped balsa-wood body has proved as good as any and better than most – with a tiny rubber or linen thread stop on the line. Avon trotting floats are useful at other times. Also, it is as well to increase line test to 5 lb in deep water, especially in places where mullet can run and foul the tackle, such as boat moorings, bridge and pier supports and the like. Striking firmly enough to hook fish in deep water, and at long range, can break 3 lb (1·3 kg) line surprisingly easy. The amount of lead on the line may need to be in-

A fine specimen thin-lipped grey mullet so typical of the shoals that run up the eastern Rother in Sussex, one of the most famous rivers for this species. On light tackle these fish are dynamite.

creased to two to three swan shots for proper tackle control, too.

Depending on whether the saltwater location is a busy resort marina or port, a pier with a café, or a tiny cove in Cornwall, Devon or Ireland where a few inshore boats land fish and throw the offal into the sea, the bait may be fresh bread-flake, red ragworms, small cubes of skinned mackerel flesh, or tiny strips of skin and flesh cut from mackerel, herring or garfish. Cubes of flesh can be about ¼ in (6 mm) square or as big as ½ in (12 mm) square; strips of fish may be about ¼ in by about 1½ in (6 mm by 40 mm).

Thick-lipped mullet will also take small pieces of shellfish, especially mussels and cockles, and in places where these shellfish are landed and cleaned, the shells and some of the contents being returned to the sea or creek, mullet come in and are caught quite readily on these baits.

Where creamery waste is discharged to sea or estuary, as in a number of well-known places in Ireland famous for mullet fishing, cream cheese makes a good bait. A wisp or two of sheep's wool or 'cotton-wool' is whipped to the hook just below the eye to give the soft cheese something to which to cling, else both water action and mullet can take it off, the latter sometimes without getting the hook into their mouths.

Des Brennan, the Irish Inland Fisheries Trust Angling Manager, who is a mullet addict, reported in *Mullet* (Osprey Anglers series) that he had caught mullet feeding wildly on creamery waste on a hook adorned only by cotton-wool, or anything else white!

Imagine a day for thick-lipped mullet from a pier or wall where the fish take bread. It is usual to fish at times and in places where tidal flow is minimal, so that the tackle fishes in a small area where mullet congregate or can be gathered together: at slack tide, or before and after it when there is little ebb or flow, and then usually around the high water period rather than the low; or in places away from the main tidal stream, such as occur where pierheads have T-shaped sections, or where harbour walls that project out to sea have strengthening abutments, or inner harbours where the water is smooth and slow-moving.

Often, when the weather is sunny and the water calm and clear, a look along the projections, especially with the help of polarising spectacles, will reveal mullet swimming slowly to and fro. The first thing to do is find a fishable spot where the fish are, or to which they may be lured. Then lower down an onion bag or something with similar size holes, containing several stale loaves which have been well soaked and mashed up. The bag or bags must just touch the water surface, so that any rise and fall washes out bits of bread; failing that, give the bag a shake on its cord occasionally. Don't forget to raise and lower the bag with the rise and fall of the tide!

Soon, however, mullet should begin to shoal around the bag as the water turns milky with the mashed bread breaking up. Simply lower the float tackle gently down beside the bag and let it waft around. Fish are likely to be taking any bits from the bag as they sink slowly, and so the bait should also sink slowly. This means that the shot should be at least 2 ft (70 cm) from the hook, when fishing less than 3 ft (91 cm) deep, although any attempt to fish the slowly sinking bait with the float much more than 4 ft (1·2 m) above the bait will result in fish taking the bread without registering very much on the float.

Avoid as much as possible making surface disturbance. Watch the bait as it sinks slowly; it is possible to see the fish move up to take the bread before the float shows anything. It is best, however, to await the float going down before striking quickly but gently.

If the fish will not take the slowly sinking bread in the first 3–4 ft (91 cm–1·2 m), then increase the fishing depth by a foot at a time. Once the fishing depth exceeds the length of the rod it is necessary to use the sliding float. It is seldom necessary to fish the bread deeper than half the depth of the water.

Usually a pinch of flake ½ in (12 mm) square on a size 6–8 hook will be about right, but if many bites are missed, or bites are finicky, try smaller pieces on a size 10 hook.

If float-fished bread fails and the mullet below your stance persistently swirl on the surface or swim with their backs out of the water round the bread bag, it is well worth trying floating bread crust, just as when freshwater fishing for carp, chub and so on. Only the hook is used and baited with a piece of crust ½–¾ in (12–18 mm) square; unless it is necessary to cast the crust any distance, in which case a bubble-float with some water in it for weight, or a short piece of balsa, with a swan shot pinched on either side of it, is threaded on the line to remain about 4 ft (1·2 m) from the bait.

When a mullet cruises slowly up to the bait, swims round it, backs off, returns and then sucks it in, do wait a second for the fish to turn down before pulling in the hook.

Usually one finds that on seaside piers, as well as in tidal reaches of rivers, thick-lips will accept both bread and float-fished red ragworms, perhaps taking both baits on the same day in the same general area. However, with ragworms on the hook and from the comparatively deep water off piers, harbour arms or bridges, it usually pays to fish the bait deeper than one would bread: for example, in water 15 ft (4·5 m) deep the best results with ragworm would be likely with the bait 8–12 ft (2·4–3·6 m) below the float. That does not apply in the river, where tactics as for thin-lips in freshwater apply.

One of the most highly respected mullet-men in the United Kingdom, Gerry Green, showing a fine fish from the Sussex Cuckmere.

There is one advantage in fishing bunches of red ragworms from piers etc. It is that mullet often take them in a more leisurely way than they do bread, which gives a better rate of hook-ups to strikes.

This rate can be improved upon in fishing harbours where the thick-lips feed on fish offal. Mullet seem to eat fish flesh and guts – often rotting fish flesh, too – more deliberately than they do most foods, perhaps because it has to be dealt with in a tougher manner than pulpy bread or soft worms, which are sucked in. Mullet can often be seen feeding on fish carcases littering the bottom among moored trawlers, standing on their heads or driving themselves into the pile with vigorous tail-wags. It was in such a situation that the author saw the two biggest thick-lipped mullet he had ever seen. It was in the harbour at Dingle, Co. Kerry, and the fish were at the end of the fish pier, the bigger, at a conservative estimate, 12 lb (5·4 kg), and the smaller one about 9 lb (4 kg).

Float-fishing with fish strips or cubes or pieces of gut at various depths, from near the surface to just off the bottom, will work when the fish are prepared to co-operate. When fishing very close to weed-covered walls or rocks, or among moored boats, it sometimes pays to paternoster a fish-bait rather than fish the float, using two hooks on nylon snoods about 4 in (10 cm) long, the first about 18 in (45·7 cm) above the small pear-shaped lead, the other about a foot (30·4 cm) above the first. This technique is good when the water is rough and in cold weather, when the mullet tend to go deep.

Simply lower the gear down and touch bottom, then lift it about a foot (30·4 cm). Hold the line just ahead of the reel, and feel for the bites; they are normally very gentle, sucking bites and the rod should be lifted sharply at any signal that perceptibly lasts a little longer than the norm.

If bites are not forthcoming at a foot above the bottom, raise the baits another foot or so, until mid-water is reached. Then begin again near the bottom. For fishing close to walls or among moored boats, the short spinning rod may be found more useful than the Avon rod used for most mullet fishing.

Mention of the spinning rod brings us to the final technique in this chapter and one which for sheer light-tackle enjoyment may well be the best of all. However, it works only in a few selected locations, and there appears to be no common ground on which to base the decision of the fish to react or not. The method is spinning.

The trout spinning rod, fixed-spool reel with 3–4 lb (1·3–1·8 kg) test line and a tiny bar-spoon is required, together with some red ragworms or even red worms from a farmer's dung-hill. The method usually works only for thick-lips in estuarine waters, and especially those in which there is a walking-pace current, and where the mullet are seen swirling, *whelming* and actually jumping clear of the water.

The French do quite a lot of this type of fishing and perfected a small bar-spoon backed up with a single hook for the worm instead of the usual treble hook. The spoon is aptly termed the Muge, and is about ¾ in (19 mm) long. Other good spoons include Mepps, Veltic, Droppen, and any other similar bar-spoons up to ¾ in (19 mm) in spoon length may be used. Silver seems a little better than gold. The trebles may be left on or changed to single hooks, about size 8 or 6, which should sit approximately an inch (2·5 cm) behind the spoon.

The cast is made across the area in which the mullet are seen and the lure wound back as near to the surface as is possible; the rod tip is kept high to keep the spinner an inch (2·5 cm) or so under the water.

When first done successfully, this technique is a revelation to the angler who has erstwhile taken mullet – that shy, gentle-mouthed grey ghost – float-fishing or on floating bread: the fish chase the spoon and take it with a thump as hard as any other European saltwater predator.

At times when the mullet are a little choosy the ragworm on the hook is essential (or an ordinary red worm from a dung-hill, as mentioned above, will do instead). At other times the bar-spoon alone will be taken; maybe the day will begin with the need for the baited hook, then develop to the stage where the un-baited spinner is taken.

Whatever method the mullet falls to the fish will fight hard – always. Much has been said about the fish's soft mouth and how hooks tear out easily if the fish is held too hard. While it is true that the prehensile part of the mouth, the front lip and its connecting membrane, will tear easily if the hook penetrates there, it is also true that most mullet are hooked farther back in the mouth, and that part of the fish is as tough as that of any other fish.

Mullet have to be played firmly, and in tight spaces – like around moored boats or snaggy pier stanchions – may have to be held hard. The Avon rod will take a lot of the shocks in such cases, and the trout spinning rod will also help a lot, unless one of the tip-action types is chosen. An easy action, though not a sloppy one, is best.

Use the rectangular dropnet from high vantage points, a round-framed landing net 2 ft (60 cm) in diameter with a deep bag net from places that can be reached with a 6 ft (1·8 m) handle.

A coarse fisher once hooked a mullet by accident while trotting bread flake for roach in the lower reaches of a tidal river. His remark as the fish tore off 40 yd (36·4 m) of line is unprintable. His commentary as the fish rushed up and down the stream for nearly ten minutes included 'bloody great bass' . . . 'foul-hooked a seatrout' . . . 'must be a stray carp'. And when finally he slid the net under a mullet of about 3 lb (1·3 kg) the comment is again unprintable.

Mullet do that to people. The angler fished for nothing else and in no other river for the next 15 years or so, after which he had to stop fishing anyway!

Just to prove those earlier pictures were not of the odd lucky fish. . . . Father and son with thick-lipped mullet from Christchurch Harbour. On 3–4 lb (1·3–1·8 kg) lines these fish will make runs of up to 50 yd (45·7 m).

# 13

# Ballan wrasse

Unless one is exceptionally fit, 50 is the usual age beyond which the best of ballan wrasse fishing from the shore must remain unattainable. Indeed, the climbs necessary to be able to fish most of the really good wrasse spots deter many young and agile anglers the first time they are taken to view the locations.

This is not a criticism of those anglers who just will not go down to wrasse spots: the author knows many a brave man (with military medals for gallantry, even) who just cannot face precipitous rock faces and cliffs.

It is not fear but the honest recognition that such climbing is beyond one's capabilities and that one would be a risk to other members of the party.

And wrasse fishing from precarious, wave-washed ledges at the base of sheer cliffs, such as there are in Devon, Cornwall, parts of west Wales, Scotland and the south, south-west and western coasts of Ireland, must be carried out in properly planned groups, preferably three or more anglers travelling together. Never, ever should an angler go down a cliff onto

It is necessary to watch for extra-big waves when perched on rocks just above the water. Here a wrasse is swung out.

wave-washed wrasse rocks alone; even with one companion the climbing and carrying and the landing of fish is arduous work. A slip, either down the rocks or cliff, or, worse perhaps, into the water could result in broken bones, or very likely be fatal; with two anglers there is somebody to give first aid, rescue or go for help. But many locations demand the use of ropes and anchoring stakes at cliff tops, plus food, tackle and other supplies to be lowered or passed down and up in stages from ledge to ledge. It is then that three to six anglers can make the trip safer, more successful and more enjoyable.

A ballan wrasse weighing well over 6 lb (2·7 kg), caught in Ireland by Cornishman Stan Hoskin. The fish was killed in this instance and found to contain hundreds of tiny mussels. Wrasse lose their colours somewhat after death.

Ballan wrasse

A rope being used to reach a ballan wrasse spot safely.

Ballan wrasse are among the most colourful salt-water species in these islands. They can vary in the same locality from a rich orange-brown, through red-brown, to a chestnut hue and a lovely dark green, sometimes with blue overtones. Some are delicately spotted with lighter markings, others may have blotches of irregular size, or vertical stripes, and perhaps the most beautiful of all is the fish with chestnut back, reddish sides marked with light spots and blue sheens, the belly being bright orange and the fins edged with bright green, the rest being either orange or yellow.

The fish tend to shoal in sizes, and in the very best places, such as some rugged holes in Cornwall and west and south-west Ireland, nearly all the wrasse taken will be 3–4 lb (1·3–1·8 kg) with several over 5 lb (2·6 kg). The author has fished in Ireland when fish over 5 lb were fairly common and several over 6 lb (2·7 kg) were caught. No doubt the species reaches 10 lb (4·5 kg).

Ballan wrasse like warm Atlantic water and the normal fishing season lasts from mid-May to mid-October. Rocks of a hard nature, such as various forms of granite and volcanic material, are the usual composition of good ballan wrasse ground, which is an advantage, since this rock is usually safe for hand and foot holds, whereas softer rocks can appear firm but are in fact treacherous as they crumble when weight is put on them. Also, the hard rocks do not form discoloured water as do some softer rocks which are eroded by wave action.

Although wrasse may be caught in calm water conditions, there is little doubt that the fish's feeding activity is increased when rough water crashes into the base of the cliffs and surges among the jagged, weed-covered rocks. Obviously such a pounding dislodges crustaceans from their holds and batters and confuses small fish, sand-eels and crabs. The wrasse make hay at such times.

Ballans eat lots of tiny mussels, where they exist in large colonies, and these and small limpets are bitten from the rocks by the fish's ivory-white front teeth – massive in comparison to the size of the fish, and very powerful too. Anybody who gets a finger bitten by a big ballan will not be ignorant of this fact. Ballans also eat whole small hardback crabs, prawns, barnacles and marine worms, both lug and rag.

As far as bait goes the fish will accept lugworm as well as any other, usually, and since lug is fairly easily obtained it is an obvious choice. But small hardback shore and hermit crabs are also fairly easy to find. Mussel flesh is excellent and slipper and ordinary limpet flesh works, too, though less well than lug.

It is obvious that in some areas especially, the larger ballan wrasse feed heavily on sand-eels when they are shoaling thickly. The author has caught large numbers of big ballans on Red Gill rubber eels when fishing with friends in south-west Ireland, and the fish somehow managed to engulf the whole eel so that the hook was well back in the mouth! The artificials had to be fished at high risk, just bumping over the odd big rock. Other anglers simultaneously using spoons did not catch any wrasse, only pollack and mackerel.

Before dealing further with the actual business of catching wrasse on lightish tackle it is necessary to say something about the requirements of a party going down a cliff or over treacherous rocks. Although some advice has been given in the chapter dealing with fishing for shore pollack, the extent of climbing and risk when attaining some ballan wrasse spots is quite a lot higher.

In some places the access to low rock ledges may be quite easy, simply a series of ledges leading down to just above sea level. In such cases the only thing to watch is that footwear is suitable, both for getting a good grip on the rock and for a degree of ankle support. Fellboots or climbing boots are naturally excellent, but some can be very expensive. Leather, strong rubber or synthetics may all be used as uppers, but the soles had best be good thick rubber, well moulded with gripping tread. Metal studs are effective on wet and weedy rock, provided the studs are constantly renewed so as to be really sharp; blunted, worn studs can be very dangerous.

The author has worn felt-soled and rubber-soled training shoes on rough volcanic rock, but when the rock is wet they do not serve well and a slip can mean a broken ankle or a bad sprain. Also, rock surfaces are very rough, knife-edged and the foot arch does need good support, else a day's wrasse fishing can be agony.

If the access means descending any sheer faces, especially when drops of 30 ft (9 m) straight down have to be negotiated, with the total cliff height perhaps 150 ft (45·7 m) or more, a rope of climbing quality nylon and of adequate length to cover the total drop must be used to avoid unnecessary danger. If there is no firm tree or rock at the cliff top to which the rope can be firmly anchored then carry several lengths of angle iron or aluminium alloy angle, the faces of which should be at least 1½ in (4 cm) across and the length about 2 ft (61 cm). One end is sharpened to a point and the other is drilled through the apex of the triangle (that is, the hole passing through two sides) to which is fixed a strong steel welded ring, or a rigging clip (used for sailing) to which the rope is tied.

Test all ropes and fittings regularly for top security.

When climbing, especially the first drop which is often soft topsoil with rock in it, never put any weight, by hand or foot, on any projecting stone or rock that has not been given a good strong pull to establish if it really is part of solid rock or just a lump of rock embedded in the soil. The author once fell 20 ft (6 m) down a face to a ledge, where he was caught by a companion who had gone down first; had he continued over an overhang to crash 60 ft (18 m) onto fanglike rocks in the water below, death or terrible injuries would have been inevitable.

Once on the lower rocks and ledges from which fishing is to be done, ensure a comfortable stance, well above the reach of the occasional big wave, and keep all the tackle together well back on dry rock platforms. Tie the bags on if necessary on a windy day. Keep the bait in a bag round your neck and spare nylon, weights and hooks in pockets. The dropnet should be tied to a rock at the distance it will easily reach the water and there should be a net between every two to four anglers, who usually fish together in small areas. Each angler needs long-nosed pliers or

This close-up photograph of the head of a large Irish wrasse clearly shows the beautiful colours and markings that has earned the species the title of Britain's most colourful sea fish.

A husky wrasse for Ian Gillespie, well known angling writer, taken on float-paternoster on the Dingle Peninsula, County Kerry.

The dentition of a ballan wrasse. These teeth can rip shellfish from their anchorages on the rocks and crush limpets, barnacles, mussels, crabs — and an angler's finger if he's not careful!

stout artery forceps in his pocket with which to remove hooks from the rubbery mouths of the wrasse.

All the above is aimed at avoiding unnecessary clambering about on the rocks. Advice is often given, not to venture at all on to wet rocks; it is sound advice but anglers ignore it when they have travelled long distances for a wrasse session and it is raining, or spray has wet the rocks. The author and his friends do fish on wet rocks, but it is imperative to be twice as careful when moving about as when the rock is dry and footholds safe.

And now to the fishing.

Apart from spinning with Red Gills, which is done in exactly the same way as for pollack, except that the lure is fished even more at risk, touching rock, and with the double-handed spinning rod, multiplier or fixed-spool reel loaded with 8–10 lb (3·6–4·5 kg) test line, there are two basic techniques for ballans: paternoster and float-fishing, and the float-fishing may be with a form of paternoster rig or more conventional float gear.

Because these fish live in jumbled rocks and deep in tiny crevices and caves, all weedy, in the ground right below your feet or a yard or so out, tackle must be simple, cheap and easily made up, because losses may be high.

For the paternoster system use either the bass surf-casting rod with 12 lb (5·4 kg) line or the double-handed spinning rod with 10 lb (4·5 kg) line, depending on the average size of fish and the ruggedness of the underwater terrain. The line tests might seem excessive to anybody who has yet to tangle with ballan wrasse, but the idea is to yield as little line as is possible to the fish, else it will get into a hole or crevice and either hang on until you pull for a break or cut the line on the sharp rock.

Tie a blood-loop about 18 in (45·7 cm) above the end of the line. This takes a snood about a foot long, made of the same line as the reel line, and with a strong size 1–1/0 eyed hook. Yorkshire Stronghold hooks have proved excellent, as have several long-shanked strong trout lure hooks with forged bends.

To the very end of the line now tie either a small split ring or plain brass ring, or form a small loop. This takes a length of about 4 lb (1·8 kg) nylon, to which is tied the weight, consisting of any object that weighs between 1–2 oz (28·3–56·6 g), such as old bolts and nuts or strips of lead or whatever. The length of the weak link to the weight should be about 3 ft (91 cm).

Examine the water below. If it has areas flecked with foam, where great rocks and caverns and cracks are revealed as each rise falls away, lob the tackle to the edge of the foam. Immediately the weight touches bottom, stop the reel, keep the line just taut without moving the weight if possible, and hold the line in front of the reel. If the ballans are around and feeding, a bite will usually come within a minute or so: a sharp pluck or two, then a strong pull. Strike and begin lifting the fish simultaneously in one smooth movement.

The first dive of a ballan wrasse of 3 lb (1·3 kg) or so will astound newcomers to the sport: the fact that the fish are hooked right at their own front doors, as it were, makes it easier for them to get 'home', of course; but even so, it is a fact that such a calibre of fish can easily break 10 lb (4·5 kg) test line with the shock. Some fish, like some pollack, will give up after that first dive, but others will fight on, diving several times. Bringing a big ballan to net in the surges of Atlantic water that can rise and fall 10 ft (3 m) on fair days it quite an art. The net and the fish have to rise and fall at the same time, and this takes some tricky arranging.

If you do hook one of the really big old fish there is no way, even with 15 lb (6·8 kg) line, that the first dive will be severely curtailed. Line must be given, grudgingly, but if the fish is determined to get deep into the kelp and rocks it is better to risk it becoming inextricable or wearing through or cutting the line on rock than to break off in mid-dive. There is a small chance that the fish may be fooled into leaving its holt by slackening off tension for a few minutes.

The weight will often be lost – one every two casts is average – and it is an unfortunate fact, too, that a fair number of hooks are also sacrificed by wrasse hunters: the hook is bound to snag as often as the weight. However, the fact is that the bigger wrasse invariably seem to be winkled from deep fissures running way back into the rock, or kelp-draped caverns that have been gouged out of the lower ledges by the gnawing waves.

Some anglers delight in making big bags of wrasse and eschew the light tackle to do so. The bass rod is used and the line increased to 15–18 lb (6·8–8·1 kg), the fish being skilfully lifted on to the fishing platform instead of being netted. The weak link to the weight is retained. And even with these strong lines the bigger specimens can actually impose such an impact strain on the line on a dive that breakages occur fairly often!

When a wrasse is landed it is a good idea to have a damp towel available in which to hold the fish cradled under and along one's arm while the hook is removed with pliers or forceps: wrasse have exceptionally tough mouths and are slippery customers as well. When putting them back try to drop them head-first, and do it when a swell comes up the rock, to minimise the drop of the fish. If the fish is just thrown back from a height and hits the water with its flank, the impact can daze it sufficiently for it to be incapable of diving, the result being a battering against the rocks. Some fish may drift on the surface for several minutes before suddenly recovering and swimming down.

The float-paternoster method is basically the same hook and weight set-up, with the addition of a sliding 'float' above the ring or loop connecting main line with weak link. In fact, the thing that keeps the tackle upright in the water and to an extent allows it to drift around, the weight bumping against the rock, is a lump of cork, a proper cork stopper from a big wide-topped jar, or a piece of white expanded polystyrene.

A ballan wrasse has lots of fin area to help it force the issue in a rough-and-tumble battle.

Cliff climbing is an essential part of ballan wrasse fishing as the best places are usually remote and inaccessible. Here a group are descending Clogher Head in Ireland's Dingle Peninsula.

Ballan wrasse come in a wide variety of colour combinations and markings, and all these specimens were taken at the same place. The author shows a dark green specimen before returning it alive; there is a fish with a dark back and reddish mottled flanks; a 'patchwork' fish of chestnut and dull orange . . . and a varied trio.

To stop the sliding 'float' running down on to the hook snood some form of stop must be used if a loop and not a ring connects main line and weak link. A swan shot or a bead will do. A swivel would do the job, too, but is more expensive to lose.

The cork or polystyrene must just support the weight used, and polystyrene about 2 in (5 cm) square is about right. A number 8 swivel may be attached to the float by lashing with nylon, cord or wire; or by softening the wire of eyed or ringed hooks (sizes 1/0–2/0 are recommended) and then pushing the barbed end into the cork or plastic foam. The swivel can be fitted into the opened eye or ring, after which it is closed again with pliers.

The usual stop on the line is made and the tackle does to an extent help to avoid snagging, since the weight is supported and has less tendency to drop down into cracks in the rock. It also can be allowed to drift around with currents or wind action. Strike when the float goes under.

Finally, it really is amazing where big wrasse will make their homes. The author has several times in Ireland winkled them from cracks in rocky ledges several yards back from the seaward edge of the ledge on which he stood and only 18 in (45·7 cm) wide at the top! The paternoster was lowered carefully down the crack until it touched bottom, the water depth apparently being about 15 ft (4·5 m), and almost immediately the rod thumped down and some exciting battles ensued; it is peculiar playing a strong fish down a crack – a bit like fishing in a street drain! There are obviously wide caves at the bottoms of such cracks.

Of course, the fish has to be lifted up the crack unless it can be guided along to the seaward opening.

# 14

# Black bream
# and red bream

Black bream.

Round about late April – the exact time of year depending on the warmth, or coolness of the water – vast shoals of black bream turn up in the eastern part of the English Channel. They spawn between mid-May and July, mostly on the rough ground interspersed with sandy patches known as the Kingmere Reef off Littlehampton.

In fact, this little harbour on the estuary of the River Arun is the mecca of black bream angling and many anglers, both regular sea anglers and coarse fishermen filling in the gap due to their close season, converge there between May and mid-June.

Black bream obviously winter in deep water, though it is also believed that some fish migrate to the Channel from the Mediterranean. Having turned up in spring off the Sussex coast, the fish later spread out, and by June can be caught just south of the Thames estuary and along the coasts of Hampshire, Dorset, the West Country and Wales, but very rarely in the North Sea. However, Sussex is by far the best fishery. Black bream occur only occasionally in Ireland.

Typical of the sea breams, the black bream has a small mouth, small teeth and deep body with plenty of fin area. The spined dorsal fin is beautifully constructed and can be retracted into a channel along the fish's back, to reduce drag and increase swimming speed. It fights extremely hard and since it averages about $1\frac{1}{2}$ lb (600 g) and is caught to 4 lb (1·8 kg) or so most seasons, it is an ideal light tackle species.

A good 95 per cent of black bream fishing is done from boats since it occurs 1–6 miles offshore as a rule. However, some are taken from the shore, especially in the Selsey area of Sussex and Devon and Cornwall, and occasional specimens turn up from South Coast piers. Shore captures are usually made in late summer, even in autumn in the West Country. The bass casting rod, 10 lb (4·5 kg) line and a single-hook nylon paternoster is right for shore bream.

Black bream, as one might expect, are not black! They are usually a steely blue on the back, shading to purple, with flanks of silvery grey or pink-hued with streaks of metallic gold-brown below the lateral line.

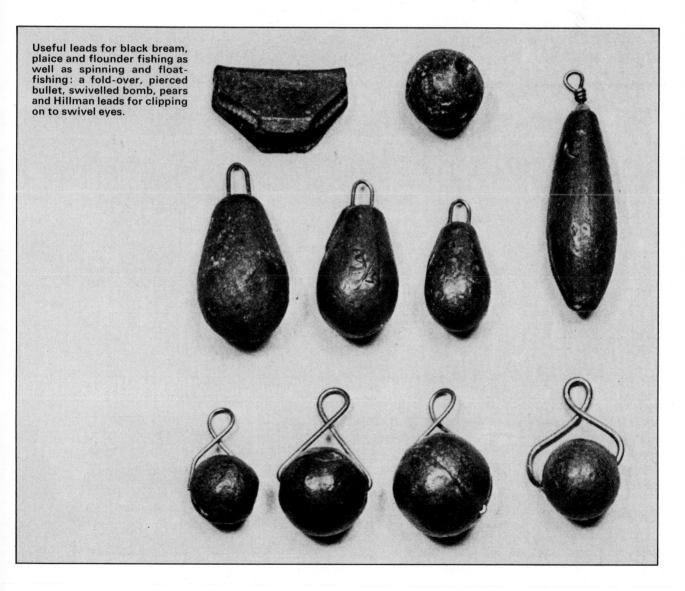

**Useful leads for black bream, plaice and flounder fishing as well as spinning and float-fishing: a fold-over, pierced bullet, swivelled bomb, pears and Hillman leads for clipping on to swivel eyes.**

# Black bream and red bream

**Black bream are caught from the shore in summer and early autumn. This is a Selsey (Sussex) specimen caught by John Cooper.**

The red bream's big eye marks it as a fish of deep water, where light gathering qualities in the eye are of great importance.

Some have vertical bars of dark grey or blue, and mostly these turn out to be the cock fish.

They are active feeders and are found in shallow water – most good Sussex fishing takes place in 4–6 fathoms (9·1–10·0 m) over chalk rubble inshore or over the reef farther out. The tackle for shallow water bream can vary, depending on preference, but line of 3–5 lb (1·3–2·6 kg) is always adequate and fishes nicely with leads varying in weight from about 1–2½ oz (28–71 g). The rod can be a crank-handled baitcaster of 6–7½ ft (1·8–2·1 m) and of the type designed for very light weights, or the trout spinning rod or the double-handed spinning rod, although the latter overguns bream of average size.

The reel for the baitcaster is obviously the small multiplier; the same can be used on the spinning rods, although the centrepin reel will provide better sport and more direct contact with tackle and fish. Some anglers use fixed-spool reels for black bream when fishing from a boat, but since no casting is done the reel has tackle control disadvantages due to its construction.

There are two basic black bream techniques: a paternoster let down and fished sink and draw for 100 yd (91·4 m) or so downtide of the anchored boat and, for the slack water period (when the fish go off the feed and require a moving bait to attract them) float tackle is used.

First the paternoster. The author's type is of variable setting and has proved very successful, as well as tangle-free. First push up the line a ¼ in (5 mm) length of nylon tube – ballpoint pen ink-tube is all right – then a number 10 swivel, followed by another piece of tube. A tiny piece of matchstick is pushed from the sides opposite the link swivel into the bits of tube, thus jamming them in position on the line with the swivel between. The lead goes on a number 8–10 link-swivel on the end of the reel line and the hook trace to the free eye of the swivel that is between the jammed tubes.

The usual distance to set the swivel from the lead is about 6 ft (1·8 m), but if this does not catch fish well, it may be reduced to a yard (1 m) or raised to 10 ft (3 m). The hook trace, of the same nylon as the reel line, is never less than 6 ft (1·8 m) and often as long as 15 ft (4·5 m). This will be wafted enticingly in the tide, lifting and falling as the angler fishes the bait down the tidal stream.

Premium positions in the boat are at the stern, but the other anglers will still catch fish, and there should be a change-over of positions every two hours to give everybody aboard a fair turn. The bait – on a sharp number 1–2 hook – can be lugworm, or slim strips of squid, cuttlefish or fresh mackerel. A workable size is ⅜ in (1 cm) wide by 4 in (10 cm) long and the hook should be nicked through once very close to one end. That way the bait flutters attractively in the water but has no tendency to spin and cause line kinks.

The gear is dropped overboard and once the lead taps bottom, it is lifted about a yard and line spilled off the reel as it drops down again. After a few seconds

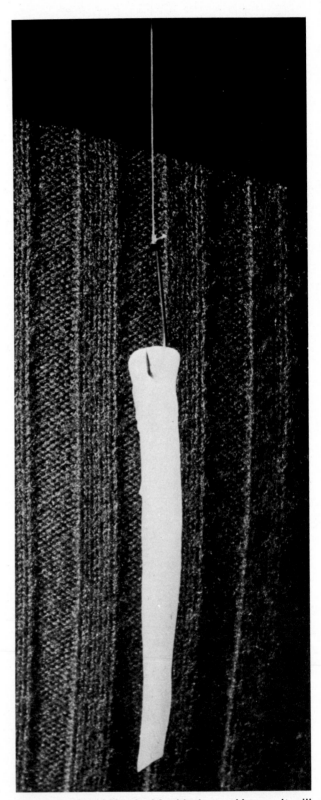

Slim strip of squid hooked for black or red bream. It will also catch plaice when moved along the seabed.

repeat the lift and drop, but never lift too high and never spill more than a yard or so of line, else the tide will billow the line downtide and lift the lead, the whole gear becoming deadened, and bites cannot be felt.

Done properly, the technique results in the bait fluttering up and down and dropping downtide from the boat, covering plenty of ground and behaving in a manner very attractive to black bream. It is essential to be able to feel the lead tap bottom occasionally. Then, even 100 yd (91·4 m) back of the boat the bites will be distinguishable.

Bites usually take the form of a light pluck or two followed by a sensation of the tip becoming heavy. Never strike a black bream bite in the accepted sense of the word. You must do the same as suggested for pollack: lift the rod and take a turn or two on the reel; the fish seems to make a firm grab, feel the hook go home and turn to dive. Just hold firmly and the hook will penetrate.

The fish will dive, pull, make runs of up to 20 yd (18·2 m) if it weighs 3 lb (1·3 kg) or so and is hooked well back of the boat with a good tide running, and even when it has been pumped and battled to the boat it will still have the energy to scuttle deep in a wavering motion that never fails to impress. Holding bream too hard will result in line (trace) breakages; they really can pull and impose sudden shocks on the gear with end-swapping direction changes.

Good boatmen will have a bucket of squid, cuttle or mackerel with them and chop it up into small pieces to feed over the side. This stream of groundbait will keep a shoal feeding behind the boat or make it feed more readily if things are slow. When the tide is running hard, however, the bait is washed away too fast to do any good for the boat, but it might help another boat anchored 200 yd (182·8 m) downtide!

A big net, not too deep, and bag-shaped rather than deep and pointed, is best for bream, and the mesh need be no more than ½ in (2·25 cm). The fish should be netted from the stern of the boat and the angler must back up the boat to get the fish on his long trace in reach. The best of the Littlehampton skippers like each angler to retain only six fish to take home and put the rest back – a very sensible conservation measure because the fish have been reduced drastically in recent years, and there have been disgusting scenes with unwanted dead fish drifting in scores down the Arun estuary from the charter-boat moorings.

The bream usually stop feeding properly at slack water and it is then that the odd fish can be lured into taking by using float tackle. The ideal rod for this is the Avon rod used for the mullet: in fact, the sliding float set-up for mullet in deep water adequately serves for bream.

Try to get the bait to swim about 4 ft (1·2 m) above the seabed and use any wind or slight tidal flow to get the float away from the boat.

Bites are signalled by a couple of preliminary bobs, then the float dives sharply; some fish will take it under without any preliminaries.

Bonus fish when black bream fishing include garfish and mackerel, of which more later, whereas pouting and lesser-spotted dogfish are regarded to be a nuisance.

Red bream are similar in general outline to black bream. They are a beautiful red or orange hue, dark on the back, shading to a silvery pink belly. Like the black bream, the red bream is a great fighter, but the bigger fish are found in much deeper rocky water offshore, or around wrecks, which means heavier tackle is usually necessary.

Red bream are far more widely distributed than black bream, inhabiting the western end of the English Channel, the neighbouring Atlantic and the south, south-west and western coasts of Ireland. Only rocky, reefy areas or wrecks on sand or mud are home to adult red bream, although little fish of under 8 oz (226·7 g), called chad, are taken from shallow water – under 20 ft (6 m). The worthwhile specimens of 2–5 lb (900 g–2·6 kg) usually come from depths of at least 15–20 fathoms, which is 90–120 ft (27·4–36·4 m) and although the species has been caught to nearly 10 lb (4·5 kg) in the western Channel, these larger-than-average bream nearly all come from more than 200 ft (60·96 m).

However, red bream can fight all the way to the boat because they suffer little from the decrease in pressure. This makes up for the slightly heavier tackle needed in deep water.

The baitcaster or the double-handed spinning rod will do fine, with 250 yd (228·5 m) of about 8 lb (3·6 kg) test line on the small multiplier or centrepin reel. A blood-loop is tied in the line about a yard (1 m) from the end, to which is attached a snood of the same nylon about a foot (30·4 cm) long ending in a 1/0 or 2/0 hook. A lead of 3 oz (85 g) will take the tackle down to the depths quickly enough, most times.

Deep water red bream fishing is rarely made a deliberate session, for the expense involved in getting out to distant wrecks and reefs has to be borne in mind. Therefore breaming is usually indulged in for perhaps an hour during slack water and when the big fish-baits meant for conger, ling and so on are being torn off in minutes by hordes of red bream.

Baits of lug or king ragworm, small sand-eels, slivers of mackerel, squid or cuttlefish are all acceptable and the strip baits may be larger than that used for black bream – say about ¾ in (2 cm) wide and 5 in (13 cm) long.

A system that works well is to let down the tackle until it taps bottom, leave it there a second or two, then lift the rod tip slowly, and reel in a yard or so of line, also slowly. Often a fish will attack with sharp jerks. Reel in, and at the same time lift the rod tip back quickly, for a red bream is adept in ejecting the bait or stripping it from the hook without getting 'spiked'. If the lift brings no response, drop the bait and lead down again and repeat the exercise.

The red bream fights in a way that is very similar to the black, but it tends to lift in the water more than the black, often giving the angler the feeling that the fish has broken the line or shed the hook. When this slack line is followed by a shuddering power-dive the impact on the rod and line is very considerable and it pays to have the clutch set very finely on the multiplier.

Like the black bream, the red has a spiny dorsal fin and should be handled with care, the damp towel coming in useful again. Red bream are good to eat but, once more, conservation should be borne in mind: six fish per angler should be plenty to take home. Red bream appear to be capable of regaining great depths, from which they are often brought, after being put back in the water, though some drift away on the surface out of sight of the boat, so some perhaps do expire.

The season for red bream usually lasts from mid-June to mid-October.

In the West Country, where most of the good catches of red bream are made, black bream are often caught in great depths of water on the offshore wrecks, alongside the red bream. The fish are no bigger than those taken in the Sussex shallows earlier in the summer, and are probably fish that have moved away from Sussex having spawned.

In the deeps the same tackle as for red bream is justified, of course, with the resulting loss of the fish's full fighting potential. The author would never deliberately fish for black bream in the deeps since, if the fish cannot be caught on the ultra-light gear mentioned, then it really isn't worth fishing for at all. As an aside, the black bream just appears to have the edge, so far as fight is concerned, over the red, comparing both fish on the same gear from the deeps.

In the Sussex shallows the black bream is one of the top-rated fighters; but if the red bream could be caught in the same area and on the same tackle, maybe . . .

**The black bream is not black, of course, but steely blue, silver and white. This fish is a female.**

In places black bream may be caught from the shore. Plump specimens like this Channel Islands fish provide superb sport on light tackle.

# 15
# Mackerel and garfish

Alive, the mackerel is one of the prettiest fish in British saltwater, with its iridescent pearly sheen and shades of green-blue-red and mauve, crossed by black bars and scribbles.

Very few anglers appreciate how well both these species can fight on light tackle because very few anglers bother to seek them with light tackle, only regarding them, mackerel especially, as baits for bigger fish.

Certainly they reach no great size in British and neighbouring waters: mackerel rarely exceed 2 lb (900 g) and garfish rarely 1½ lb (600 g), although mackerel over 5 lb (2·6 kg) and garfish to nearly 3 lb (1·3 kg) have been recorded.

The season for these two species, which may fairly be dealt with together (since fishing for one will as likely as not yield some of the other, and are widely distributed round most of the coastline of Britain and Ireland) lasts from late May to late September in general.

Both may be taken from the shore, especially from any projections giving access to deep water, such as piers, harbour arms, breakwaters and rocky promontories, during late June to early autumn, and in boats offshore about a month earlier; in some circumstances, there are 'jumbo' mackerel runs deep down, in the autumn months.

From late June until mid-September, when the weather has been settled and calm and warm for a week or more, mackerel and garfish shoals move inshore, often right on to the beaches, herding small fry. At such times the newspapers report fish leaping on to dry land and holidaymakers harvesting mackerel with buckets.

At such times the trout spinning rod, fixed-spool reel and 3–4 lb (1·3–1·8 kg) line with a slim, heavyweight wobbling silver spoon, such as a Condor, Toby, Koster, Krill and similar designs, will prove a killer. Cast to the edge of the milling shoal and recover quickly. No trace is necessary: tie the line to the nose swivel of the lure; the Condor needs split-ring and swivel to be attached since this lure is sold without.

Keep testing the knot on the swivel since constant casting of these heavyweight lures of around ¾ oz (21 g) can weaken such delicate lines; in fact, if constant long casts of 40 yd (36·5 m) are necessary to reach the shoals, tie on a leader of 6–7 lb test (2·7–3·1 kg) monofil to absorb casting shocks and help hauling fish ashore. It should be long enough to take three to four turns round the reel with the bait hanging about 2 ft (60 cm) below the rod tip.

From piers, similar projections or an anchored boat, especially a dinghy in calm inshore water, there is great sport with both mackerel and garfish with either the trout spinning outfit or, better still, the Avon rod, centrepin or fixed-spool reel and 3 lb (1·3 kg) line. A sliding float similar to that used for mullet and which will support either 1, 2 or 3 swanshot will usually be found about right. The hook, a fine-wire eyed number 1, is baited with a thin sliver of mackerel or herring, cut across the flank, or squid, cuttlefish or tiny sand-eels.

Blind-fishing where mackerel are supposed to be is all right, but the sport is best when the conditions are fairly calm and the fish are seen boiling on the surface. Garfish often leap clear of the water as they chase fry and they also do this when they play around flotsam in the water – such as a plank, raft of weed or an old container. From a boat the delicate tackle justifies the use of a landing net; trout size is sufficient, or roach size, if coarse fishing is also done! From piers etc use the dropnet.

The bait is nicked through one end and then the float is allowed to drift away with the tide or wind. Starting depth can be about 4 ft (1·2 m) if the fish are seen on the surface, but if no bites are forthcoming increase the depth by a yard (91 cm) at a time until fish are found, or the boat is moved to a new location, or you change position on the pier.

It pays to reel the bait back quite slowly, when a fish will often grab it.

Although mackerel pull hard and swim fast, they lack any 'plan of campaign' and instead of long runs, simply indulge in their characteristic jagging fight, driving down and dashing round in circles. However, on the light tackle this can be good fun. Garfish, on the other hand, are spectacular fighters, and are often more out of the water than in it, greyhounding across the surface and tail-walking just as their bigger brethren, the big game billfishes do. A fair number of garfish will come unhooked due to the difficulty of finding a hook-hold in the hard bill.

In the autumn, when the whiting are moving inshore, very big mackerel, called 'jumbos' by anglers, swim among them, both species obviously feeding on the migrating shoals of small fish of that season's breeding. Quite often the first indication of these big mackerel – running 2 lb or more, maybe up to nearly 4 lb (900 g–1·8 kg) – is when one is taken on lugworm or herring strip being fished for the whiting, just off the bottom. For a real slogging battle, the trout-spinning rod is brought into use and employed with 3–5 lb (1·3–2·6 kg) line and a single hook on a yard (1 m) trace fished about 2 ft (60 cm) above the minimum size of lead that will take the gear down and keep contact with the seabed. Often an ounce (28 g) will do; sometimes 2 oz (56·6 g) is necessary. In strong tides fishing this way will not be possible for very long, only near the slack periods.

Strangely, these 'jumbo' mackerel will often prefer lugworm to fish strip, even though their very presence is to feed on small fish.

Finally, when the sea is calm and the whitebait are showering from the water as the mackerel and/or garfish attack, as occurs on many a summer dawn or evening period, the fly rod used with a sinking line, from shore or small boat, can produce wonderful fishing, the garfish being especially acrobatic on this gear. The 'fly' need be nothing more elaborate than a reservoir trout-fisher's White Lure on a number 6 long-shank hook or on a tandem system, both hooks facing down. The easy way to make such a fly is to wrap the shank of the hook with broad silver tinsel – or thread on a suitable length of Mylar silver tube,

tied back and front for security – and add a wing of white goat hair or deer tail hair.

Garfish seldom grow longer than 3 ft (91 cm) and are very slim, but the author once thought he had the 'mother and father' of them all when fly fishing for bonefish on the flats off North Andros, Bahamas. The bonefish fly was taken with a great pull and a vast 'garfish', apparently 4 ft (1·2 m) long leapt high out of the water, went back in and proceeded to scream away with line, leaping every 2 yd (2 m) or so. In fact, the fish turned out to be a houndfish, or that's what it apparently was. It's a billed species very similar to the gar, except that it grows to about 8 lb (3·6 kg).

It's a pity garfish and the common mackerel do not grow to about 10 lb (4·5 kg). If they did they certainly wouldn't be considered only as baitfish, nor hauled up six at a time on feathers!

**Previous page:**
**The garfish is a mini-marlin and if it grew any bigger – even by a few pounds – it would rate one of the top three places in the United Kingdom sport-fishing honours.**

# 16

# Flounders and plaice

These two species of flatfish are widely distributed in the British Isles and if they are found in areas where the tidal conditions permit light tackle to be used, both can produce good fishing.

Both species are happiest over ground that consists of a mixture of sand, mud and fine gravel, but the flounder has a penchant for brackish water, especially in its youth, and spends a fair amount of time (up to palm-of-hand size) in pure freshwater. The plaice, however, likes the real salt, but also inshore and offshore grounds and banks where loose, coarse sand

harbours sand-eels; or grounds where low ridges of rock abutting sand provide rich feeding on small mussels; as well as sand that is the home of razorfish, lugworms, cockles, various other bivalves and the ledges of soft rock or peat that contain the boring piddocks.

Both flounders and plaice also have a yen towards moving baits, and for that reason many of the techniques used to catch them hinge on the fact that a visual attraction can lead to final engulfing of the baited hook.

**A flounder and a codling. Also some good flounder baits: the bivalve that is often washed ashore after gales and known to anglers as 'butterfish'.**

Flounders and plaice

Believe it or not, this is a flounder, not a plaice. It was taken from a Kent beach on razorfish and weighed about 4½ lb (2 kg). On a baitcaster from a boat such a fish would be a real handful!

Many areas that were once great plaice grounds, where good bags could be caught from the shore, now no longer exist. Trawlers and trammel nets have not only ravaged the stocks, but have used chains and heavy weights on the trawls to tear up the very grounds that harboured the fish: mussel-beds, cockle-beds etc.

Even the so-called protected areas – which include the nurseries of valuable food fish – have been plundered, perhaps because the British Government's fishery protection organisation has proved to be less than adequate.

Two examples come to mind. Foreign and British trawlers have for years plundered the Skerries bank off Dartmouth in Devon, an area where trawling is

**Trawling and trammel netting have ruined many places where good bags of plaice could be caught. But there are times and places . . . and this angler knew where to go and when, and reaped his reward. Such bags are rare from the shore today.**

expressly forbidden, yet the boats get away with it repeatedly in broad daylight! Thus for years has Britain been seen as the lion with no teeth. The Common Market agreement has without doubt signed the death warrant of many flatfish-producing grounds. Another example, of which there is ample knowledge, is the Rye Bay area of Sussex where the greedy trawlers from Hastings were not content to have a decent yearly return but felt obliged to get 'the lot' before visiting trawlers got it. The result was annihilation of the mussel-beds which attracted the plaice in the first instance: trammel nets were set and trawlers went up and down between them, dragging tons of ironmongery that broke up the mussel-beds, tore up the sand and stones, and sent the plaice into the waiting nets.

But the plaice have never re-colonised the area. All this, and more, has gone on under the eyes of the local fisheries inspectors. Almost every tide, Hastings trawlers make that last sweep and end up landing tons of undersized fish which are left to rot on the beach in full view of anybody who cares to look! Just over the back of the beach trippers can buy plaice, dabs and other illegally landed *undersize* fish from men who can sell them at bargain prices. Even photographic evidence and dates and times published of the offences have failed to get any reaction from the authorities.

So what follows concerning plaice and flounder fishing in a sporting manner is advice on the fishing as it has been, still is in a few places, and could be were it not for government complacency.

First, the plaice. It's a well-known food-fish and a favourite in the fish-and-chip shops. In actual fact its popularity with the public stems from a mixture of good public relations in the fish trade and ignorance of other good and more tasty flatfish. Widely distributed, as has been said, the plaice is a sucker for sandbanks and sandy ground among rock round most of Britain and Ireland.

Any disturbance of the sand makes it curious and it will move to investigate. So, anglers have devised methods of disturbing the seabed to get the fish's interest, and these include drifting with special rigs from boats, and moving baits by reel and rod action from the few shore places that have not been ruined by commercial fishing.

From the shore, depending on the depth, strength of tidal current etc, be it from pier, rocky promontory, shingle or sand beach, the bass surfcasting rod, or the double-handed spinning rod may be used, with 2–3 oz (56·6–85 g) lead (or lighter) and 6–10 lb (2·7–4·5 kg) line. A trace of 4 ft (1·2 m) minimum is best, ending in a number 2–1/0 hook baited with the bait that locally does best: this can be lugworm, razorfish, mussel, soft or peeler crab sections, cockles, butterfish (shellfish), ragworms of big and small varieties, piddocks, or sand-eels, to name some.

The lead, fixed via a small link-swivel running on the reel line, is augmented by a barrel or spiral lead of about 1 oz (28·3 g) set about a foot (30 cm) ahead of the hook, or with a small fluttering bar-spoon, set at the same distance from the hook, give or take an inch or so. Many books advise a big spoon, 2½–3½ in (65–90 mm) long, but a spoon 1–2 in (25–50 mm) will do just as well. Its job is to create flash and sand/mud disturbance, and the smaller spoon helps casting to greater range when necessary.

Having cast the tackle to the required area, the lead is allowed to touch bottom, when a few turns are made on the reel, at the same time swinging the rod smoothly away from the sea and low – almost parallel with the beach. A pause of a few seconds is made, followed by another few turns on the reel and a sweep of the rod. The take, when it comes, occurs most commonly as the reel begins to move the tackle along the seabed after a pause. A plaice really wallops a bait fished in this way and fish of 2 lb (900 g) or so can really put a bend in the rod, fluttering and pulling with a surprising strength. Even the bass rod can take a thumping from a good plaice, 3 lb (1·3 kg) or so.

In some areas the only plaice left by the inshore trawlers are those that inhabit narrow drifts of sand between rocky ledges and outcrops, and in such places the only method for the angler is to note the positions of the sandy patches and channels at low water, then cast accurately the lightest running paternoster – made up as for bass but even lighter in test. Such places often produce best results during evening flood tides, the chance being at peak following a moderate onshore wind.

There are still a few places, notably in Ireland and western Scotland, where shallow bays still host good stocks of plaice that the commercial fishermen have not found. If rocks or a pier give way to reasonably deep water – 6 ft (1·8 m) or so – float-fishing in a way that permits use of the Avon rod, 4–5 lb (1·8–2·6 kg) line and a light barrel lead just dragging the bait over the bottom can be very killing.

Basically the same methods work for flounders from the shore, except that they are much more plentiful than plaice and found in quiet creeks, estuaries, and harbours, the species being happy over mud or sand, even fine gravel.

Of course, both species are taken on normal heavy casting tackle from open beaches, specially after gales when razorfish and other shellfish and worms are being washed up by the waves. But as a pure sport-fishing exercise, there is little in it. The bait or baits are simply legered and bites awaited, as in cod fishing.

The very best plaice and flounder fishing is from boats, especially in the case of plaice on offshore banks (often not much more than two miles out, perhaps) where the depth is only 3–5 fathoms (5·4–9·1 m). For flounders the same areas can be fished, though estuaries and creeks are usually more accessible, and, maybe, more rewarding.

The boat is drifted over the ground, the baits being dragged behind, with either spoons, barrel or spiral leads, a few coloured plastic beads stopped from running right on to the hook eye by a swan shot, or a metal button threaded on the trace and stopped in the same way – all 6 in–1 ft (15·5–30·4 cm) from the hook.

For plaice the baitcaster and small multiplier is a good choice, although the longer spinning rod is also suitable. In shallow, calm estuarine water, the trout spinning rod and 3–4 lb (1·3–1·8 kg) line on centrepin or fixed-spool reel will let even 1 lb (400 g) flounders give a reasonable account of themselves and allow bigger fish to put up real battles.

Both plaice and flounders can dive in a most spectacular manner when suitably light tackle is used and a landing net is necessary to avoid losses by last minute struggles.

Plaice will accept avidly a strip of squid dragged behind a fluttering spoon or other sand-stirrer, whereas flounders rarely do. It really pays when seeking both these flatfish to make enquiries in the area to be fished in order to establish the best local bait. Both fish have localised tastes and plaice in one area may be on lugworm, while in others it will only accept razor-fish or mussel. Flounders, likewise, may be locally fond of rag or lug, usually the former, but more likely take razorfish, cockles, butterfish or pieces of peeler crab, among others.

Some anglers have pointed out the importance of ensuring that the baited hook trailing behind a flasher spoon, barrel lead or other form of attractor, does not spin, but the author has had perfectly good results without fitting any swivels at all between the back of the hookless bar-spoon and the bait. Each angler must rig his tackle in a way that suits him and gives him confidence, however, and if you think swivels will help, use them. A good light hookless bar-spoon for bait fishing is made by Mepps; another good one for the job is the Normark Vibro – an oldie with a good reputation.

Naturally, when boat fishing there is no need to drift all the time. The boat may be anchored and casts made over the ground with spoon, lead or beads attractor and bait, or with float tackle run down the tide. The boat may be moved if nothing happens within about an hour.

Plaice are usually in poor condition in April and May when they return to inshore waters after spawning offshore, but they soon put on weight and by the early summer have become fat. The migration for spawning usually runs from around January to March, inshore fishing not usually being very rewarding at that time.

Flounders also migrate offshore to spawn, usually from late February to May, but through most of the summer and up to January are catchable well up estuaries, in creeks or in the sea proper. A favourite sport in parts of Wales and in many parts of the south coast of England from East Anglia to Devon, is fishing tidal creeks and rivers with freshwater tackle, legering as if for chub or roach, the lead being an Arlesey bomb of maybe ½–1½ oz (14–42 g) stopped about 18 in (45·7 cm) from a size 6–8 freshwater hook.

The bait is usually small ragworms, red or white, lugworm or (in areas of brackish or nearly fresh water) garden lobworms or red worms from a farmer's manure heap.

The rod is placed in a rest or rests, just as in freshwater legering, and bites signalled by the pulls on the rod tip, striking being timed to coincide with a long pull on the tip that holds it round.

On the conventional boat and beachcasting tackle used by most sea anglers, both plaice and flounders are of little account, sportwise. But by treating them almost as freshwater fish, and dropping down the tackle to that level, they compare very favourably with such freshwater species as tench, perch, carp and fast-water roach, size for size.

And few anglers denigrate them.

**In addition to spinners, spoons and leads ahead of the baited hook for flounders and plaice, coloured beads also prove very successful. The bait should be moved along the seabed with such a rig.**

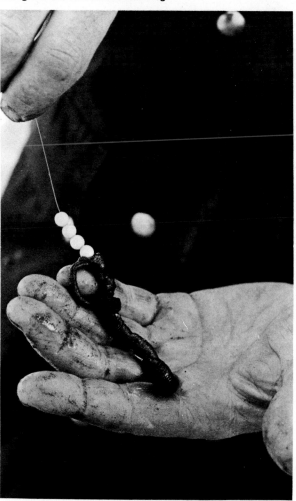

# 17
# Twaite shad and allis shad

A nice allis shad taken float-fishing with herring strip in the estuary of the Ouse at Newhaven, Sussex. The other fish are horse mackerel, also called scad. Shads are declining in numbers due to pollution and obstructions in many rivers which prevent access to the fish – which is illegal, anyway.

These two herring-like fish are taken from time to time in the sea, particularly in the English Channel, the Bristol Channel and the south and south-west of Ireland. It is when the fish run into certain rivers in May and June to spawn, however, that most captures are made.

The allis shad is the larger of the two, and the twaite shad is immediately distinguishable by six or seven dark spots in a line running from behind the upper rear edge of the gill covers.

Shads are very active fish on the hook, leaping clear of the water and capable of sustained speedy bursts.

The allis swims farther upstream in rivers to spawn than does the twaite, but both may be taken on trout spinning outfits and small bar-spoons fished fast, especially where the fish congregate at weirs. The Rivers Wye and Severn offer good shad fishing of this type; in Ireland the Munster Blackwater, Suir, Barrow and Slaney have runs.

In saltwater, most shads are taken by anglers using light float tackle for mullet, school bass etc. The mullet float technique works well and on the hook, a size 6, should be a slim strip of fresh mackerel, herring or squid, although the shads will accept bunches of red ragworms, a live prawn, several bunters or sea slaters, which are woodlouse-like creatures that live in cracks in wooden piles, jetties or concrete structures.

There is little angling interest in the shads, probably because they are not so plentiful as they were even 50 years ago, which marine biologists blame on various barriers placed across rivers which prevents access to the fish for reproduction.

Although the allis is said to reach 8 lb (3·6 kg) few over 2½ lb (1·1 kg) have been recorded; the twaite rarely reaches 2 lb (900 g) but is far more common.

Parts of the Kent, Sussex and Hampshire shoreline can produce reasonable shad fishing, Deal, Newhaven and the Solent area being especially reliable, the Kent and Sussex ports fishing from the pier and harbour arms respectively.

The float should be set at about half the total water depth – usually about 10–12 ft (3–3·6 m) – and the bait allowed to drift on the tide, being checked every few yards so that it rises and falls attractively.

Since the fish do not reach a great size line of 3 lb (1·3 kg) test will be adequate, but unless there are reports of shad captures, in good numbers, along the coast (as opposed to the much more reliable spinning for them in the rivers) there is little hope of contacting fish by fishing at random. Late June to early September are the best months to fish shad in the sea.

# 18

# The International Game Fish Association and British Anglers

The IGFA is allegedly an international organisation which sets out to encourage light tackle fishing and lists authenticated captures of what the association considers to be 'game' fish. Unfortunately, IGFA, based in Florida, appears not to want to accept on its list many of the fish found in British and north-west European waters.

Only seven of the 50-odd species on the IGFA list are found in British waters, of which sharks (blue, porbeagle, mako and thresher) form four and another, the bluefin tuna, is considered so rare as not to be worth the expense of hunting any more. The others are cod and pollack, except that there is some more confusion about the last-named species.

As already mentioned in these pages, the Americans call coalfish pollock and don't have our true pollack over there. But IGFA, in its truly strange fashion, agrees to accept from Britain entries of either pollack or coalfish in its pollock category. Two species entered as one!

At the same time IGFA has turned down the idea, put up by the British Conger Club, that conger should be included on the list. Why? Probably because those sun-bronzed wealthy game fishermen don't relish a big, slimy eel sullying the list, but the reason given was that conger is not widely distributed. Well, Britain's sea is not exactly bursting with tarpon, striped and channel bass, swordfish, wahoo, marlin, bluefish and bonefish, is it?

Over the past few years a new organisation, The British Light Tackle Club, has made an effort to get more British species on IGFA's list, so far without much success. The BLTC is affiliated to IGFA but at the time of writing is setting up its own list of British light tackle records.

IGFA was responsible for setting up line classes and prescribing certain lengths and designs of rods, reels, lines and hook arrangements as acceptable in the sporting capture of game fish of the oceans. As such, it has done a very good job, to the extent that even in the United Kingdom and its environs, it is possible to buy off-the-peg rods that are built to IGFA specifications, opening up world records to those who may catch a big fish on such a rod.

In spite of the fact that IGFA has inspired great deeds of light tackle skill, which to many is much better than the sort of thick-eared angling mentality one finds too often in Britain, there are obvious loopholes that make a mockery of IGFA's *raison d'être*. Some of the alleged light tackle captures are obviously impossible if something a bit odd is not done: like chasing a fish with the boat to drive it into shallow water where it can be vanquished without being able to sound; dropping a bait into the mouth of a fish that has been chummed to within a yard or so of the boat, then gaffing it immediately the hook is pulled home without ever bending a rod in battle. . . . Long traces can be grabbed very quickly when necessary.

At present, then, the IGFA and its list of so-called game fish is a sore point in this country. It is quite obvious that a number of British and European species should be included if the set-up is to meet the description 'international'. For example: bass, grey mullets, smooth-hounds, tope and conger.

In spite of the problems, Britain does hold a number of IGFA world records, including porbeagle shark, cod and 'pollock' (actually pollack).

The best solution appears to be for the British Light Tackle Club to prosper, but that organisation has found it difficult to put itself in a strong position, partly due to poor public relations, partly to lack of interest in the promotion of sporting angling principles by many anglers.

Until there is better news of the sport-fishing scene in Britain, it is necessary for individual anglers to fly the flag, to think and talk about the new enjoyment of catching a few fish rather than boast of having caught 'a ton of fish' in a day, or having won a car for catching a 2 lb (900 g) school bass!

Fishing for the love of the sport rather than for personal gain, either in cash realised from the sale of fish or prizes won, has got to be the way to a better outlook on saltwater angling in Britain.

# Fishing to International Game Fish Association rules

The 'angling rules', so called, of the IGFA cover some 19 points, but the basis of the system – as has already been illustrated in these pages – is one of light and balanced tackle used 'in accordance with sporting ethics and customs'.

Most of the rules apply to boat fishing tackle and methods in the line classes which run as follows: 6, 12, 20, 30, 50, 80, 130 lb (2·7, 5·4, 9·0, 13·6, 22·6, 36·2 and 58·9 kg). Lines must test, when wet, up to and including these weights. In addition to the records for these classes, the IGFA lists an all-tackle section for the heaviest fish of each listed species taken on any tackle class (only certain selected fish are eligible for IGFA world records).

When applying for a world line-class record, not only must the angler have been using tackle acceptable by IGFA but he must also have followed the procedure set by the organisation. For example, for 50 lb (22·6 kg) class and below, a 50 ft (15 m) sample of the actual line used, plus 2 ft (61 cm) of leader or trace must accompany the application. For classes above 50 lb, the 2 ft of trace must go in, but the length of line is increased to 80 ft (24 m) and if a double line was used (as in shark fishing, for example) the double line is included in the length.

It is interesting to note that if a fish is taken on two lines of different tests knotted or spliced together, the catch will be classified under the heavier of those two lines, samples of both having been submitted for testing.

The amount of double line and leader allowed is also controlled: on all weights up to and including 50 lb class 15 ft (4·5 m) of leader and 15 ft of double line may be used. For heavier tackle the double line must not exceed 30 ft (9 m), neither must the leader.

Rods must also measure up. The tip, measured from a point directly beneath the centre of the reel, must be a minimum of 50 in (127 cm) long. The butt, measured from the same place on the reel, must not be more than 27 in (68·5 cm) long. These figures do not apply to surfcasting rods 'used in surfcasting' and are intended to outlaw freak rods, obviously to preserve the sporting aspect and to protect anglers in combat with big fish.

Reels, too, must be 'in accordance with sporting ethics and customs'. Mechanical reels of any kind, including power-assisted reels, are banned. Strangely, so are reels with double handles! There seems no logic in such a rule. For example, our British centrepin mullet reel has two handles and is fitted out with light line: yet were our mullet to be listed by IGFA as a sporting species, captures on a centrepin reel would not be accepted.

Fighting chairs used for big fish must have no mechanical device which helps the angler fight his fish; and the only butt gimbal permitted (to take the extreme butt of the rod) is one which swivels in a vertical place only. That is to prevent an unscrupulous angler just jamming his rod in a fixed gimbal and letting that take the strain!

Were one to catch a cod using the wire line technique mentioned, that fish could not be entered as wire lines, including lines with metal cores, are prohibited.

When using natural bait, no more than two single hooks may be attached to the trace, and then only if they are both attached to or imbedded in the bait. The eyes of the hooks must be no less than a hook's length apart, and no more than 18 in (45·7 cm) apart. On artificial lures, the eyes of the two hooks must be at least a hook's length but no more than 18 in apart; the trailing hook may not extend behind the lure for more than a hook's length. No swinging or dangling hook is permitted. This is to prevent foul-hooking of fish, of course.

Treble or double hooks on plugs are permitted, but they must be limited to a maximum of two hooks – meaning two doubles, two trebles or two singles – are eligible. When casting a lure from a boat the boat must not be under any form of propulsion. And any record claim made for fish caught by plug fishing or lure fishing must be accompanied by a photograph of the plug or lure.

Two-hook bottom rigs are permitted so long as the top hook is far enough away from the bottom hook so as not to hook into a fish taken on the bottom hook – or vice versa. Again, a photograph or sketch of the tackle must accompany record claims.

The use of floats, other than a small balloon, bladder or cork, is prohibited. This is to prevent large buoyant devices being used to tire fish which would have to tow such heavy floats under the surface and through the water. Floats are solely for the purpose of drifting the bait while suspended in the water; the release balloon mentioned in the shark chapter certainly fulfils those demands.

A gaff up to 8 ft (2·4 m) long may be used to secure a fish on a boat, and it may be attached to a maximum of 30 ft (9 m) of rope. Longer gaffs may be used for bridge or pier fishing. The angler must hook, play and bring the fish to the net or gaff unaided. If anybody else touches the tackle during the period after hook-up any record claim is outlawed.

The rod must not be rested on the gunwale while fighting a fish, but a harness attached to the reel and a belly-pad are permitted. An angler is not allowed to change rod or reel, or to splice, or in any way add to the line during the period a fish is being played.

The following acts and situations also disqualify a fish: Failure to comply with the rules or tackle specifications. A broken rod, including a broken butt. Any person touching the tackle during play, except that one person is permitted to hold the trace when a fish is being boated. Shooting, harpooning or lancing any fish. Any fish mutilated, either by sharks during play, or by propellers that remove or penetrate its flesh. Old scars or marks caused by line or trace during the fight are not considered to be disqualifying injuries. Chumming (rubby-dubby) with flesh, blood, skin or guts of any mammal; chum must be consistent in size with that of the bait being used. Beaching or driving fish into shallow water, after hooking it from a boat, so as to deprive the fish of its normal ability to swim.

In addition to all the above, record applications have to be made on special forms and a great deal of information and verification is required. For example, photographs that clearly show the physical features of the fish, plus the tackle used, have to be submitted. The angler must be photographed with the fish; also the scales on which it is weighed. For shark records detailed photographs of the head, especially dentition, are required.

All claims from outside the United States of America must be received by IGFA within 60 days of the fish's capture. Entries of fish caught elsewhere must be received within three months of capture.

To replace a record for a fish weighing 100 lb (45 kg) or more, the new record must exceed the existing record by 1 lb (450 g); a fish weighing less than 1 lb more will be considered to tie with the record. For records weighing less than 100 lb (45·2 kg) similar conditions apply, except that the stipulated weight difference is half a pound.

Finally, no officer of the IGFA may hold a world record for a line class.

The address of IGFA is 3000 E. Las Olas Boulevard, Fort Lauderdale, Florida 33316, USA.

# Glossary

## A

**ABU** A Swedish manufacturer of tackle, with a branch in Glasgow. Famous for its reels and lures.

**Anodise** A method by which aluminium and its alloys are colour-coated to prevent corrosion and used as a form of decoration.

**Araldite** An epoxy-resin adhesive first developed for gluing aircraft frames together. This two-part adhesive is much used in rod making.

**Avon-type rod** Basically a freshwater rod with a flexible middle and top section, capable of subduing big barbel or tench and good for mullet, bass, etc.

## B

**Backing** Line used behind the main line as a reserve for playing fish, or for building up the line level to aid casting.

**Backlash** Line over-running during a cast with a multiplier or centrepin reel and winding itself in tangles the wrong way round the spool or drum. A surfcaster's nightmare!

**Bag-net** A landing net that ends in a U-shape at the base when suspended from the frame.

**Balsa** A soft, buoyant wood used in float making.

**Bar-spoon** A spinning lure on which a spoon- or willow leaf-shaped blade revolves round a wire bar when pivoted from its front end.

**Berkley** American fishing tackle makers of Spirit Lake, Iowa. They make excellent swivels, rods and nylon lines.

**Beta-light** A light, the power source of which is based on atomic reaction between tritium gas in a glass tube lined with a phosphorescent coating.

**Bickerdyke (John)** 19th Century angling writer who was best known for his love of pike fishing, but who also enjoyed sea fishing.

**Big-game fish** Usually such species as marlin, broadbill swordfish or bluefin tuna, but in British waters including the sharks.

**Blank** A glass-fibre or carbon-fibre tapered rod, hollow or solid, from which a fishing rod is constructed; or a day's fishing during which no fish are caught.

**Boatcaster** A rod made for casting and legering from an anchored boat.

**Bonefish** A streamlined, fast-swimming sportfish found in shallow tropical and sub-tropical oceans.

**Boom** A rigid bar from which a hook link or trace is fished so as to help avoid tangling with the main line. Also, an attachment for a lead which runs on the line as in tope or skate fishing.

**Break-off** Line breakage while casting or when fighting a fish.

**Brennan, Des** Organising Controller of the Inland Fisheries Trust Inc. of the Irish Republic and a respected sea angler.

**Broken** Word used to describe losing a fish by line breakage: 'I was broken by a big cod.'

**Bronzed hook** A steel hook protected by a bronze coloured lacquer.

**Brooks, Joe** A famous American angler who pioneered saltwater flyfishing among other aspects of the sport. The late Joe Brooks was an all-round angler.

**Butt** Thicker end of the rod near the handle; the lower joint of a rod. Also used in flyfishing: the thickest part of the leader where it joins the flyline.

## C

**Caged drum reel** A centrepin reel – for trotting or flyfishing usually – on which the drum is enclosed within a two-sided frame with crossbars.

**Carbon fibre** A modern material, very stiff for its weight and used in making expensive rods. It is produced, in simple terms, by burning special textile manmade fibres in the absence of oxygen.

**Cast** Excreta of a worm (lugworm) deposited on the surface of sand and mud shores below high water mark; also the action of projecting tackle to reach the fish.

**Charter-boat** An angling craft which may be hired by the day or for longer periods. It can be obtained with a skipper – and sometimes a mate – to position anglers over fish and assist in boating them.

**Check** The audible ratchet mechanism on a reel that clicks as line is drawn off the spool or drum. Used to signal bites, at times, and to judge rate at which line is being drawn off.

**Chumming** American term for rubby-dubby – the minced and cut fish used to attract fish to an angling boat. In Britain used to describe cut chunks of fish rather than minced fish and oil.

**Clutch** Braking mechanism on a reel, also called a drag.

**Collet** A device rather like the chuck of a drill that holds the drilling tool; it holds the tip of a baitcasting rod in the cranked handle, usually, by screwing up against a tapered tube.

**Collyer, Dave** Well known English freshwater angler and flydresser.

**Corrosion** Destruction by chemical action, especially by the action of acids, rust, etc. upon metals; in saltwater angling usually caused by salt deposits on reels and other metalwork on tackle.

**Crank (or cranked) handle** Short handle on a baitcasting rod which retains a reel, usually a small multiplier of closed-face spinning reel, at a low centre of gravity and lying in a U-shaped clip.

231

**Crimp** Describes the act of crushing a metal ferrule on to a wire-to-hook joint or wire loop with a special pair of pliers.

**Custom-built rod** A rod that is made by a craftsman to the special order and specification of a customer.

# D

**Dingle** Peninsula in south-west Ireland famous for its saltwater angling, particularly bass in the surf, pollack and wrasse from the rocks.

**Doubled line** Used in the capture of large fish, such as sharks and tropical water game fish. The end of the line is doubled for 15 ft (4·5 m) or so, both to resist abrasion weaking the line and provide a means of pulling the fish to the side of the boat by handling the doubled line.

**Drag** See clutch.

**Drum** Cylinder holding the line, usually on a centre-pin reel. On multipliers and fixed-spool reels the term used is spool.

**Dressing** Describes style and materials such as feathers, hairs and tinsel used in the manufacture of flies.

**Dropper** Term most used in fly fishing to describe a fly (or hook) on a short piece of nylon fixed above the terminal fly (hook) and usually projecting at a right angle from the line or leader.

# E

**Estuarine** Description of any fish, habitat, etc. in the vicinity of tidal mouth of large river.

# F

**Feathering** Term to describe catching fish, such as mackerel or pollack, on traces bearing a number of feather-decorated hooks. Also a method of slowing down the rate of line leaving the spool of a fixed-spool reel by letting a fingertip just touch the coils as they come over the front lip.

**Fight** The duel between angler and hooked fish.

**Flats** Term to describe flatfish, as opposed to round-fish, i.e. plaice or flounders. Also very shallow, sandy or muddy areas of sea, particularly in tropical and sub-tropical areas such as the Caribbean and Florida Keys, but also in the United Kingdom, especially the Essex coastline.

**Forged hook** Hook on which the area of the bend has been hammered flat to better resist distortion when a fish is hooked.

**Foul-hook** To hook a fish, accidently or purposely, usually in the body or around the head, without it having taken a bait or lure.

**Forrest, Nigel** East Coast angler and expert tournament surfcaster. Co-inventor with Ian Gillespie, of the Breakaway lead.

**Free-spool** System on a multiplying reel whereby the spool may be freed from the recovery gears system, for casting or lowering tackle to fish. Most are lever- or button-operated.

# G

**Gaff** Steel hook with a sharp point used to haul a large fish into a boat or on to shore.

**Gammon, Clive** Angling journalist and sports writer and until late 1976 a columnist in *Angling* magazine; now in America as a staff writer on *Sports Illustrated* magazine. A keen conservationist.

**Gillespie, Ian** Respected angling writer, *Angling* magazine columnist of long standing, and tackle innovator (see Forrest).

**Gimbal** Slotted device built into the butt cap of boat rods which locate in the bar of a belly-pad and prevent the rod turning when fighting a fish.

**Greyhounding** Term which describes the action of a fast-moving fish leaping forward at a low angle from a water. Usually applied to sailfish and marlin, but sometimes to garfish and even stingrays.

**Ground** Term used to describe the seabed configuration relative to the types of fish sought, i.e., rough ground, smooth ground.

# H

**Hands** The ability that comes with experience which tells an angler when to be gentle with a fighting fish and when to be firm. Cf. 'good hands' – as in horsemanship.

**Hardy** Hardy Brothers of Alnwick, Northumberland, world renowned tackle makers.

**Hold, holding** Term used to describe whether the leaded tackle will remain in position on the seabed . . . 'Are you holding?'

# J

**Jig** A heavy metal lure (sometimes adorned with feathers, hair or other fibres) which is fished in an up-down motion near the seabed. To jig: to fish a lure in an up and down motion.

**Jumbo mackerel** Very large mackerel which run westwards, very near the seabed in British and north-west European waters – usually in late summer and autumn.

# K

**Kelp** Rubbery, ribbon-like fronds of weed that grow in relatively deep water with a rocky bottom. Cod fishermen, who have to fish into it, often lose both tackle and fish as a result.

# L

**Lead** The moulded piece of lead used to sink, project, anchor or otherwise help present a bait or lure to a fish.

**Leger** To fish a bait anchored to the seabed by a lead; also sometimes used to describe such a lead.

**Line capacity** The amount of line a reel will properly hold.

**Line-class** A term used by the International Game Fish Association to classify various tackle systems. Lines in various classes must be tested to break at no more than the various figures listed, when the line is wet. For example, line for 20 lb (9 kg) class is usually made to break at about 17 lb (7·7 kg).

**Linnane, Kevin** Sea Angling Officer of Ireland's Inland Fisheries Trust. This respected sea angler is also an active conservationist.

**Lip-hook** Definition of having hooked a fish by the lip; also to describe method of using a live and dead fish, so hooked, as a bait.

**Lesser-spotted dogfish** A bottom-dwelling scavenger of no sporting value, but a valuable fish-and-chip shop food-fish.

**Longline** A long line of baited hooks used to catch big fish such as cod and halibut commercially.

# M

**Mark** Location at sea where there is good fishing; found either by radar navigation systems or by lining up on landmarks.

**Memory** Quality of a line which enables it to stretch, then return to its former position, as curls remain in monofilament nylon.

**Milbro** Tackle company based in Motherwell, Scotland.

**Mincing-machine** Slang name for a fixed-spool reel, used mainly by those who do not like using it.

**Mitchell** Famous French reel-making company; also make other tackle.

**Moncrieff, Leslie** Known as the 'Gentle Giant', the pioneer in Britain of long-distance surfcasting techniques.

**Monel-metal** A malleable material, used to make wire fishing lines, which does not corrode.

**Mylar** A bright plastic material, resembling shiny metal; often made into a braided tube and used to make flies.

# N

**Neap** A tide where the rise and fall between high and low is at a minimum.

**Neish, Don** Casting expert and tackle dealer of Edmonton, North London.

# O

**Over-run** Line coming from the spool too fast (usually of a multiplier or fixed-spool reel), then getting caught up by winding itself round the spool the wrong way. Also backlash.

# P

**Paternoster** Method of fishing with one or more hooks above a lead weight, the hooks on short links projecting from the main line at right angles.

**Pirk** A heavy metal or plastic/metal lure fished up and down, usually from a boat; used for predatory fish, such as cod, pollack and coalfish.

**Play** Similar word to fight – to battle with a hooked fish.

**Policansky** Name of a lever-drag reel made in South Africa.

**Pump** The action of lifting a fish by raising the rod, then winding in slack line rapidly as the rod is lowered again.

# R

**Ratchet** Same meaning as check.

**Recovery rate** Of reels: The amount of line rewound on the spool or drum for one turn of the handle.

**Reverse taper** Feature of a rod on which the part below the reel tapers in the opposite direction to that of the rod. It was produced by Leslie Moncrieff to help people cast long distances without over-runs or back-lashes.

**Rig** Name for terminal tackle.

**Rings** Fittings on the rod through which line runs and is supported.

**Roller** Revolving bollard in the pick-up arm of a fixed-spool reel to reduce friction; also parts of roller-rings used on boat rods.

**Run** The action of a hooked fish swimming away from the angler; also the movement of migratory fish to and from a region at a particular season of the year.

# S

**Set** Bend that remains permanently in a rod after stress; also the action of sinking the hook in a fish's mouth.

**Sink and draw** Lift and fall action of fishing a lure or bait.

**Sound** A fish diving towards the seabed.

**Spade-end** A hook with a spade-shaped flattened end to its shank and which holds a whipping-knot firmly.

**Spring tide** A tide where the rise and fall between high and low is at a maximum; the opposite to neap tide.

**Star-drag** Capstan-shaped wheel, like a ship's helm, by which the drag on a reel can be adjusted.

**Steep-to** Description of a beach that slopes steeply from the water level.

**Stop** A knot or some other form of method by which a lead or a sliding float is fixed on the line at the correct fishing depth.

**Swash** The shallow water left to recede after a wave has run up a shallow surf beach and expended its energy.

**Swivel-chair** Fixed to a boat's stern from which an angler plays a big fish.

# T

**Tailer** Rope used to secure large fish, like sharks, by putting a noose over the tail.

**Take** Action of a fish grabbing a bait or lure.

**Test** The amount, expressed in pounds or kilograms, to which a line will resist linear elongation.

**Test curve** Optimum bend in a rod for safety, by which safe casting weight and safe line test to be used can be evaluated.

**Thumb** Action of braking a multiplier reel spool, when casting and fighting a fish.

**Tournament casting** Casting on a field for distance and accuracy. (Some tournament casters do not go fishing at all!)

# W

**Whelm** The disturbance visible on the surface caused by a mullet moving fast deep down and changing direction.

**Work-harden** Means by which the molecular construction of a metal – such as a line – is altered and made brittle by constant friction over another unresistant surface.

# Y

**Yorkshire Stronghold** Brand of high carbon steel hooks marketed by a company called Mackenzie-Philps of Sicklinghall, near Weatherby, Yorkshire.

# Index

*Index compiled by H. Jolowicz*

# OTHER GUINNESS SUPERLATIVES TITLES

## Facts and Feats Series:

**Air Facts and Feats,** *2nd ed.*
John W R Taylor, Michael J H
Taylor and David Mondey

**Rail Facts and Feats**, *2nd ed.*
John Marshall

**Tank Facts and Feats,** *2nd ed.*
Kenneth Macksey

**Car Facts and Feats,** *2nd ed.*
edited by Anthony Harding

**Yachting Facts and Feats**
Peter Johnson

**Business World**
Henry Button and Andrew
Lampert

**Music Facts and Feats**
Robert and Celia Dearling
with Brian Rust

**Animal Facts and Feats**
Gerald L. Wood FZS

**Plant Facts and Feats**
William G Duncalf

**Structures – Bridges,
Towers, Tunnels, Dams . . .**
John H Stephens

**Weather Facts and Feats**
Ingrid Holford

## Guide Series:

**Guide to Bicycling**
J Durry and J B Wadley

**Guide to French Country Cooking**
Christian Roland Délu

**Guide to Freshwater Angling**
Brian Harris and Paul Boyer

**Guide to Mountain Animals**
R P Bille

**Guide to Underwater Life**
C Petron and J B Lozet

**Guide to Motorcycling,** *2nd ed.*
Christian Lacombe

**Guide to Formula 1 Motor
Racing**
José Rosinski

**Guide to Water Skiing**
David Nations OBE and Kevin
Desmond

## Other Titles:

**The Guinness Book of
Answers**
edited by Norris D McWhirter

**The Guinness Book of
Records**
edited by Norris D McWhirter

**The Guinness Book of 1952**
Kenneth Macksey

**Universal Soldier**
Martin Windrow and Frederick
Wilkinson

**History of Land Warfare**
Kenneth Macksey

**History of Sea Warfare**
Lt-Cmdr Gervis Frere-Cook
and Kenneth Macksey

**History of Air Warfare**
David Brown, Christopher
Shores and Kenneth Macksey

**The Guinness Guide to
Feminine Achievements**
Joan and Kenneth Macksey

**The Guinness Book of
Names**
Leslie Dunkling

**Battle Dress**
Frederick Wilkinson

**100 Years of Wimbledon**
Lance Tingay

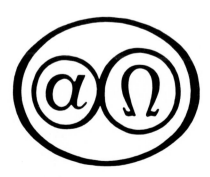